TREASURES OF
Virginia

Monticello, home of Thomas Jefferson

by Damon Neal

a part of the Morgan & Chase Treasure Series
www.treasuresof.com

MORGAN & CHASE PUBLISHING INC.

Published by:
Morgan & Chase Publishing, Inc.
531 Parsons Drive, Medford, Oregon 97501
(888) 557-9328
www.treasuresof.com

Printed by:
Taylor Specialty Books - Dallas TX

First edition 2007

ISBN: 978-1-933989-11-2

THE
TREASURE
SERIES

I gratefully acknowledge the contributions
of the many people involved in the writing and production of this book.
Their tireless dedication to this endeavour has been inspirational.
—William Faubion, *Publisher*

Managing Editor:
John Gaffey

Senior Story Editor:
Gregory Scott

Senior Writer:
Megan Glomb

Proof Editors:
Avery Brown, Clarice Rodriguez, Robyn Sutherland

Graphic Design:
Confluence Book Services

Image Coordinators:
Wendy Gay and Donna Lindley

Website:
Molly Bermea, Ben Ford

Morgan & Chase Home Team
Cindy Tilley Faubion, Emily Wilkie, Pam Hamilton, Heather Allen , Virginia Arias, Ray Ackerman,
Danielle Barkley, Anne Boydston, Sue Buda, Casey Faubion, Shauna O'Callahan, Cari Qualls, Terrie West
C.S. Rowan, Tamara Cornett , Michael Frye, Jesse Gifford, Jacob Kristof, Mary Murdock, Chris Rose-Merkle

Contributing Writers:
Dusty Alexander, Cory Bernhardt, Carol Bevis, Mark Allen Deruiter, Claudia Van Dyke, Lanette Fadley,
Dori Graham, Paul Hadella, Mary Knepp, Lynda Kusick, Mary Beth Lee, Nancy McClain, Maggie McClellen,
Sandy McLain, Kevin Monk, Damon Peterson, Susan Vaughn, Todd Wels

We believe that enlightened people strive to create beauty from chaos and understanding from tragedy. In that spirit we respectfully dedicate this book to the students, families, and staff at Virginia Tech University.

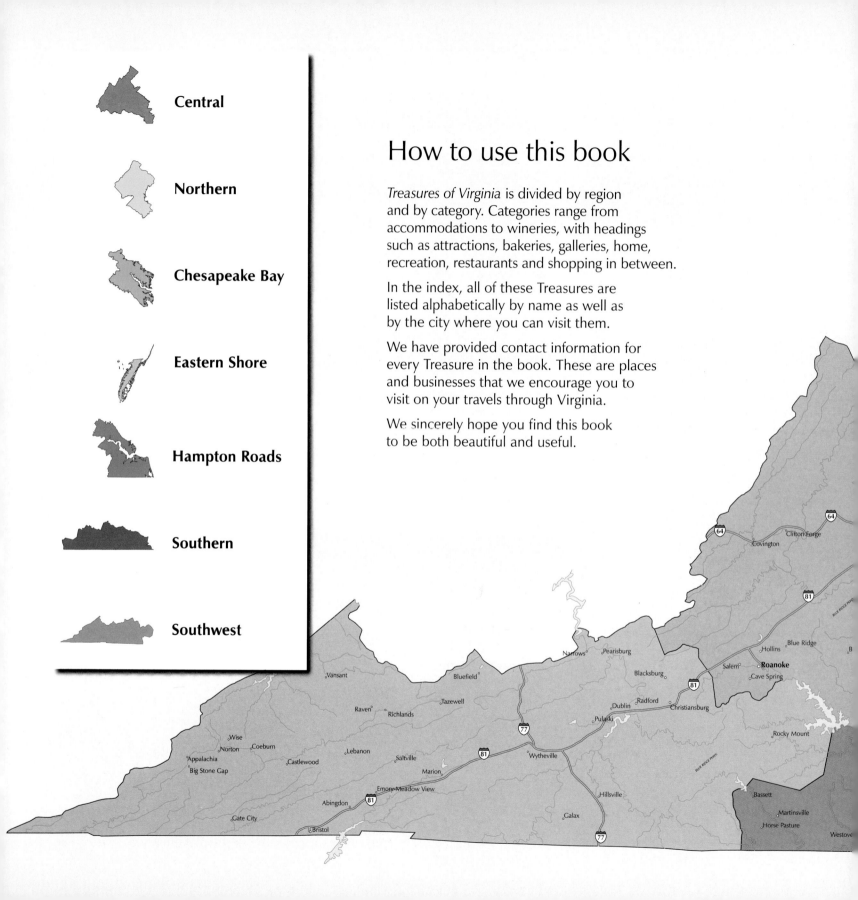

Central

Northern

Chesapeake Bay

Eastern Shore

Hampton Roads

Southern

Southwest

How to use this book

Treasures of Virginia is divided by region and by category. Categories range from accommodations to wineries, with headings such as attractions, bakeries, galleries, home, recreation, restaurants and shopping in between.

In the index, all of these Treasures are listed alphabetically by name as well as by the city where you can visit them.

We have provided contact information for every Treasure in the book. These are places and businesses that we encourage you to visit on your travels through Virginia.

We sincerely hope you find this book to be both beautiful and useful.

VIRGINIA FACTS:

Admitted to the Union: 1788, the 10th state

Population (2006): 7,642,884

Largest City: Virginia Beach, 447,000

Largest Metro Area: Hampton Roads, 1,600,000

Highest Mountain: Mt. Rogers, 5,729 feet

Bird: Cardinal

Dog: American Foxhound

Fish: Brook Trout

Fossil: *Chesapecten jeffersonius*

Insect: Tiger Swallowtail

Motto: *Sic Semper Tyrannis* (Thus Always to Tyrants)

Nickname: Old Dominion State

Tree: American Dogwood (*Cornus florida*)

Foreword

Welcome to *Treasures of Virginia*. This book is a resource that can guide you to some of the best places in Virginia, one of the most beautiful states and surely the most historic state in the Union. Virginia is geographically diverse, extending from the Ridge-and-valley Appalachians to the Tidewater. The Old Dominion was the first of the 13 colonies, and from Yorktown, where America won its independence, to Manassas, where the Blue and Gray first met in battle, the state breathes history. With so many battles fought on its soil, it's only natural that Virginia should be the home of the U.S. military, with the Pentagon in Arlington and the world's largest naval base in Norfolk.

Though the past is everywhere in Virginia, the present and future are more exciting still. The state today is growing rapidly, as more and more citizens and immigrants discover its mild climate, lush green vistas, warm and easy style of living, and above all, its enormous economic vitality. The bustling metropolises of Northern Virginia, Richmond and the Hampton Roads are as cosmopolitan as any places on earth.

Countless attractions await visitors to Virginia, home of presidents. See George Washington's mansion at Mount Vernon and Thomas Jefferson's Monticello. Come to Williamsburg, once the capital, or Yorktown, either of which boasts some of the nation's greatest collections of historic sites, as well as fabulous places to lodge, dine and shop. Enjoy the Nostalgiafest celebration in Petersburg, join the Peanut Festival in Emporia and tour the museums of Newport News.

Virginia is home to the nicest people you'll ever meet. In preparing this book, we talked to thousands of business people about their products, their services and their visions. We visited art galleries in Alexandria and shopped for antiques in Midlothian. We watched the cars zoom past at Virginia International Raceway near Danville. We dined on seafood in Virginia Beach and slept at bed-and-breakfasts everywhere. You are holding the result of our efforts in your hands. *Treasures of Virginia* is a 342-page compilation of the best places in Virginia to eat, shop, play, explore, learn and relax. We did the legwork. All you have to do now, is enjoy.

—John Gaffey

Central Virginia

Accommodations

Virginia Cliff Inn

Follow Thomas Jefferson's path down Mountain Road, the nation's second oldest road, and you will find not only a passage steeped in history but also The Virginia Cliff Inn. This stately manor, completed in 1974, sits just 350 feet off of the famed road. The manse was modeled after the Morris-Jumel Mansion, the place George Washington used as his New York headquarters during the Revolutionary War. Innkeepers Margaret and James Clifton purchased the six-acre plot in the early 1950s and, after being unable to remodel the existing 100-year-old farmhouse, decided to build their dream house instead. After visiting New England on vacation and staying exclusively in bed and breakfasts, the couple realized that the venue would be an ideal inn after their retirement, and the rest is history. The Clifftons pride themselves on offering guests a relaxing and enjoyable bed-and-breakfast experience with a focus on service and hospitality. The Clifton's family members, including their children and grandchildren, help run the inn, making this truly a family affair. It is their hope that when you look back on your Virginia vacation, your most outstanding memories will be those of the gracious service you received. The Virginia Cliff Inn is Henrico County's first and only bed and breakfast. It offers four beautiful suites and a cottage, lush grounds and wonderful breakfasts. The inn is also the ideal place for hosting weddings, and brides will love the beautiful garden gazebo that James built over 25 years ago for his daughter's wedding. Experience gracious living at its best with a stay at The Virginia Cliff Inn.

2900 Mountain Road, Glen Allen VA
(804) 266-7344 or (877) 254-3346

The Babcock House

Voted Best Evening Cuisine by the *Inn Traveler Magazine* two years in a row, The Babcock House is the only bed and breakfast in the county that offers evening dining. They also offer a catering service that catered 52 weddings in 2005. Located 30 minutes east of Lynchburg and 90 minutes west of Richmond, The Babcock House is on two acres in the second oldest home in town. The home was built in 1884 and still has the original pine wood floors. It is furnished with period antiques making for a beautiful setting where you can sit back and stay awhile. The Babcock House is also the only bed and breakfast in town that has a AAA three diamond rating. They have six guest rooms and a restaurant that you will love. The menu is noted for the spinach crab bisque and, although they have been repeatedly asked, they will not give out their secret recipe. Since it is located in a quiet town with a population of 1,800, you can relax on the porch swing without distraction. Approximately 250,000 tourists travel to this town each year because of the rich civil war history. It is located less than three miles from the Appomattox Courthouse National Historic Park where General Robert E. Lee surrendered the Army of Northern Virginia to General Grant. The inn is also at the center of the 19th Century Homes Walking Tour. The Babcock House is always very clean and comfortable, so make your reservations today.

250 Oakleigh Avenue, Appomattox VA
(434) 352-7532
www.babcockhouse.com

West Manor Bed & Breakfast

From the gracefully appointed 1800's Manor House to the 600 acres of lush meadows, wood and mountain views, West Manor Bed & Breakfast aims to pamper you. The Lester family and their experienced staff handle all the details that create the fairy tale event. Since this former dairy farm opened as a Bed & Breakfast 12 years ago, it has steadily been making a name for itself as a breathtaking wedding and event site. Greg & Sharon, with the help of their children, Aaron, Jordan, Bethany & John, tailor each event, including entertainment, decorations, setup and delectable cuisine. The Grand Ballroom, sunlit conservatory with wood carved full service bar and enchanting gardens with gas lanterns and a gazebo, are all idyllic for any special event. Guests may enjoy any of the beautifully decorated guest rooms with fireplaces, jetted tubs and peaceful sitting areas. Become part of another era—just 20 minutes from downtown Lynchburg.

3594 Elkton Farm Road, Forest VA
(434) 525-0923
www.westmanorbb.com

Photos by Stoneblueproductions.com

Federal Crest Inn Bed and Breakfast

It was love at first sight for innkeepers Ann and Phil Ripley when they discovered a 1909 Georgian Revival mansion, in the Federal Hill district of Lynchburg, in 1994. The Ripleys renovated the 8,000-square-foot home and now proudly welcome guests to stay in their distinctive bed and breakfast with uniquely decorated bedrooms and suites. Phil previously owned a publishing house and sold real estate in northern Virginia and Ann was a high school teacher and gymnastics coach with a strong art background. Today, Phil indulges his hobby of attending antique auctions, Ann finds excuses to add artistic embellishments to her stately home and both enjoy serving their diverse clientele. The inn features mahogany paneling in the library and dining room and a grand central staircase flanked by columns. Guests appreciate seven gas log fireplaces, overstuffed chairs and period furnishings in spacious guest rooms. Gourmet breakfasts are served by candlelight, on Limoges china, with Ann's hand painted crystal goblets. Every room comes with a snack basket, monogrammed robes and down comforters. One guest bathroom boasts a Jacuzzi tub surrounded by Ann's hand painted mural of the Blue Ridge Mountains. With formal public rooms, a third floor with a performance stage and spacious grounds, the inn makes a charming location for a wedding reception, corporate meeting, or family reunion. It is also a popular couples retreat, conveniently located near several area colleges and Civil War historic sites and with easy access to golf, hiking, wineries, and antique shops. For a retreat from the ordinary, visit the historic Federal Crest Inn.

1101 Federal Street, Lynchburg VA (434) 845-6155 or (800) 818-6155
www.federalcrest.com

The High Street Inn

The High Street Inn in Petersburg has had quite the colorful past. This elegant bed-and-breakfast was built in the late 1890s for a Petersburg merchant, J.A. Gill, his wife and their six children. After the death of Mrs. Gill, the fired brick mansion was sold to Mr. Wells. Wells turned the home into the Wells and Gould Funeral Parlor. In the 1960s, the parlor served as a VFW hall and a secret gambling den was set up in a back room that is now the laundry room. The house achieved bed-and-breakfast status in 1986 when it was sold to Mr. and Mrs. Bruce Noe. They retained the property until 1996, when it was sold to the Swensons who renamed it the Owl and the Pussycat. It was during this time that beloved actress Katherine Hepburn and her driver stayed at the inn. Today, this family inn is owned and operated by Eddie and Tina Bertenshaw and their two children. The couple has worked diligently to restore, redecorate and refurnish their beloved home. The inn can serve up to 20 guests, accommodates all dietary needs and is child friendly. Choose from several charming and elegant rooms including the Sycamore Suite, also known as the Hepburn Suite. Come discover historic Petersburg and enjoy true hospitality with the Bertenshaws at The High Street Inn.

405 High Street,
Petersburg VA
(804) 722-0800
www.thehighstreetinn.com

Ragland Mansion

The Ragland Mansion in Petersburg has been providing Southern comfort and elegance since the 1850s. A Welsh aristocratic descendent named Rueben Ragland built this exquisite 10,000-square-foot Italianate villa. Yolande Bezaka purchased the mansion in 1997 and turned the grand property into a bed and breakfast. The Ragland Mansion Guest House prides itself on both its colorful history and the fine Southern hospitality that Claudia and her staff provide. As legend has it, the daughter of one of Ragland's relatives ran away to elope with a union solider. Her grieving mother reappeared as a ghost on the top landing wearing a pink chiffon ball gown and waiting for her return. This spirited guest has not been seen since the 1950s but her spirit was just one of many visitors who have come and gone over the years. Another famed former resident was General Pershing. He was supposedly housed in what is now the Sycamore Room during the First World War while the mansion served as Fort Lee's officers' club. Eight stunning guest rooms are available, each with its own marble fireplace and elegant private bathroom. The mansion features an extensive collection of 19th and 20th century art and furnishings along with incredible plasterwork and inlaid flooring. With its large reception and dining rooms, the mansion is a fabulous place to host a gala, wedding or other special event. The Ragland Mansion Guest House is located in the historic Poplar Lawn residential district and is only a few minutes' walk from museums, parks, restaurants and shops. Ragland Mansion Guest House is an historical landmark filled with that special kind of warmth and cheer that is inherent to the South.

205 S Sycamore Street, Petersburg VA   (800) 861-8898
www.raglandmansion.com   www.ragland-mansion.com

Folly Castle Inn

In 1763, Peter Jones II, grandson of Petersburg founder Peter Jones, set aside the conventions of the day and built a grand manor, now Folly Castle Inn, using money gained from selling 28 lots on High Street that he had inherited from his grandfather. The Gregorian style manor received the name Folly Castle for two reasons. The community felt it was folly for the 28-year-old bachelor to build such a home and at the time, *castle* was a term applied to any large dwelling. Peter died at the age of 30 but Folly Castle stayed in the family for approximately 100 years. In 1928, Mary Deffenbaugh turned the stately residence into a guesthouse and tearoom where she charmed and catered to the Petersburg elite for nearly 40 years. During that time many a bride descended the lovely master staircase. The inn further served as a home away from home for soldiers and their wives during World War II. Today, Owners Jackie and Tim Graham continue this famous home's long tradition of Southern hospitality. Folly Castle is ideal for those who wish to explore the historically rich and important community of Petersburg. The Grahams also keep up the tradition of housing the military. This elegant inn is uniquely suited to housing guests for extended stays and offers military guests adjusted per diem rates. Folly Castle Inn features two fully stocked guest kitchens, laundry facilities, a full complementary breakfast and off-street parking. Let Folly Castle Inn be your place to stay while exploring historic Petersburg.

323 W Washington Street, Petersburg VA
(804) 861-3558
www.follycastle.com

Virginia Crossings Resort

Just 15 minutes from downtown Richmond is a conference facility that combines world-class technology and exceptional communication capabilities with luxurious accommodations and extraordinary leisure activities, all wrapped in a country setting. Virginia Crossings Resort in Glen Allen, under the management of Benchmark Hospitality, is the area's foremost destination for meetings with over 25,000 square feet of flexible meeting space, three executive board rooms, and a large ballroom to meet all of your conferencing needs. Gracious buildings reminiscent of Williamsburg, flower gardens and 20 sweeping acres create a serene environment while elegant guest rooms provide impeccable décor, spectacular views and many amenities like dual-line phones with data ports, voice mail and high speed Internet access. When the day is done, enjoy the fitness center, walking and running trails, outdoor swimming or the Crossings Golf Club located next door. Refresh yourself at the Glen Restaurant which provides daily breakfasts, lunch buffets and *a la carte* dinners, or watch television sports, listen to live music and play billiards at the Yellow Tavern & Grill with its tempting lighter fare and perfectly poured beverages. The building sits on the grounds of the Battle of Yellow Tavern where 800 soldiers died and Confederate General J.E.B. Stuart was mortally wounded. Plan your next conference or important meeting at Virginia Crossings Resort. With state-of-the-art technology, elegant surroundings, a responsive staff and entertainment to suit all tastes, your conference is sure to be a huge success.

1000 Virginia Center Parkway, Glen Allen VA   (804) 727-1400 or (888) 444-6553
www.virginiacrossingsresort.com

Commonwealth Park Suites Hotel at Capitol Square

Experience stately elegance and genteel hospitality at the newly remodeled Commonwealth Park Suites Hotel at Capitol Square in downtown Richmond. The forerunner of this charming hotel opened in 1846 under the ownership of Louis Rueger as a bootlegging saloon with rooms above for those who had overindulged. During the Civil War the warehouses along the James River were set afire, the wind swept the flames up Ninth Street and the Hotel Rueger was engulfed. It then stood empty for 50 years until 1912, when it was rebuilt. Over the years this handsome hotel has served as home for members of the Virginia General Assembly while in session and as the residence of Governor James Gilmore while the Governor's Mansion underwent renovations. In 1982 a new developer purchased the building and gutted the 123-room interior in order to make way for 49 luxurious one or two bedroom suites, 10 standard rooms and three banquet rooms. Further improvements over the following years included adding modern luxuries while maintaining this historic site's opulent, old world feeling. Each beautifully appointed suite offers a host of wonderful luxuries designed to pamper and indulge guests. The hotel's many amenities allow Commonwealth Park Suites to be your home away from home. Maxine's Bistro, located on-site, offers guests fabulous views along with sensational cuisine. Unsurpassed Southern hospitality is yours at Commonwealth Park Suites Hotel.

901 Bank Street, Richmond VA
(804) 343-7300 or (888) 343-7301
www.commonwealthparksuites.com

Amelia Family Campgrounds

In 1968, John and Ferne Hutchinson operated a rock shop and restaurant. The nearby Rutherford and Moorefield Mines attracted rock collectors from all over the United States and beyond. Tourists who would visit often stopped at John's rock shop and ask about overnight accommodations in the area. Amelia Family Campground was established to fill that need. Open year 'round and located on Highway 153, the campground's 59 lush acres contain all the amenities including a swimming pool, sport-fishing pond, playground and recreation room for the kids. From rock collectors to bluegrass music fans, people from all walks of life have looked to this campground for a place to stay since it opened in 1973. With the assistance of their five children, the Hutchinsons provide a clean and friendly campground with a focus on family fun. Twice a year that fun takes on the distinctive sound of bluegrass. Amelia Family Campground is home to the Central Virginia Family Bluegrass Music Festival held twice a year on the third weekends of May and August. These three-day banjo-picking music extravaganzas have been held for the last 27 years and the overwhelming success of the festivals has resulted in John being named 2006 Promoter of the Year by the Society for the Preservation of Bluegrass Music of America. Please visit the website for this year's line-up of talent or call to speak with John or Ferne with any questions pertaining to camping or the bluegrass festivals.

9720 Military Road, Amelia VA
(804) 561-3011
www.ameliafamilycampgrounds.com

Attractions

Miles B. Carpenter Museum Complex

When Donald Walters of the Abbey Aldrich Rockefeller Folk Art Center spotted a whole watermelon carved out of wood and sitting in a cart by the side of the road one hot June day in 1972, he knew he was looking at an American treasure. From that day forward, word of the 83-year-old Miles B. Carpenter's quirky wood carvings spread, making him one of the best known folk artists of our time by his death in 1985. The Miles B. Carpenter Museum Complex houses a large collection of original Miles Carpenter art as well as museums dedicated to wood products and peanuts, both Sussex County products. The complex includes the Victorian house that Miles and his wife occupied from 1912 until 1985. The kitchen contains furnishings used by the Carpenters. The site also holds a permanent collection of the artist's carving tools and memorabilia. The wood products museum sits on an old sawmill foundation, and the peanut museum uses photographs to depict early planting and harvesting techniques and showcases shelling, roasting and harvesting equipment. The peanut museum commemorates the 1842 Sussex planting of the first commercial peanut crop in the United States. This complex promotes artistic, educational and cultural interests by preserving the heritage of Sussex County. Seven visiting exhibits take up temporary quarters in the second floor gallery each year. Visit the Miles B. Carpenter Museum Complex to pay homage to the art and industry that has blossomed in Sussex County.

201 Hunter Street, Waverly VA
(804) 834-3327
www.sussexcounty.govoffice.com

Blandford Church & Cemetary

The earliest grave in Blandford Cemetery dates back to 1702, when the United States was still a British colony. The church was added in 1735 and was in use throughout the colonial period and into the early years of the new republic. By 1806, the church was abandoned. The building was left untended for more than 95 years, until 1901, when the Ladies Memorial Association, an organization of Petersburg women, had the idea of restoring the church to be used as a Confederate war memorial. The ladies solicited funds from former confederate states and in 1901, commissioned 15 stained glass windows from the world renowned art glass maker Louis Comfort Tiffany. The first of the Tiffany windows were completed and unveiled at a ceremony in 1904. Eight years later, the last of these fabulous stained glass windows were installed in the renovated Blandford Church. The cemetery surrounding the church is known for its diverse array of gravestone sculptures, tombs and funerary art that spans the 18th, 19th and 20th centuries. It is also home to the graves of more than 30,000 Confederate soldiers. Walking tours are offered year-round and for those who prefer a little fun with their hallowed history, there is an educational and popular Halloween cemetery tour. Whether you are a Civil War buff, an admirer of fine art glass or just interested in American history, a trip to this 300-year-old landmark is for you.

111 Rochelle Lane, Petersburg VA
(804) 733-2396
www.petersburg-va.org/tourism/blandford.htm

Mount Vernon Estate & Gardens

Located just 16 miles from Washington, D.C., George Washington's Mount Vernon Estate preserves both George Washington's home and his place in our hearts. Henry Lee eulogized Washington as "first in war, first in peace, and first in the hearts of his countrymen," a riveting description that explains the attraction of Washington's home. Since 1860, more than 80 million visitors have toured the estate, making it the most popular historic home in the country. The Mount Vernon Ladies' Association owns and operates the property. The association, founded in 1853, is the oldest national

Photos courtesy of Mount Vernon Ladies Association

preservation organization in America. Come by car or let the Potomac Riverboat Company in Old Town transport you here by boat. A visit includes opportunities to tour the main mansion, several outbuildings, Washington's tomb and a four-acre demonstration farm complete with a re-creation of Washington's 16-sided treading barn. Four gardens showcase heirloom plants that thrived here in the late 1700s. The new visitor facilities, the Ford Orientation Center and the Donald W. Reynolds Museum & Education Center, opening in 2006, house 25 galleries and theaters that will revolutionize your experience here with state-of-the-art interactive displays, movies and more than 700 artifacts. Make a day of it with a relaxing meal at the Mount Vernon Inn and shopping at the Shops at Mount Vernon. For a breathtaking look backward at the life and times of our nation's first president, visit George Washington's Mount Vernon Estate.

3200 Mount Vernon Memorial Highway, Mount Vernon VA (703) 780-2000 *www.mountvernon.org*

Nostalgiafest

It's a celebration. Nostalgiafest is a great way to spend a weekend. This three day festival of family fun fits perfectly into the historic setting of Old Towne Petersburg. Each year on the first weekend in October, the area's biggest street festival takes place amidst a burgeoning environment of artist galleries, distinctive boutiques, shops and restaurants within historic buildings that are being wonderfully restored. Nostalgiafest itself offers a wide variety of music and great food in addition to craft, art, antique and specialty vendors. In celebration of Petersburg's past, present and future, the festival showcases the City's many important attributes with historic tours that include tram rides on the scenic Appomattox River Heritage Trail. And since no festival is complete without entertainment for children, one of the highlights of Nostalgiafest is the Kids Zone. This is an environment for children of all ages with crafts, games, magician performances, a petting zoo, clowns and a variety of children-friendly rides—all free of charge. Petersburg is a city being re-discovered for its architectural and historical riches spanning three centuries. The City is steeped in hospitality and Nostalgiafest is one way Petersburg is showcasing that hospitality. Come stay in one of the area's bed-and-breakfasts and enjoy an exciting weekend that will become a favorite memory.

Downtown Petersburg Incorporated, Petersburg VA
(804) 732-0700
www.downtownpetersburg.net

Centre Hill Museum

Have you ever wondered what life was like for our founding fathers or wanted to walk in the footsteps of presidents? At Centre Hill Museum, you have the opportunity to do both. Called a symbol of the grandeur that characterized the aristocracy of Virginia in the 19th century, Centre Hill allows visitors to experience a slice of American history first hand. Built in 1823, this home contains stately examples of Greek revival architectural features that take you back in time. Built by Robert Bolling IV, this residence symbolizes his family's economic and social stature as members of Virginia's gentry. The house remained a private residence until 1936. Distinguished guests included President Abraham Lincoln in 1865 and President William Howard Taft in 1909. In 1972, the building was acquired and restored by the City of Petersburg. This historical gem was turned into a museum and its doors were opened to the public. One interesting feature is a tunnel constructed in the 1840s. This 100-foot long passageway (originally 300 feet long) provided access into the house for the Bolling family's slaves. Learn the interesting and illustrious history of this grand old home on a guided tour. A popular annual ghost watch is held every January 24th. Will you see the ghosts of Civil War soldiers who once marched up and down Centre Hill's halls? There's only one way to find out. You'll just have to see for yourself at Centre Hill Museum.

1 Centre Hill Court, Petersburg VA
(804) 733-2401
www.petersburg-va.org/tourism/cntrhill.htm

Chesterfield Berry Farm

The fourth generation, family owned and operated Chesterfield Berry Farm in Moseley offers wonderful fun for the whole family. This popular destination farm has been in the Goode family for nearly 100 years, originally serving as a top-notch dairy farm until 1993 when the current generation decided to switch gears and create a pick-your-own place that sells strawberries and pumpkins. Chesterfield Berry Farm also provides a great way for younger children to become familiar with farm life by letting them explore the tractors, visit with the animals and soak in some clean, fresh air. During the May strawberry festival, everyone can join in on some old fashioned fun highlighted by scrumptious treats. Festival events include strawberry wine tasting and the strawberry slingshot game where you use a slingshot to fire a pint of strawberries at a designated target for prizes. Chesterfield Berry Farms is also an ideal place for school, church or other group field trips. Located on Pear Orchard Road, this is a terrific place to take the family for some simple down home fun and fantastic produce, so grab the kids and come on down to Chesterfield Berry Farm.

26002 Pear Orchard Road, Moseley VA
(804) 739-3831
www.chesterfieldberryfarm.com

The National D-Day Memorial

The National D-Day Memorial is a monument for all seasons. Dedicated to the valor, fidelity, and sacrifice of the Allied forces on D-Day, June 6, 1944, the National D-Day Memorial stands to ensure that the lessons and legacy of the turning point in World War II are not forgotten. The Memorial was dedicated on June 6, 2001. The National D-Day Memorial Foundation is a not-for-profit educational foundation established by Congress. On three levels, the Memorial takes visitors through the planning, execution and victory of D-Day. It is a place that, once visited, will never be forgotten. Enter through the triumphal arch inscribed with Overlord, the Allies' code name for the Normandy landing. View the displays, statuary, and plaques recognizing all service branches and Allied nations that participated in the Allied Expeditionary Force. Learn why Bedford, Virginia was selected as the sight for the Memorial. The National D-Day Memorial not only pays tribute to those who died on D-Day, but also to those who lived to secure the beachhead and carry freedom inland. Walking tours and shuttle-cart tours are offered. The Memorial is wheelchair accessible, and wheelchairs are provided free of charge for those who need them. Group tours and school programs are available. The monument includes a Memorial Store that is open daily. The National D-Day Memorial Foundation welcomes you to come and learn about the valor and sacrifice of our nation's heroes.

202 E Main Street, Bedford VA
(540) 586-3329 or (800) 351-3329
www.dday.org

The Lynchburg Museum System

The Lynchburg Museum System provides numerous portals to the past. The Museum is housed in the 1855 Old Court House, one of the most visible landmarks in Lynchburg. This Greek Revival treasure is seated high above the James River, with a vista leading down Monument Terrace to the site of Lynch's Ferry, started here in 1757. Inside its walls you will find treasures such as rare early photographs, fine furnishings and historic costumes. Lynchburg has a fascinating history that involves Native American tribes, Quaker settlers and the reign of King Tobacco. The museum gives you the chance to relive the bloody struggles of the Civil War and the birth of the new South. After a visit here, continue your journey to Point of Honor, named for duels fought for honor near this Virginia historic landmark at 112 Cabell Street. Built in 1815 for Dr. George Cabell, Sr., Point of Honor has been carefully restored. Enjoy the views of the James River from its windows while admiring the period antiques and the *Monuments of Paris* mural wallpaper. Visit the Gift Shop in the Bertha Green Webster Carriage House and see an authentically restored plantation kitchen. Luxuriate in the beautifully recreated landscape sponsored by the Garden Club of Virginia. Get to know the City of Lynchburg past and present, with a visit to The Lynchburg Museum System.

Lynchburg Museum System Box 529, Lynchburg VA 24505
(434) 455-6226
www.lynchburgmuseum.org
www.pointofhonor.org
www.ci.lynchburg.va.us

901 Court Street, Lynchburg VA
(434) 847-1459
www.lynchburgmuseum.org
www.pointofhonor.org
www.ci.lynchburg.vaus

Celebrations at the Reservoir

Turn your wedding or other significant event into the occasion of a lifetime at Celebrations at the Reservoir. This 125-acre, magnificently landscaped facility offers five distinct man-made and natural settings that make ideal backdrops for weddings, commitment ceremonies and other special moments of your life. Additionally, Celebrations offers three fabulous and individualized reception sites that reward guests with spectacular views of the 1,700-acre Swift River Reservoir. Situated within easy reach from Richmond, Tidewater or Northern Virginia, this elegant venue features a lovely Plantation-style home along with a giant gazebo. Another delightful feature is the Shimizu Tea House, a hand-crafted art piece that was named for its gifted designer, Osamu Shimizu, and hangs suspended over an Oriental garden pool. Celebrations Owner Lori Caudill, along with her husband Steve and her parents Jim and Paulanne Thacker, is committed to ensuring that your planning time and special day are stress-free and filled with nothing but fond memories. To this end each client is given personalized attention and event coordinating services. Celebrations can assist you with everything from ordering the invitations to planning the meal in order to make sure that your event is perfect. With so many different settings available, Celebrations can help you make your dreams come true, whether you want an intimate indoor ceremony and supper for 25 or a spectacular occasion set against nature in its glory. You are invited to celebrate the special moments of your life in grand style with Celebrations at the Reservoir.

4801 Woolridge Road, Moseley VA
(804) 739-9015
www.celebrationsatthereservoir.com

Celebrations
at the Reservoir

Southampton Agriculture & Forestry Museum/Heritage Village

The opportunity to explore the heritage and artifacts of a bygone era await you at Southampton Agriculture & Forestry Museum/Heritage Village. In 1987, residents of Southampton County began to wonder what to do with the abundance of old farm equipment from this predominantly agricultural area. The Southampton County Historical Society organized a committee of interested volunteers led by William B. Simmons and, after countless volunteer hours fundraising, collecting and cleaning old equipment, the Southampton Agriculture & Forestry Museum opened its doors in 1991. The museum preserves the items necessary for survival in everyday life during the 18th and 19th centuries. Among the exhibits are several items that are the first of their kind, including the first Franklin logger. The Peanut Building showcases the prized Virginia legume's old-fashioned planting and harvesting equipment. After seeing the exhibits inside the museum, explore Heritage Village, consisting of authentic stores and buildings from the 1800s that have been moved to the site. This is a place where younger crowds may imagine the unthinkable—a life without cell phones, stereos or email. At the country store, customers purchased five-cent candy bars and steaks costing 16 cents a pound. The pre-Civil War one-room schoolhouse reveals original blackboards and schoolbooks. Be sure to peek inside the sawmill, four-seater outhouse and blacksmith's shop, too. For a fascinating look at the lives and tools of our forefathers, visit the Southampton Agriculture & Forestry Museum/Heritage Village. Open Wednesday, Saturday and Sunday, from one to five PM, March thru November.

26135 Heritage Lane, Courtland VA
(757) 653-9554

Photos by Anne W. Bryant

The Poe Museum

The Edgar Allan Poe Museum is a retreat into the world of the author of such classic tales of terror as The Tell-Tale Heart and The Cask of Amontillado. This four-building complex boasts the world's largest collection of Poe-related artifacts and memorabilia including the writer's boyhood bed, his silk vest and even a lock of hair cut from Poe's brow at the time of his death. The Poe Museum takes visitors back in time to the early 19th century by bringing together furniture, paintings and building materials from the buildings in which Poe lived and worked. Bricks from Poe's place of employment, the Southern Literary Messenger Building, were used in the construction of a Poe shrine which stands amidst an enchanted garden inspired by Poe's love poetry. Displays of his letters and manuscripts demonstrate the thought process of a gifted author who nonetheless struggled to make a living, on the verge of starvation. Virginia Poe's portrait and trinket box serve as reminders of Poe's devoted wife and cousin who married him when she was 13 and died 11 years later of tuberculosis. A photograph of Poe on display once belonged to Sarah Elmira Royster Shelton, the Richmond woman who was twice engaged to Poe but never married him. Come visit the Poe Museum where guided hourly tours bring Poe's story to life and end with a presentation of Poe's most famous poem, The Raven.

1914 E Main Street, Richmond VA
(804) 648-5523 or (888) 21E-APOE
www.poemuseum.org

Black History Museum and Cultural Center

By the end of the Civil War, the Richmond area known as Jackson Ward had so many African American business and property owners, it was locally known as Little Africa. Called the birthplace of Black capitalism thanks to five Black-owned banks that started between 1888 and 1930, this city within a city was home to 93 percent of Richmond's black population by 1920. The Black History Museum and Cultural Center of Virginia was created to showcase the works and histories of regional African Americans. Carroll W. Anderson Sr. founded the center in 1981. Museum-owned collections are exhibited in a mansion that was built in 1832. These displays teach visitors about the legacy of Jackson Ward's banks, boutiques and the popular 2nd Street area known as The Deuce. More than 100 artifacts represent six countries and 13 ethnic groups.

The museum also displays historical papers, photography, journals of Black newspapers and 20th century art. In addition, the museum presents four to six changing exhibitions each year as well as hosting a variety of educational programs. The center provides outreach through loan programs, visitation and community activities. The Black History Museum and Cultural Center is a must-see cultural experience that commemorates the lives and accomplishments of Blacks in Virginia.

00 Clay Street, Richmond VA
(804) 780-9093
www.blackhistorymuseum.org

Meadow Farm Museum

Discover what life was really like in rural Virginia during the late 1800s with a visit to the Meadow Farm Museum, where history comes alive. The Sheppard family, who acquired the acreage during the 1700s, were the original property owners, and seven generations of Sheppards were born and raised on the farm. John Mosby Sheppard (1817 to 1877) lived at Meadow Farm for most of his life, leaving to obtain a medical degree from the University of Pennsylvania in 1840 and to marry Virginia Ann Young, the daughter of a wealthy plantation owner from Caroline County, in 1846.

Meadow Farm was donated to Henrico County in 1975 by Elizabeth Adam Crump, wife of Sheppard Crump, the last adjutant general of Virginia. The estate was then made into a living museum where visitors can experience Virginia life circa 1860. The farm is listed in the National Register of Historic Places, and general admission is free. Costumed interpreters beautifully emulate characters of the past. From speech patterns to hairstyles and proper attire, these talented workers will take you back in time and leave you feeling like you have just stepped onto a working 1860s Virginia farm. Each season at Meadow Farm offers visitors a new and exciting experience. The museum offers numerous weekend programs and special events, including needlework, old-fashioned baseball games in the spring and the annual holiday Yuletide Fest. Get a taste of the good old days with a visit to Meadow Farm Museum.

3400 Mountain Road, Glen Allen VA
(804) 501-5520

Siege Museum

In 1864, the Civil War came to Petersburg in the form of a 10-month military siege that left city residents deprived of basic necessities. The story of the siege and its effects on daily civilian life is told through artifacts and writings in a permanent exhibition housed at the Siege Museum. This historic building, built circa 1839, was originally constructed as an agricultural exchange building, one of the few that still stand in the United States today. The impressive two-story rotunda was used as the main auction area with the bidders standing above the balcony. After the agricultural exchange folded in 1845, the Greek revival style building was used by various civic and commercial organizations. The city of Petersburg restored and opened the building as the Siege Museum in 1978. The permanent exhibition includes civilian and military period objects related to the ordeal of the city and life in Petersburg immediately before and after the siege. Three new, lower level galleries feature changing exhibits on 19th century history. Visitors can also view the powerful film The Echoes Still Remain, narrated by Joseph Cotton, an actor born and raised in Petersburg. Come experience the dramatic impact of the Siege Museum first-hand.

15 W Bank Street, Petersburg VA
(804) 733-2404
www.petersburg-va.org/tourism/siege.htm

The Richmond Braves—
The Diamond

Since 1966 downtown Richmond has been a place for fun family entertainment at The Diamond. Come watch the Richmond Braves play 72 home games from April to Labor Day in a stadium that seats 12,166 screaming fans. Originally called Parker Field, it was renamed The Diamond in 1985. The Richmond Braves are owned by the Atlanta Braves and are the only Triple A team owned by their parent club. They have been affiliated with Atlanta since the stadium was built. The Diamond features an old time family atmosphere, with low ticket cost and run around buses on Sundays. Some major players who have come through the Richmond Braves are Dale Murphy, John Smoltz, Chipper Jones, and Ryan Klesko. You can enjoy fireworks on the third and fourth of July every year, a salute to Hispanic Baseball Night and a salute to the Negro League's traveling museum. The Diamond is also the home of the VCV Baseball Field. General Manager Bruce Baldwin invites you to come to The Diamond with your friends and family to enjoy an exciting game played by the Richmond Braves.

3001 N Boulevard, Richmond VA
www.rbraves.com

Metro Richmond Zoo

Discover the wild on an unforgettable adventure to the Metro Richmond Zoo. Originally built and developed by an individual family who held educational programs for schoolchildren, the zoo has grown to national status. It is currently situated on 70 acres with over 160 animals including 20 on the endangered species list. Metro Richmond Zoo provides educational entertainment in a clean and wholesome atmosphere for kids and adults of all ages with a commitment to conservation. It boasts one of the largest primate collections in the country with more than 27 species. Visitors get close contact and interaction with a host of different animals and you can even feed and pet a giraffe. You can also watch animals being fed throughout the day or hop aboard the tram ride for an aerial view. The habitats are large and naturalistic and many contain multiple species, allowing for hours of viewing. Along with the primates, Rajah the white tiger is one of the most popular residents. Zebras, cheetahs, pink flamingos, rhinos and lemurs are just a few of the many animals you'll see at the Metro Richmond Zoo. Walk through an aviary for a rare view of exotic birds. The many educational programs featuring a multitude of animals offer fun and exploration in the exciting animal world. The Metro Richmond Zoo is continually growing, so gather the family and come to the zoo for a truly wild adventure.

8300 Beaver Bridge Road, Moseley VA   (804) 739-5666
www.metrorichmondzoo.com

Stingray Point Marina

Deltaville is one of three sailing centers on the Chesapeake Bay. The Stingray Point Marina is Deltaville's premier sailboat marina. Home to the Sting Ray Harbor Yacht Club, the Stingray Point Marina is located near the Mouth of Broad Creek, providing immediate access to both the Chesapeake Bay and the Rappahannock River. Built and founded by Billy Norton, The Stingray Point Marina offers 240 slips for sailors to lease on an annual basis. Owners James Rogers and Brent Halsey are dedicated to providing a quiet, scenic and secure environment in which slip holders enjoy a residential

atmosphere void of commercial intrusions. The Marina is now also home to the legendary Stingray Point Lighthouse Replica, located just a mile and a half from its original location. The first Stingray Point light was automated in 1950 and the cottage was dismantled in 1965. The replica was created from the drawings of the 1858 original and is a painstakingly exact, full-scale re-creation. The Lighthouse mini-museum is open to the public during office hours and is available to slip holders for special occasions.

PO Box 527, Deltaville VA
(804) 776-7272
www.stingraypointmarina.com

Bakeries, Coffee & Tea

Java Mio Coffeehouse and Bistro

Delectable European pastries beckon from their glass cases as you enter Java Mio Coffeehouse and Bistro. These treats are the creation of Pastry Chef Scott Davison, whose career has taken him from humble pot cleaner to Gold Medal winner at the Eastern European Culinary Olympics. In the interim, he learned his art working as an apprentice for master pastry chefs in the United States and Europe. He continues to use premium imported ingredients and has found out how to address customers' special dietary needs and extra-healthy lifestyle concerns without compromising authenticity or taste. Co-Owner Dave Cislak brought Scott and his bakery into his established coffeehouse/bistro to help bring to life his own vision of a true neighborhood gathering place: a comfortable spot for all in Petersburg's Old Town District. In the midst of an ever-changing art exhibit, local college students hang out and study or access the Internet through Java Mio's free wireless system, while working people and travelers enjoy a well-prepared meal and coffee roasted right on the premises. Java Mio is on Petersburg's Friday for the Arts gallery tour with wine-tasting available throughout the evening. Step inside Java Mio Coffeehouse and Bistro for breakfast or lunch or relax in the beautiful Old World-style courtyard while savoring what a local reviewer called, "scrumdiliumptious pastries."

322 N Sycamore Street, Petersburg VA
(804) 861-2700
www.javamio.com

Yankee Coffee Shop

The historically rich community of Petersburg offers visitors and locals alike a plethora of shopping, educational and recreational opportunities. However, no one can shop and explore forever without refueling at the neighborhood favorite Yankee Coffee Shop. This lively and charming restaurant has been open since 1976 and is currently owned by Louise and William Isham. The Yankee Coffee Shoppe serves up delicious daily specials and hearty breakfasts and lunches. Catering mostly to downtown businesses and government offices, this area favorite has served such regulars as the former mayor of Petersburg and Johnny Oates, former manager of the Texas Rangers. Much of the community considers The Yankee Coffee Shop a Petersburg institution. The friendly, cheerful staff and terrific food are consistent and the atmosphere is warm and welcoming. It does not take you long to see why the Yankee Coffee Shop is the perfect place to enjoy a flavorful meal and a great cup of coffee while taking the time to catch up with friends.

2557 S Crater Road, Petersburg VA
(804) 861-4990

Sideline Café

First and foremost, Sideline Café is a neighborhood restaurant that serves everything from freshly made burgers to she-crab soup. It's also a place with great music on the jukebox, exciting games and constant entertainment. In the evening after mealtime, Sideline becomes a true sports bar with big televisions and seats with a good view for everyone. In 2005, Sideline was a runner-up in the State Chili Cook-off. It features a large and lively menu with daily specials, homemade desserts and choices just for kids. A broad range of diners find favorite foods to enjoy in this comfortable restaurant where the chef invites customers to make special requests. "We treat you like family, but come on in anyway," jokes Owner Peggy Sanders who has continually looked for ways to improve Sideline's appeal since the restaurant opened in 1994. In addition to the televisions, dartboards and video games, she offers weekly entertainment and white tablecloth dining on Fridays and Saturdays. NASCAR is a big hit on Saturday nights and Sundays during the season. Customers also enjoy weekly karaoke and Sideline's Cruisin' Car Show, an outside exhibit of antique cars located in the restaurant's parking lot. Whether you've come to watch a football game or celebrate a special occasion with the family, Sideline will put you at ease and earn your loyalty. Visit Sideline Café and discover the delights of a restaurant that caters to the desires of its customers.

10348 Iron Bridge, Chester VA
(804) 748-4786

Chester Perk

If you're looking to liven up your day and put a spring in your step, then head to Chester Perk for a cup of fabulous coffee and a dose of great conversation. This spirited and inviting coffee house opened in September of 2005 to almost immediate success. Owner Shari Wilbur Bancroft set out to create a place where the art of conversation could be reinvented and chatty patrons could trade news over decadent desserts and distinguished coffees. She succeeded magnificently. The menu features freshly baked cookies and desserts that are created on-site in a customer visible setting and served in consumer friendly portions along with specially made, delicious chicken and seafood salads. Everything is made to order including their super smoothies and their wonderful, decadent hot chocolate, featuring homemade whipped cream. All of the coffee is shipped directly from a farm in the Dominican Republic that Shari and her husband found while on their honeymoon. Chester Perk has been featured in numerous area publications and is a favorite with local businesses as a place to hold meetings and parties. Surround yourself in Chester Perk's warm and relaxing atmosphere while enjoying its exclusive blend of coffee as well as a variety of espresso based beverages, non-coffee beverages, smoothies and teas. Treat yourself to a light fare breakfast, lunch or dinner including homemade chicken salad, seafood salad and daily soup selections. Complete your experience with an assortment of petite eats of fresh-baked cookies, cheesecake bites, brownies, breads and much more to please the palate. Come out on select Friday nights for live acoustic music. Perk up your day and connect with your neighbors at Chester's hottest new java joint, Chester Perk.

11884 Chester Village Drive, Chester VA   (804) 425-8109
www.chesterperk.com

Rostov's Coffee & Tea

Coffee and tea have been staples of numerous cultures for thousands of years. For the past quarter century, Rostov's Coffee & Tea has been at the heart of Richmond's caffeine culture. The store was originally known as Carytown Coffee and Tea but was renamed by owner Tammy Rostov in honor of her father and Rostov's founder Jay Rostov. Upon entering the store, your senses will be enveloped by the aroma of over 50 varieties of coffee cascaded along the wall. These coffees are roasted daily on the premises by a specially trained master roaster. As you delve deeper into the store, you will find a selection of premium loose teas. Rostov's offers over 60 tea varieties, among them the famous Richmond Blend tea which has been served for afternoon tea at the exclusive Jefferson Hotel for over a decade. For those who wish to sample some of the brews or simply get a cappuccino, step up to a fully equipped coffee bar with rotating coffees of the day and tea available by the cup. Rostov's also offers a wide array of accoutrements, such as teacups, coffee mugs, tea infusers, grinders and syrups. The store offers colorful gift boxes featuring their various coffee and tea products. For those that can't make it into the store, Rostov's products are available through its mail order department. Tammy and her staff are incredibly knowledgeable about all of the store's offerings. This helpful staff can aid both the beginner and the aficionado in finding the perfect brew or accessory.

1618 W Main Street, Richmond VA
(804) 355-1955 or (800) 637-6772
www.rostovs.com

Kari's Café

If you're looking for a fresh cup of coffee in Richmond, then follow your nose down Main Street to Kari's Café. Since 1998, Kari's has been providing patrons with the sustaining juice known as coffee while also offering fabulous service, friendly smiles and scrumptious baked goods and pastries. The café menu contains wonderful breakfast and lunchtime favorites such as savory homemade soup and a choice selection of gourmet sandwiches. While the coffee and espresso bar keeps corporate Richmond alert at their desks, that's not all that keeps folks going back to Kari's Café time and time again. The warm and happy atmosphere is the ideal place to escape from a hectic day and grab a relaxing lunch with co-workers. You can also sit back and rest in a cozy corner and enjoy the peace that comes from being surrounded by fresh baked cookies. Owners Kari and David Lege are focused on the continual growth of their customer base so that they can continue to keep everyone in Richmond both caffeinated and full of fresh goodies. Store Manager Shelia Wright and her cheerful staff arrive early to bake their filled croissants and pastries, usually sold right off their hot trays, fresh from the oven. Smell and taste the difference that freshness makes with the tasty delights awaiting you at Kari's Café.

801 E Main Street, Richmond VA
(804) 225-8299

Baker's Kitchen

Long ago in Rome, fertility cakes were broken over a new bride's head on her wedding day. Later, in England, new couples attempted to establish good luck by kissing over stacked cakes without knocking them down. A sympathetic visiting French chef developed the tiered cake after witnessing this ritual. Although cake decorating has evolved into an art form, there is a lengthy tradition throughout history of using the cake as a centerpiece of celebrations. Cecil Wills was no doubt aware of this when he founded Baker's Kitchen. More than a quarter of a century later, Baker's Kitchen continues to offer customers the best Mercken's chocolate, candy oils, ingredients and supplies, a variety of flavorings and custom cakes for all events. They carry an extensive inventory of Wilton cake-decorating supplies. The professional design staff at Baker's will insure a memorable creation for any occasion. Their cakes not only look divine, but taste wonderful as well. Baker's Kitchen developed a technique with a cream frosting that has the look of a smooth fondant, but with the delightful taste of butter cream. Bring them your challenge and they'll make your best dreams a reality. To make your decision easier, Baker's Kitchen offers consultation appointments to taste samples of their cakes and browse the catalog of designs. Choices can be made from the catalog, or it can be used as inspiration for an original idea. Custom designs are always encouraged at Baker's Kitchen.

3503 Courthouse Road, Richmond, VA
(804) 745-0441
www.bakerskitchen.com

Shockoe Espresso

It's time to wake up and smell the coffee, because Shockoe Espresso in Richmond has all your caffeine needs. Featuring 20 original and seven custom coffee blends, coffee and tea connoisseurs will find all their wants fulfilled here. Shockoe's location has been used for coffee blending since 1865. Roasting is done in-store at least twice a week by a highly trained roaster using select, top quality green beans. This ensures that the beans you buy are always fresh and pleasing to your taste buds. Shockoe Espresso is a member of the Mill Mountain Coffee and Tea family of gourmet coffee shops, offering a selection of coffees from Latin America, Indonesia and Africa as well as American blends. In addition to its coffee selection, Shockoe carries 40 types of tea and fresh, gourmet baked goods. Serving breakfast, lunch, dinner and dessert, Shockoe Espresso is a perfect place for meeting friends old and new. Bring your own laptop for free Internet surfing. Shockoe Espresso features live music Friday and Saturday nights. You can also purchase coffee directly by phone. Come on in and join the fun at Shockoe Espresso.

104 Shockoe Slip, Richmond VA
(804) 648-3734

Fashion

Saxon Shoes

It all started back in 1953 when, with not much more than a few dollars and a dream, Jack and Gloria Weiner opened a tiny shoe shop. Today Saxon Shoes is still owned by the same family, but has grown to be one of the largest full-service shoe and accessories stores in the country. Jack and Gloria held on to solid values and a strong commitment to service and selection. Those same values and commitment to service and excellence continue on today, through son Gary Weiner and daughter Susan Adolf. When fire destroyed their store in 2001 the Saxon family saw it as a call to action. Within months, a temporary store was opened. Like a Phoenix rising from the ashes, Saxon's superstore was rebuilt and reopened. The store now has a staff of more than 100 and nearly 80,000 pairs of shoes. With more than 200 brand names to choose from for men, women and children, there's a wider selection of shoes and styles than you would find in 10 typical shoe stores combined. And now, there are two floors of shoes, handbags, gifts and accessories in the new store. At Saxon's, their customers always come first and their team of dedicated professionals will do whatever it takes to make your visit as productive and satisfying as possible. Saxon's is well known for having hard-to-find sizes for people of any age. Stop in at Saxon Shoes, one of the largest shoe stores in America, for the ultimate shoe experience.

Short Pump Town Center
11800 W Broad Street, Richmond VA
(804) 285-3473 or (800) 686-5616
www.saxonshoes.com

Photos by Dwight Jarratt

Bygones Vintage Clothing

Established in 1979, Bygones Vintage Clothing is Richmond's favorite throwback clothing store. Bygones is located in Richmond's premier shopping destination, the Carytown district, next to Byrd Theatre, a historic movie palace. Specializing in clothing for men and women as well as fine and costume jewelry from the 1900s to the 1970s, Bygones offers a unique selection that will fascinate shoppers young and old alike as they explore the world of nostalgic chic. Bygones Vintage Clothing offers the finest attire from the jazz age to the summer of love. From gowns to gloves, tuxedos to tiaras and fishnets to fedoras, the ever-changing inventory encompasses a sentimental world of romantic regalia. An extensive selection of period jewelry is also offered with many signed pieces and suits made by famous collectible designers. Bygones is a sparkling well-organized boutique with everything categorized by era so you can easily find the treasure you're seeking. Whenever possible, an article's provenance is retained, so don't be surprised to find a note with your dress stating it was worn to an Inaugural Ball in 1938 or an Elvis concert in 1961. People come from miles away to see the window displays. Each one is a beautiful, often whimsical, diorama allowing Owner Maynee Cayton to use her personal collection of vintage mannequins. Opened by Maynee and her mother Barbara Church, Bygones Vintage Clothing has received accolades from many sources including *Southern Living* magazine. The friendly and knowledgeable staff will be happy to help you find the perfect piece for your collection, party, play, movie or wedding. Whether you are searching for a specific item or just looking to add a little charm from yesterday to today's life, you'll love Bygones Vintage Clothing.

2916 W Cary Street,
Richmond VA
(804) 353-1919
www.bygonesvintage.com

Ciao

If you're tired of carbon copy styles and uninspiring frocks, then take a trip to Ciao in Richmond. Owner Cathy Redding and her partner Patty Gray have created a fun and classy boutique featuring European lines, fabrics and designs that you just can't find anywhere else. They carry choice clothing selections designed for ladies 40 and up that are versatile and appropriate year-round. Ciao doesn't stock the frumpy and fashion-deficient fripperies of yesteryear, but instead provides a resource for sophisticated, fashionable and sexy clothing for today's woman. Ciao has many loyal customers who return often, knowing they will find the best selection and honest advice about what styles work on their figures. Since the shop opened in 2002, many of the customers have become like an extended family for Cathy. "No one here will tell you something looks good on you unless it truly does," says Cathy, who prides herself on providing exemplary and honest customer service to all the ladies who stop in. Ciao's inventory runs the gamut from jeans and t-shirts to ritzy cocktail dresses. Cathy renews her inspiration semiannually with a trip to the Coterie show in New York City, where European designers go to show off their latest creations. She also makes sure to stop by SoHo and Greenwich Village, where she can keep her finger on the pulse of fashion. Add color, whimsy and style to your wardrobe with a visit to Ciao.

3313 W Cary Street, Richmond VA
(804) 342-7422

Shoe Box

It seems like fashion trends change by the week these days, and it can be very difficult to keep up with what's hot and what's not. Luckily, The Shoe Box, located in The Shops at Libbie and Grove, has a wide selection of elegant and classic footwear and decorative accessories that will make any outfit shine. President Roma Marshall has an inherent flair for fashion and has enjoyed a long career in the fashion industry. The Shoe Box opened in 1995 and has since gained a loyal following of faithful customers. Part of the reason for her extended popularity is due to the fact that Roma is diligent about service, comfort and fit, therefore she is always happy to spend the extra time it takes to ensure that you have exactly what you need. Many of the ladies who come to the shop will bring in an entire ensemble or wardrobe so that Roma can help them to choose the ideal shoes and accoutrements. In conjunction with the shop's extensive selection of footwear and both fine and costume jewelry, The Shoe Box further offers a wide range of great handbags and purses that are as practical as they are stylish. Roma feels that it's important to sift through the ever-changing trends and focus instead on what works for you. With help from Roma, that advice is easier than ever to follow, so come by today and find your style at The Shoe Box.

401 Libbie Avenue, Richmond VA   (804) 288-2303

Lex's of Carytown

Fun, funky and affordable designer clothing is what you will find at Lex's of Carytown. After years of visiting the New York garment district, Owner Lisa took her vast knowledge of fashion and opened her own location. Taking fashion from Los Angeles to New York and settling it all in one store, her clothes come directly from the runway to the rack. Lex's is filled with bright colors, unusual designer clothing and selections that change constantly to ensure no one else has your style. This is the height of fashion, from prom gowns to cocktail party dresses. These are the kinds of clothes you can express yourself in and still stay elegant. While visiting Lex's be sure not to pass up their array of accessories to complement your attire. Show off your imagination and create your own custom handbags or choose from the wide selection on-site. Complete your ensemble with shoes, wraps and jewelry. Let Lex's of Carytown be your guide in the world of fashion.

3020 West Cary Street, Richmond VA
(804) 355-5425
www.lexsofcarytown.com

Chic Chapeau

In some circles, the distinction between well dressed and dressed-up is ultimately decided by a hat. Chic Chapeau in Richmond provides fabulous hats in an endless array of creatively embellished and fashioned headwear. The milliners of Chic Chapeau have designed head adornments for such personalities as a princess in Granada and cousins of the Queen of England, as well as the hat-wearing public at home. The premise behind Chic Chapeau goes beyond making hats to sell. The hats are a statement of the wearer's personality and a means for expression. A hat can project a strong presence by its design and the materials used in its creation. The first hat sold here was the Duchess, a fancifully gilded, extremely slanted, wide-brimmed piece of lavish feminine coquetry. The maker of the Duchess is fulfilling her personal destiny with each newly fashioned headpiece. As a child, the inspired designer concocted hats from anything she could find, including Clorox bottles, burlap bags and brown paper bags. Chic Chapeau boasts two gifted milliners and with designers of such devotion, their results are superlative. Whether you are a regular hat wearer or new to the experience, Chic Chapeau is the place to find your own signature design.

200 E Grace Street, Richmond VA
(804) 643-3399

Monkeys

In a historic house in the West End of Richmond, you will find a unique women's clothing boutique named Monkeys. A Richmond tradition, Monkeys has been stylishly outfitting women for more than 21 years. The boutique, which specializes in fashions for all ages, is well known for its distinctive sportswear and eveningwear. The knowledgeable staff will solve any fashion need and are eager to specially design a look, order in any size and fit you for every event. Monkeys also carries locally designed jewelry, fetching shoes, tasteful lingerie and an assortment of handbags and accessories. Whether you are looking for a gift or something to shake up your wardrobe, stop by and let the Monkeys staff help you select something special that will set you apart.

**306 Libbie Avenue,
Richmond VA
(804) 228-3131**

Wagner Jewelers

Wagner Jewelers in Ashland has been creating one-of-a-kind, custom pieces since 1981. They know how to make your jewelry dreams into a reality of precious metals. With a combination of skill and imagination they creatively solve any challenges their customers bring to them, whether it's designing a whole new piece or changing an existing one. These ingenious crafts-ladies will draw sketches, brainstorm, create and then fabricate amazing new pieces that come to life in a three-dimensional form. The atmosphere is fun and playful with music in the background that enhances the creative process and inspires the customers and jewelers alike. Mirrors abound throughout the store allowing customers to "play" and try on jewelry to their hearts content, while sharing their ideas with the jewelers and owners Susannah Wagner and Elizabeth Spahr. This allows for the customer and designers to make the best choices of materials and design concepts to suit each individuals needs. The ladies will even create custom ring settings with botanicals, fish, hunting dogs, deer or car gears for men's wedding bands. They have also made landscapes using colored diamonds for streams running through the trees of a forest. Additionally, they take themes from nature, hobbies, or careers and make special occasion items such as retirement gifts. Wagner Jewelers can work with almost any idea and make it a beautiful and lasting piece that will be enjoyed for years to come. Several times per year the owners throw an open-house party to display new collections. Let your imagination soar and then take your jewelry design challenges to Wagner Jewelers.

107 Hanover Avenue, Ashland VA   (804) 798-5864

Galleries & Fine Art

Brazier Fine Art

Brazier Fine Art is Richmond's gallery of original realist and impressionist oil paintings and sculpture. The gallery represents more than 40 nationally known artists from across the country as well as Russia, Canada, Mexico, Hungary and Spain. Works include landscape, figure, interior and still life paintings as well as bronze sculpture. New exhibitions are presented throughout the year featuring one or more artists, but works by all of the gallery's artists are on view at all times. The gallery is divided into room-like sections, all painted a different color and accessorized with antiques and furnishings to give it the appearance of a home or office setting. The studio of award-winning painter and portrait artist, Loryn Brazier, is housed within the gallery. Her works are in major collections including the Smithsonian National Portrait Gallery. However, you can say you saw it first when you visit Brazier Fine Art.

3401 W Cary Street, Richmond VA   (804) 359-2787
www.brazierfineart.com

Melinda's

Do you have a great old painting or a new addition to your collection? Melinda Tennis can make your artwork look its best. Melinda's can turn your artwork into an heirloom you will be proud to pass on to your children. Melinda takes extraordinary care with each object she frames. She uses archival quality materials for matting, framing and glazing. Melinda is an expert in French line matting, a style that is contemporaneous with the 18th and 19th century art she often frames, which can enhance the presentation of the work. An enormous selection of frame corner samples are arrayed on the walls behind the design table. In addition to framing services, the shop is a gallery. When you walk through the door, you see a full wall of original paintings and watercolors by local artists. On the other wall is a display of antique prints, matted and framed in different styles to show the many possibilities available. Melinda's offers 19th century *Vanity Fair* lithographs from England, copper engravings from the 17th to 20th centuries and architectural engravings. Other holdings include 19th century botanical engravings and lithographs, as well as 18th and 19th century maps. Melinda's is located in Historic Downtown Lynchburg, in an 1880s building she has almost finished renovating. Come to Melinda's and let her add beauty to your life.

1019 Church Street, Lynchburg VA
(434) 528-1329
melindasframe@earthlink.net

Rentz Gallery

People can pass by the picture windows that wrap around the Rentz Gallery only so many times before they're compelled to stop in. Rentz Gallery Director Jennifer Glave Kocen attests that every day a new patron walks through the front door and compliments the exhibit and the space. This inspiring contemporary art gallery specializes in sculpture, glasswork and paintings. Since its inception in 2003, the gallery has become prominent in the Richmond art community due to a magnificent partnership between Kocen and Robert Rentz of Robert Rentz Interiors. Although 1700 square feet is dedicated exhibit space, the gallery includes additional space where Kocen and Rentz work together pairing art with handmade furniture and accessories. This section is constantly updated, making it worthwhile to visit the gallery often. Featuring both established and emerging artists, Rentz Gallery displays work from around the globe. Among the featured artists is Sheep Jones of the Washington D.C. area. Her oil and mixed media works have been exhibited on both the East and West Coasts, and she received The Torpedo Factory's Artist of the Year award and was included in its New American Paintings magazine. Primitive figurative sculptor Mark Chatterly hails from Michigan and was recently the subject of a PBS documentary. He says of his work, "I am looking for visual speed bumps, images that slow me down to take a closer look, work that allows me in without explaining everything at first glance." Mark's enchanting work and many others will entice you to take a closer look at the Rentz Gallery.

1700 W Main Street, Richmond VA
(804) 358-5338
www.rentzgallery.com

Friday for the Arts!

The secret is getting out. Petersburg is more than an historically-rich and architecturally-graced city on the banks of the beautiful Appomattox River, it's home to *Friday for the Arts!* This monthly arts gala transforms the evening of the second Friday of every month into a standing date to be in Old Towne Petersburg. From six until 10 pm, art lovers from Petersburg and throughout the regional community make downtown Petersburg their destination. From the Petersburg Regional Art Center, which represents the talent of 70 artists in studios on several floors of the former Butterworth's building, to the Petersburg Area Art League, a gallery and studio representing area talent since the 1930s, there is quality art for every taste. The settings for the art are as varied as the art itself. From the environment of a warm and eclectic coffee house, which provides wine tastings beginning at five pm, to the beauty of a quality antique shop in the setting of an early 19th century Federal building; from the gallery space in the William R. McKenney Library, to the palette of soft patina plasterwork and warm-hued brickwork in a prominent, landmark building (incorporating both gallery, shop, restaurant and jazz club), the evening provides an energized and festive atmosphere. You can leisurely stroll amongst the various venues, perhaps catching the mellow sounds of the saxophone performed by local talent, or take a seat on the free Arts Bus which offers easy transportation between all participating locations. The wide selection of artistic styles is complemented by an international selection of dining options and a wide variety of live musical performances. Come and experience the pulse of an arts community in the heart of an historic setting and realize a true renaissance at *Friday for the Arts!*

400 E Washington Street, Petersburg VA
(804) 733-2400
www.petersburg-va.org

Judy Newcomb Gallery Fine Art and Framing

Judy Newcomb Gallery Fine Art and Framing in Richmond was created to champion creativity by providing value-conscious high quality custom framing, oil painting and frame restoration, quality art and prints. The gallery is owned and operated by Judy Newcomb and her husband Don. The first location opened its doors in 1996, and they now have two locations to serve their customers' needs. Judy Newcomb Gallery's friendly and knowledgeable staff is

always on hand to assist you in creating designs that will complement your decor and express your individual style. Judy, a well-known Richmond artist for more than 30 years, displays many of her paintings along with other prominent local and national artists. Judy Newcomb Gallery was voted The Best in Richmond for quality custom framing, consultation and art design. This popular neighborhood business is also highly involved in the community and donates to many local charities. Although Judy and Don have endured setbacks, including a fire that destroyed all but one of her original paintings, they continue to strive toward enriching the lives of their neighbors and community by offering the very best in products and service and by reaching out to those in need. Life is a journey that is best enjoyed one moment at a time. Make those moments last forever at Judy Newcomb Gallery Fine Art and Framing.

11382 Mall Drive, Richmond VA
(804) 794-6001
9125N West Broad Street, Richmond VA
(804) 527-0701
www.tgfu.com

Quirk Gallery

If you would like a fresh perspective on the gallery scene, take a walk down Richmond's Broad Street Corridor. Quirk Gallery, the latest addition to this art-filled community, offers patrons a whole new way of experiencing art. The gallery will feature exhibits by both known and emerging American and international artists. "Quirk's artists are chosen for uninhibited use of material and forms, for juxtaposition of tradition and experimentation and for refinement of vision and skill," says Gallery Director Kathy Emerson. Individual collections appear in the Cabinet of Curiosities, an idea based on a Renaissance custom of placing random, eclectic pieces together in a single display. The gallery shop offers a carefully edited selection of beautiful handmade things. Its inaugural show at the beginning of 2006 called Watt's Up? featured a fantastic collection of chandeliers created by 18 artists and proved the Quirk philosophy that play can be serious and art can be light. Quirk Gallery will participate in Broad Street Corridor's First Friday events. The first Friday of each month from September through June, all of the galleries in the surrounding urban community hold an open house where patrons can stroll through each of the galleries and enjoy everything the Richmond art scene has to offer. Explore the world of art from a slightly different point of view at Quirk Gallery.

311 W Broad Street, Richmond VA
(804) 644-5450
www.quirkgallery.com

Uptown Gallery

Uptown Gallery provides affordable art you can love and live with. Located in the uptown section of Richmond, you will find the gallery in a row of brightly painted houses. Uptown Gallery features a 19th century salon-style gallery that displays the work of local artist members. There are six shows a year in the main gallery. The shows typically feature two artists but also include many others. Additional shows in the loft feature students from the Governor's School and Richmond High School along with other special displays. Uptown Gallery sponsors workshops and promotes art in the greater Richmond area. It also provides art classes, demonstrations and studio rentals. The cooperative style of the gallery allows each visitor to both view the art and meet the artists who created it. Uptown Gallery is open Tuesday through Saturday and the first Friday evening of every month, so stop by for a truly personal art experience.

1305 W Main Street, Richmond VA
(804) 353-8343
www.uptownartgallery.com

Corporate & Museum Frame and Gallery

One of the most important aspects of displaying a painting or photograph is proper framing. At Corporate & Museum Frame and Gallery in Richmond, experts specialize in the art of choosing the proper frame. The process begins with making sure they select the appropriate materials, based on the period of the work, the culture, the medium and the skills, style and technique of the artist. Then they painstakingly create the ideal frame. The majority of their clientele are corporations and institutions. However, they also have a loyal following among serious collectors and private artists. Owner Joseph Johnson was a frustrated artist who couldn't afford to frame his own work until he realized he could do it himself. He opened the doors to Corporate & Museum Frame and Gallery in 1992. For more than 10 years he has continued to build upon his reputation for excellence. Using state-of-the-art equipment, mature framing skills and informed design styles, Johnson consistently produces top quality frames that enhance the work they surround. The gallery features world-class photography with a focus on Virginia talent. Johnson also uses his facility to teach classes on frame selection and history. He is a certified picture framer and a member of the American Institute of Conservation. Fine art and photography deserve equally fine framing so take your treasures to Corporate & Museum Frame and Gallery.

301 W Broad Street, Richmond VA
(804) 643-6858
www.corporatemuseumframe.com

Petersburg Area Art League

On November 30, 1934, Miss Anna Mercer Dunlop and nearly 20 others gathered at Miss Anna's studio to establish an organization dedicated to the promotion of art and art interests. A committee was chosen and the Petersburg Art Guild was formed. Over the next few decades both the location and the name changed and it emerged as the Petersburg Area Art League, or PAAL, in 1960. Over the years, PAAL has organized numerous art walks and shows for the community. Today, its focus is still on the promotion of artistic interests. The art league gained a permanent home in 1970 when then-president Walter H. Brown purchased an East Old Street building which he leased to the league for

99 years. Time marched on and the league sponsored many events that engaged the community and featured numerous artists. On August 6, 1993, tragedy stuck the art league in the form of a tornado that destroyed the building and the artwork housed inside. Fortunately, much of the permanent collection had been taken in for restoration, and five months after the destruction the league hosted a survivors of the tornado event. Only slightly daunted, PAAL's intrepid leaders marched on, and today the East Old Street location houses not only fabulous exhibits filled with the work of extremely talented artists, but classes for budding artists of all ages. Experience both magnificent art and an interesting history with a visit to the Petersburg Area Art League.

7 E Old Street, Petersburg VA
(804) 861-4611

Health & Beauty

Textures

Textures Salon and Day Spa in Richmond offers full range of spa treatments for the whole family. Owners, Becky Mitchell and Susan Sayle along with their professional and personable staff strive to provide nothing but the best customer service, products and treatments available. Additionally, they have a focus toward making the salon a truly fun and relaxing place to be. When you first arrive, you will be greeted at the door and ushered into welcoming environment where you will be offered refreshments and a choice selection of reading material. In the salon, you can choose from a nice selection of services including Color, Cuts, Permanent Waves, Thermal Straightening, Special Occasion Styles, Waxing, and Bare Minerals Make-Up Applications. Textures always has Redken Master Specialists on hand. Get pampered in the Spa with a Relaxing massage, Reflexology or Hot Stone Therapy. Spa Packages are also available. After your massage enjoy a pedicure and/or manicure, featuring Bella Lucce and OPI products. The Spa further offers a wide selection of Bioelements Facials that will leave your skin fresh, glowing and healthy. For the body Textures Salon and Day Spa provides a series of full body treatments such as Aromatherapist Oil Wrap, a Herbology Body Wrap that revitalizes and Trissage Body Smoothing. Don't forget the finishing touches that keep you feeling your best such as the Herbology Hand Retexturizer or Lip-Conditioning Treatments. Indulge yourself the way you deserve to be indulged at Textures Salon and Day Spa.

8320 Staples Road
Richmond, VA 23228
(804) 264-7071
www.Texturesdayspa.com

Slip Salon

You are invited to come enjoy a one-of-a-kind spa experience at Slip Salon. Located in the historic Shockoe Slip district, Slip Salon is downtown Richmond's only complete spa. Surrounded by history and culture, the salon strives to create a relaxing and soothing atmosphere from the moment you walk through the door. The spa's open space welcomes you in with a warm and inviting sense of style and a spacious waiting area that is just the beginning of your journey. By utilizing the latest in cutting edge coloring and cutting techniques for men and women, the talented staff of professionals will create a look that is just right for you whether you are in the mood for a complete makeover, a style update or anything in between. Next, slip into the spa area where the staff is ready to pamper you from head to toe. Customized facials and body treatments revitalize your skin while Slip Salon's massages, manicures and pedicures offer a refreshing release from the stress of everyday life. The salon offers complete waxing services for both men and women. Choose from one of its popular packages or create one of your own to experience the best of everything Slip Salon has to offer. An on-site wedding coordinator will also help you choose packages for the bride, groom and entire bridal party and make sure that your special day starts off beautifully. Call to make your reservation, and come and be a guest at Slip Salon.

1331 E Cary Street, Richmond VA   (804) 343-SLIP (7547)
www.slipsalon.net

Yoga Source

Richmond's premiere yoga center, Yoga Source, offers over 50 classes per week along with specialized workshops and Yoga Alliance-certified teacher training programs. Owners Anne Battle and Lynn Brooke opened the center in 2000 as a place to cultivate health, expand consciousness and facilitate spiritual and psychological growth. Yoga Source offers classes that will benefit people from all walks of life and all experience levels. The studio offers several different styles of yoga, including Anusara, which blends movement and grace with universal principles of alignment; Ashtanga, which emphasizes linking breath with movement through a set series of postures and Iyengar, which focuses on alignment and precision within the postures. Still other yoga styles taught at the studio are Vinyasa Flow, likened to dynamic dance, and Yin, a quiet practice revolving around long-held, passive poses. The studio's Kids, Tweens and Teens program is ideal for helping youngsters build focus and concentration and improve self-awareness and confidence. Yoga Source also offers plenty of beginning and introductory classes as well as prenatal yoga and periodic workshops such as Yoga for Stiff Guys and yoga for anxiety, depression and meditation. Weekend workshops with nationally and internationally known yoga instructors complement the teacher training program and provide unique opportunities for local yoga students. Find out for yourself how yoga can help to improve and add balance to your life with the classes and fabulous, professional staff at Yoga Source.

3122 W Cary Street, Suite 220, Richmond VA
(804) 359-YOGA (9642) *www.yogarichmond.com*

Home & Garden

Sutherland's Tavern Antiques

Sutherland's Tavern Antiques is located in Historic Fork Inn, a 204-year-old plantation house and tourist attraction. What better way to view 19th- and early 20th-century furniture and decorative arts than in an authentic 1803 plantation house, similar to the actual setting the pieces were first created for and enjoyed in? Perhaps none, think Darrell and Michelle Olgers, owners of one of Central Virginia's newest and most unique antique stores. They have spent a decade restoring Fork Inn, Darrell's family home, where they and their young daughter reside. After having a successful antique shop in nearby Old Towne Petersburg for five years, Darrell decided to move his business in 2005 into one half of their 14-room plantation house. He changed its name to Sutherland's Tavern Antiques to reflect one of the two names the house went by, when it served as an inn, tavern, post office and U.S. Army hospital during the Civil War. Today, Sutherland's Tavern Antiques offers quality estate items rescued from homes, barns and attics all over the East Coast. "Our goal is to maintain an inventory of furniture and decorative arts that date from the late 1700s through the early 1900s," says Darrell. "Our inventory regularly includes cupboards, desks, tables, servers, sideboards and early painted furniture. We also offer a selection of quality pre-owned Suter's and Henkel Harris hand-crafted furniture." They also have three barns packed to the rafters with furniture in the rough, early home salvage and architectural elements, including mantles, doors, door locks, hinges and hardware. An avid clock and pocket watch collector, Darrell usually has a large assortment of both for sale in the shop, along with Civil War and other military items, another passion of his. Guests are often invited in to see the rest of the house, each room furnished with late 18th-century and early 19th-century pieces. During the warmer months, Olgers Store Museum is open across the street, where visitors can experience a personal collection of oddities, historic newspapers, local memorabilia and more. Sutherland's Tavern Antiques is open Saturday from 10 am to 5 pm, Sunday from 1 pm to 5 pm and by chance or appointment. As long as they're at home, they'd be glad to show you around.

19621 Namozine Road (corner of Rt. 460), Sutherland VA 23885   (804) 943-2283
www.circa1803@hotmail.com

Green Front Furniture Company, Inc.

Known for high-end furniture, fine oriental rugs and home accessories from around the world, the Green Front Furniture Company, Inc. has 700,000 square feet of retail space. Located in the downtown district of Farmville, Green Front Furniture is not just a conventional retailer. The company is a shopping attraction with merchandise displayed in 12 buildings encompassing several blocks. Green Front Furniture carries only high-quality merchandise, and is best known for its comfortable flea market atmosphere and charming, old tobacco warehouse buildings. Fifty percent of the customers who visit Green Front Furniture live outside of Virginia. Green Front Furniture has established itself as a real shopping destination. The company also has an unbelievable selection of handmade oriental rugs at a third to half of the prices of a normal retail store. The oriental rugs are imported directly from India, Pakistan, Nepal and Iran. With more than 100 employees, Green Front Furniture also has two satellite stores located in Sterling, Virginia and in Raleigh, North Carolina. Green Front Furniture has been selling furniture since 1960 and is still growing. In recent years, Green Front Furniture has consistently ranked in the top 100 furniture retailers nationwide in gross sales according to *Furniture Today*. This company defies conventional business wisdom. In the beginning, only promotional items were sold. The company's owner, Richard F. Crallé, Jr., then discovered that the formula for success was to accept a smaller profit margin and to buy in volume, thus passing the savings on to the consumer. Customers love the ever-changing displays, relaxed atmosphere with no pressure to buy, open rooms with vast selections, and the unique mixture of products. When you are ready for deeply discounted prices on fine quality furniture, accessories and oriental rugs, come explore Green Front Furniture Company, Inc.

316 N Main Street, Farmville VA
(434) 392-5943
www.greenfront.com

Village Garden Greenhouses & Flower Shop, LLC

In the heart of Virginia lies the sleepy little tourist town of Appomattox, where our nation reunited and a young entrepreneur could build a dream. In 2000, then 17 year-old Christina opened her first of four greenhouses to the public. She envisioned a garden village filled with unique and interesting plants, trees, shrubs, herbs, water gardens and supplies in the years to come, hence the name, Village Garden Greenhouses. Attracting gardeners both far and wide, Village Garden has thrived. In 2003, her mother, Lisa and sisters, Tiffany and Whitney, all bringing different talents, joined her for an ideal family-run business. Christina and her family have proven that dreams do still come true. Today, Village Garden is a fully stocked garden center where nursery plants, a full-service florist and gift shop, garden supplies and touring gardens intermingle. Much like a small town, customers really do stroll through many distinct areas, shops and gardens. Whether by phone, e-mail, the ever-popular web, or in person, be sure to keep in touch with the friendly folks at the Village Garden Greenhouses & Flower Shop.

Rt. 3, Box #354, Appomattox VA
(434) 352-5889
VillageGardn@aol.com
www.VillageGardn.com

Lavender Fields Herb Farm

Lavender Fields Herb Farm is the ideal place to while away the hours and relax while taking in the splendor of the beautiful grounds and the refreshing scents of fresh herbs. Lavender Fields Herb Farm is owned by husband and wife team Stan and Nicole Schermerhorn on a piece of family property that was deeded to Stan's great-great-grandfather. Nicole, a native Australian, met Stan while on vacation. They got married and then decided that they would open a business where they could work and be together. Stan had dreamed of being a farmer since his youth and accredits his interest to *Progressive Farmer* magazine. In 1997 that dream became a reality and they opened Lavender Fields Herb Farm. The couple celebrated two new additions in 2003, the first being their son Luke and the second a local business named A Thyme to Plant Herb Farm, which they purchased and moved to their already existing farm. At Lavender Fields Herb Farm and A Thyme to Plant Herb Farm you will find a wide range of gifts including sculpture, artwork and pottery from local artisans and an array of other handmade items that adhere to the lavender theme. The farm carries over 200 varieties of herbs and sells flavorful honey from seven on-site hives. They also host numerous classes and special events throughout the year and have terrific shipping and mail-order services for your convenience. Please come and enjoy the world of Lavender Fields Herb Farm and A Thyme to Plant Herb Farm.

11300 Winfrey Road, Glen Allen VA   (804) 262-7167   www.lavenderfieldsfarm.com

Ladybug Cottage & Garden

The family owned and operated Ladybug Cottage & Garden offers an extensive array of home décor, garden and gift items that will add whimsy and elegance to any home. Susan Lassiter started the business in 2003 after 20 years as a window treatment designer. She works alongside family members Margie Lloyd, Sharon Boyd, Brandy Ezzell and Kay Carroll to offer only the best quality plants and products to her loyal customers. All of the plants at Ladybug Cottage come from local growers, and include rare flora and decorative trees like Japanese maples. Ladybug Cottage & Garden's gift and home décor departments offer a sizeable collection of lamps, occasional tables, figurines and other exciting treasures that come and go quickly. Ladybug Cottage & Garden also provides a full-service interior design shop that can help you with everything from elaborate window dressings to quaint dried floral arrangements. Gift wrapping is always free at Ladybug Cottage. The store's distinctive gift bags, complete with colored tissue and curled ribbons, will have friends clamoring in delight to see what's inside. The women of Ladybug Cottage & Garden will welcome you in with true Southern hospitality that includes a hearty smile and complementary coffee, iced tea or lemonade. Meet the family and explore the frequently changing wonders waiting for you at Ladybug Cottage & Garden.

606 England Street, Ashland VA
(804) 752-3510

Tom French: Flowers

Tom French: Flowers truly embodies its slogan of "classic design, Southern charm." Owner Tom Binns believes that flowers are an integral part of celebrating life and love and can provide romantic and exquisite bouquets for your memories. Tom French: Flowers does only flowers, and they are superlative in their field. The arrangements are elegant, European in design and beautiful adornments for any day. Christmas is Tom's favorite season and he loves doing special arrangements. Tom French: Flowers is a garden-inspired shop that features poetic floral arrangements, clear glass vases and delivery to Richmond and the surrounding areas. When you are looking for the finest in flower arrangements for a wedding, party or other special event, you will want to turn to Tom French: Flowers. Located one and a half blocks north of Cary Street in Carytown, Tom French: Flowers is not to be missed, whether you are looking for that perfect arrangement for your special day or a unique and beautiful enhancement for your every day.

17 N Belmont Avenue, Richmond VA
(804) 278-9420

Vogue Flowers

Richmond Magazine has chosen Vogue Flowers & Gifts as the Number One Florist in Richmond for eight consecutive years. With the kind of services Vogue provides, it's easy to see why. Steve

Papoulakos has been building his fine reputation in the flower business for 20 years and offers a number of services you're not likely to find elsewhere. His florists specialize in European floral design. They work with businesses to create interior plantscapes or custom floral and plant arrangements complete with scheduled maintenance services. Steve also has a reminder service to help clients remember important dates and events for sending floral gifts. He carries a huge variety of flowers from around the world as well as locally grown plants and imports his flowers directly from the growers so that they're fresher and less expensive. His designers can provide beautiful arrangements for any occasion. Vogue also has a large selection of gift baskets, fruit baskets and holiday decorations and works with both FTD and Teleflora for prompt delivery anywhere in the country. If you need to say it with flowers, let Vogue interpret the message for you!

(800) 923-1010
www.vogueflowers.com

Chadwick & Son Orchids

With two locations in central Virginia, Chadwick's is the largest retail orchid nursery in the state with 10 greenhouses in Powhatan County and a showroom in Richmond. The company was founded in 1989 by Art Chadwick Sr. and his son, Arthur, who purchased 18 acres of farmland and built the first greenhouse. The early success of the company can be attributed to Art Sr., who has been growing orchids since 1945 and provides invaluable cultural and hybridizing experience. His many Cattleya hybrids adorn the pages of orchid magazines worldwide and he continues to be a regular feature writer for the American Orchid Society. In 2006, his first book, *The Classic Cattleyas*, was published and he personally signs copies at flower shows. Art Jr. writes a monthly orchid culture question and answer column for the *Richmond Times Dispatch* and frequently speaks to plant societies and garden clubs. In 2005, he traveled to France to address the World Orchid Conference. Today, visitors enjoy the personalized tours of the greenhouses where they often bring friends and make a day of it. They are amazed at the enormity of the boarding operation where over 10,000

plants are currently being grown for customers. The retail store is located in Richmond's historic fan district and is a showroom of the best orchids along with tasteful botanical artwork and accessories, all in a friendly museum-like environment. Both locations offer a tremendous selection of blooming orchid plants and the knowledgeable staff can answer the most challenging horticultural questions.

1240 Dorset Road, Powhatan VA (Greenhouses)
(804) 598-7560 or (800) 771-9113
203 N Belmont Avenue, Richmond VA (Retail Store)
(804) 359-6724
www.chadwickorchids.com

Lifestyle Destinations

Woodlake Community Association

"Come home to life the way it should be" is Woodlake's motto and nearly 2,800 families do just that each day. Woodlake is a planned community unsurpassed in the range and diversity of homes it offers. Whether you're looking for a starter home, a spacious family home, or a lakefront showplace, there is something for every lifestyle and budget. Neighborhoods are nestled within 400 acres of beautiful wooded common areas that border the 1,700 acre Swift Creek Reservoir. Families enjoy the sense of community and security that comes from living in an intergenerational melting pot where singles, families, and retirees enjoy life in a neighborhood with a small town, all-American feel. Woodlake offers two award-winning elementary schools, a large daycare center, 15 neighborhood tot-lots, a community church, shopping, clubs, and organizations. An active homeowners association sponsors community events and concerts throughout the spring and summer at the waterfront pavilion and amphitheater. The community includes three outdoor pools, one indoor Olympic pool, a complete fitness center, fourteen tennis courts, nine miles of bike and jogging trails, private boating and mooring facilities, and nine fishing piers along five miles of shoreline. Woodlake was voted Best Community in America in 1990 by the Community Associations Institute and has been featured in a number of popular publications. It was named one of the 20 Hot Places to Live and one of the 99 Best Residential & Recreational Communities in America for Vacation Retirement and Investment Planning. As one of the most successful planned communities in the United States it is one of the hottest real estate values today. Whatever your heart is looking for in a home, you will find it in Woodlake.

14900 Lake Bluff Parkway, Midlothian VA
(804) 739-4344 *www.woodlakeonline.com*

Brandermill

Enjoy life surrounded by the natural beauty of woodlands and water in Brandermill, named the Best Planned Community in America by *Better Homes & Gardens*® in 1978, just four years after its inception. Since then, Brandermill has set the standard for quality living in a resort environment. Bordering the lovely 1,700-acre Swift Creek Reservoir, this sylvan community encompasses 2,800 acres and features four fabulous swimming pools, two clubhouses and a championship golf course designed by Gary Player. Conveniently located 15 miles from Richmond, Brandermill offers 3,700 distinctive homes, quality schools, fine restaurants, retail shops, churches and a retirement community. A haven for outdoor enthusiasts, the community boasts 456 acres of wooded common areas, 15 miles of nature trails, playgrounds, picnic pavilions and fishing piers as well as a sailing center with rental boats. In addition, Brandermill is home territory to blue herons, osprey, beavers and a variety of fish including citation bass. Every year, bald eagles visit the reservoir for prime fishing. The site is also home to one of Virginia's most remarkable trees, a huge swamp chestnut oak believed to be over 300 years old. Highly community oriented, Brandermill plays host to numerous special events throughout the year including concerts, plays, golf and fishing tournaments, sailing regattas, holiday celebrations and charity outreach programs. Come be a part of a nature lover's paradise and live the life you've always dreamed of in Brandermill.

3001 E Boundary Terrace, Midlothian VA
(804) 744-1035
www.brandermill.com

Beaufont Towers Retirement Community

After you have seen the apartments at Beaufont Towers, tasted the food and checked the activities calendar, you are left with one big question, is this really a retirement community, or is it a resort? Since 1982, the people behind Beaufont Towers have been providing high quality care while enriching the lives of seniors in Virginia. Yes, this is a retirement community, offering both independent, assisted living and Alzheimer's care options. However, your confusion is understandable. From the beautiful gardens to the Southern hospitality of the staff, this is fine living in an inspiring environment. Whether residents enjoy three meals per day, or decide to do their own cooking, since apartments feature a full kitchen, they are always well fed. Amenities may include weekly housekeeping, linen and personal laundry service. There is always something fun going on here. A typical day begins with exercises for the body and games for the brain. Later, a local chef might drop by for a cooking demonstration. In the afternoon, a musician might lead a Patsy Cline sing-a-long. If that is not enough for one day you could hop on the Beaufont van heading to the ballpark for the Richmond Braves' game. For a youthful approach to retirement living, visit Beaufont Towers Retirement Community today.

7015 Carnation Street, Richmond VA
(804) 320-1412 *www.rui.net*

Chippendale Retirement Center

Chippendale Retirement Center is conveniently located near major roadways, shopping and dining facilities. The Center possesses a personable, homelike atmosphere on one level, with no stairs to navigate. Each staff member is very friendly, family-oriented and personally knows each resident by name. Each resident is treated with compassion, consideration and respect. Residents are provided home cooked meals in a dining room setting. Occupational therapy, speech therapy and physical therapy are provided by home health agencies. Amenities include a 24-hour emergency call system, 24-hour supervision and personal care, total medication management, a beauty shop, complete housekeeping services and daily activities. Residential and assisted living are offered at one flat rate. The center offers the help you need, as well as the independence that you want, while maintaining your personal dignity. Families are encouraged to visit often and visitors are welcomed anytime. The staff at Chippendale Retirement Center invites you to take a tour so that you can see for yourself what makes this retirement facility exceptional.

4931 Ridgedale Parkway, Richmond VA
(804) 271-8000

Markets

Plantation Peanuts of Wakefield

In 1842 Dr. Matthew Hargis of Wakefield grew the nation's first commercial crop of peanuts, which was the onset of a southeastern Virginia tradition that lives on today. Plantation Peanuts of Wakefield, located only a few miles from Dr. Hargis' original farm, has been offering their customers an exquisite sampling of perfectly prepared, cream of the crop peanuts for more than 25 years. Owners Edwin and Tammy Goodrich, grandchildren of Gurney Goodrich, designer and patentee of one of the first mechanical peanut diggers, began as a mail-order only company in 1980 but quickly grew to include a retail store front, due to increased demand and interest from local residents. The Goodriches have since made five additions to the original building and make shipments to peanut lovers across the globe. Using only top quality, locally grown and extra large peanuts, the Goodriches hand prepare each batch to ensure an even and constant flavor. Their product line includes raw peanuts as well as those roasted in the shell, available either salted or unsalted. Additionally, they offer candied, chocolate and butter toasted peanuts as well as Virginia cashews and pistachio nuts. Visitors to the shop will also find a wonderful selection of locally made arts and crafts, Southampton and Beales Hams and a choice selection of Virginia souvenirs. Enjoy a true taste of a Virginia classic or send a sampling to your friends and loved ones with the delicious and distinctive peanuts available only at Plantation Peanuts of Wakefield.

509 County Drive, Wakefield VA
(800) 233-8788
www.plantationpeanuts.com

Chesterfield Berry Farm Market

Located just a mile down the road from the family owned and operated Chesterfield Berry Farm is one of the Moseley area's most popular shopping stops, the Chesterfield Berry Farm Market. The market was started by the Goode family in 1986 in conjunction with the farm. The market houses numerous Virginia products alongside farm fresh produce. These products include Amelia Springs Water, Virginia grown wines, Route 66 beverages and crisp apples straight from the Virginia mountains. They are also renowned for their incredible fresh strawberry milkshakes, which have been named the Best in Richmond. Other dining options include succulent barbecue and fried green tomatoes. The market came about after the family began selling their surplus produce out of roadside trailers and has expanded to become the area's favorite place to go for the freshest and tastiest produce and other fresh products. Chesterfield Berry Farm Market also offers wonderful seasonal gifts including garden flags, novelty items, gift baskets and homemade wreaths during the holidays. The market is also the ideal place to pick out a superior selection of homemade jams and jellies for your pantry. Taste for yourself the difference that care, quality and freshness make with the fine products available at the Chesterfield Berry Farm Market.

20800 Hull Street Road, Moseley VA
(804) 739-3831
www.chesterfieldberryfarm.com

Photos © 2005 Chip Mitchell

The Caboose Wine and Cheese

Ian Kirkland earned a degree in art with plans of becoming an illustrator. However, his desire to work for himself and his passion for unique beers and wines drove him to open his own store in 1997. The Caboose Wine and Cheese offers connoisseurs and newcomers alike a terrific venue in which to sample and purchase a variety of distinguished wines and beers from small vintners and microbreweries all across the globe. The focus of The Caboose is to introduce people to a greater scope of wines and beers than what is available at local pubs and grocers. You will find numerous niche brands and creative brews that will surprise and delight the average taster. The Caboose features a tasting every Friday evening, where patrons can sample a delicious array of wines along with assorted cheeses selected to follow the evening's theme and complement the chosen beverage. Ian's sister, Shannon Cooke, fondly known as the Duchess of Cheese, handles the shop's specialty food department where she reigns over a kingly assortment of olives, sausages and cheeses along with dips, oils and spreads. Additionally, Ian, Shannon and the other staff members are experts in helping you select the ideal spirit for your next party and they offer cheese platters designed for any budget. Expand your horizons and your palate with the tempting array of fine wines, excellent beers and great specialty foods available at The Caboose Wine and Cheese.

108 S Railroad Avenue, Ashland VA
(804) 798-2933
www.thecaboosewineandbeer.com

The Peanut Patch

If you think of peanuts as simply an afterthought sprinkled on top of an ice cream sundae, a visit to the Peanut Patch will change the way you look at these tasty morsels forever. More than 30 years ago, several members of the Riddick family came together to open a small gift shop selling Virginia peanuts and other local specialty items. Today, the Riddick family is still producing award winning, locally grown peanuts, carefully roasted in small batches, but they call their product by a new name. The FERIDIES® brand name is a combination of the last names of all of the people integral to the success of the store—the Shaffers, Riddicks and Fries'. The FERIDIES® line includes a mind-boggling number of peanut flavors that go beyond the traditional salted or honey roasted varieties to flavors like wasabi, cajun and garlic peanuts. The peanut butter fudge, chocolate peanut brittle and butter toffee peanuts offer a winning combination of sweet and salty. The FERIDIES® brand also extends to cashews, pecans, pistachios and other gourmet nuts. The extra big peanuts in FERIDIES® salted Virginia peanuts made it on *Food & Wine* magazine's December 2005 list of most spectacular holiday gifts, while the wasabi peanuts were mentioned in the July 12, 2006 issue of the *New York Times* as *tantalizing*. The shop carries other Virginia specialties, including jams and jellies, wine and maple syrup. The Christmas Room puts you in the holiday spirit year-round, with ornaments, Christmas collectibles, nativity figures and other seasonal decorations. Visit the Peanut Patch, where a longstanding product line and a new brand name make a prize winning combination.

27478 Southampton Parkway, Courtland VA
(757) 653-2028 or (866) 732-6883 *www.feridies.com*

Carytown Wine & Beer

Located about four blocks off Interstate 195 in Richmond, Cary Court Shopping Center is home to the popular Carytown Wine & Beer. Owner Malcolm P. Moore opened the doors of this full-service shop in 1992. His extensive selection includes an inventory of more than 1,400 fine wines and 400 different beers from at least 15 different countries. Brands include St. George, Bear Republic and Weyerbacher. The shop also carries a choice array of popular cheeses that are an ideal nosh to complement any bottle of wine. Carytown Wine & Beer is also a great place to stock up on wine accessories or pick up a new set of Reidel glassware. The soft, gentle music that plays in the background is soothing and creates a relaxed shopping experience. During the holiday season, Moore uses his shop to host various wine tasting events. Moore and his friendly staff are very knowledgeable about their stock and are happy to help patrons pick out something new. With reasonable pricing and a fabulous selection Carytown Wine & Beer is the place you should go for hard-to-find beers and classic wines.

3144 W Cary Street, Richmond VA
(804) 257-5910
www.carytownwineandbeer.com

River City Cellers

The informal atmosphere and a highly knowledgeable staff are the first clues that you have stumbled onto an unusual gem at River City Cellers. Owner Julia Battagilini stocks an electric selection of sophisticated small productions wines, artisan cheeses, microbrews and imported beers using local and international manufactures. The shop offers a variety of services to discrimination patrons, including rental options for a redwood locker that stores 16 to 20 bottles of wine, aging them to perfection in the best possible climate controlled room before you ever take them home. River City Celler hosts wine and cheese pairing classes and free weekly wine tastings. Educating the public about the cheese, beer and wine sold here is part of the overall mission of this quality celler and various events are regularly planned to achieve this end. Its specialties are Italian, Spanish and French bottles. There are over 500 wines in stock and two-thirds are kept at under $20. Julia is proud of the under $10 rack, known as the you-can't-go-wrong rack and there are no sub-standard wines in stock. The staff will help customers create custom gift basket and also stock instant wine tasting party sets that include everything but your friends. Wine is meant to be shared and pairing it with food creates a warm communal atmosphere, so come by and join the crowed.

2931 W Cary Street, Richmond VA
(804) 355-1375
www.rivercitycellers.com

Magnolia Foods

Come and visit Magnolia Foods, Lynchburg's premier gourmet deli, specialty food and wine shop. Magnolia Foods is known across Central Virginia for delicious sandwiches, bag lunches, decadent desserts and breathtaking wedding cakes. Come browse the store located on Rivermont Avenue near Randolph College (formerly RMWC) and see the fantastic array of craft beers and handpicked wines. In a hurry? They offer a large selection of choices for fresh meals-to-go. Hobby chefs will enjoy browsing through the selection of organic, gourmet and hard-to-find ingredients to complete their favorite recipes. Magnolia Foods offers wine tastings on Saturdays or you can check the schedule of cooking and wine classes. Entertaining is easy with Magnolia Foods' huge imported and domestic artisan cheese selection, frozen appetizers and a variety of chips and salsas. They offer a wide assortment of products made in Virginia. Stop in and pick up a custom gift basket, freshly prepared dinner to-go or let them help you with appetizers, dinner and dessert for your next party. Magnolia Foods has everything you need to make life delicious.

2476 Rivermont Avenue, Lynchburg VA
(434) 528-5442
www.magnoliafoods.com

Padow's Hams & Deli

Visitors to Richmond come to Padow's for their famous Virginia hams, bacon and peanuts, along with their award winning Deli sandwiches. Customers can order Genuine Smithfield, country or honey glazed hams, and have them shipped to their friends and families around the county. Plan to stop for lunch and have Richmond's finest, made-to-order deli sandwiches, homemade soups, salads and desserts. For a unique treat, try the House Special, a combination of Padow's Country Ham, Padow's Turkey Breast, and American cheese served heated on a sub roll with lettuce, tomato and mayonnaise. For over seventy years the Padow family has provided Richmonders with the best hams and deli favorites. George Padow started in 1936 with a small market in the Jackson Ward district of Richmond. Today, his sons Eddie and Sidney preside over a franchise network of fourteen delis throughout Virginia. Padow's also provides catering, take-out and delivery. If you can't make it to Richmond, visit the Padow's Hams & Deli website.

9864 W Broad Street, Glen Allen VA
(804) 965-6262 or (800) 344-4267
www.padows.com

Recreation

Woodlake Swim and Racquet Club

Are you ready to explore everything Woodlake Swim and Racquet had to offer? Start with the fact that Woodlake Swim and Racquet Club's first commitment is to their community and its families. Since 1985, the developers of Woodlake Swim and Racquet Club have focused on listening to their members and giving them the amenities and services that they want in a swim, tennis and fitness club. The facilities, staffing and programming are all designed to meet the varied needs of the community they serve. The club's setting is beautiful, situated on a 1,700-acre lake, and you'll always feel welcome at Woodlake. Everywhere you look there are smiling faces. Woodlake is perfect for families and individuals alike to enjoy a wealth of activities and amenities designed to bring people together for fun and fitness. Woodlake Swim and Racquet Club has four outstanding pools: an Olympic sized heated indoor pool with high and low dives, three outdoor pools with a 60-foot waterslide, mushroom feature and low and high dives. Tennis enthusiasts will find 12 clay courts and four hard courts with eight lighted for evening play. Year-round swim and tennis lessons are available for all ages and all levels. The fitness center has the latest equipment including free weights, circuit and cardio equipment, plus certified personal trainers and fitness instructors. There are over 200 land and water fitness classes offered each month for every fitness level. Other amenities include massage therapy, children's fitness programs, regulation basketball and sand volleyball courts, babysitting and a playground and tyke track for the little ones. In addition, the club has a huge social and events calendar for all ages year round. Stop by and let one of the club's terrific staff guide you through one of this area's finest treasures as Woodlake Swim and Racquet Club continues to build on their foundation of putting families first.

14710 Village Square Place, Midlothian VA
(804) 739-9095
www.woodlakesrc.com

Richmond Raft

Believe it or not, there's a place where you can go rafting down through the center of a large metropolitan city! That city is Richmond, and the company that can arrange the adventure for you is Richmond Raft. Incredible as it sounds, it's really true. The Saint James River runs directly through downtown Richmond for a seven mile stretch and is known for being the best urban whitewater in the United States. The river drops 105 feet on its journey through town and creates class I to IV rapids, which translates to lots of fun and adventure. Don't worry if you're faint of heart, there's a variety of trips you can take that range from mild to wild. If you're not familiar with the numbering system of rapids it's based on a scale from I to VI with VI being the most diffi cult. You'll encounter class IV rapids as you pass through Richmond's city limits. All trips are professionally guided

by skilled and knowledgeable river guides and Richmond Raft has an excellent safety record. Don't worry if you've never done anything like this before, you don't need any previous experience. All the trips begin with getting outfi tted with all the necessary safety gear and a safety briefi ng. After your trip they have showers and changing rooms available for your convenience. Stop in at Richmond Raft, where they can help you decide which adventure is right for you!

4400 East Main Street, Richmond VA
(804) 222- RAFT (7238) or (800) 222-7238
www.richmondraft.co

Virginia School of Sailing

Get ready to fall in love, because you're sure to be smitten with sailing after a class at the Virginia School of Sailing. Let Master Captain Tom Landers get your feet wet while you learn the basics. Tom can also help the more advanced sailor prepare for a sailing certification. With 40 years of experience to his credit, Tom uses knowledge, good teaching skills and a sense of humor to put his students at ease. He understands the importance of being thorough and learning within your personal comfort zone. Watch as Tom runs a boat aground only to illustrate how to get it free. He's ready for every contingency and has taught sailing for the U.S. Navy and belongs to the U.S. Coast Guard Auxiliary. He also teaches sailing at the University of Richmond's School of Continuing Education. The American Sailing Association voted Tom instructor of the year on three separate occasions in addition to a school of the year award in 2003. Private instruction is available and convenient, with locations in Deltaville and Richmond. Let Tom share his love of the sport with you as you enjoy the thrill of your first sail and revel in the peace and relaxation that sailing offers. When you are ready to sail the sea, get your sea legs at the Virginia School of Sailing.

9501 Kennesaw Road, Richmond VA
(804) 674-6500
www.sail-school.com

Restaurants & Cafés

Mi Hacienda

Mi Hacienda offers patrons an expansive menu filled with both traditional favorites and contemporary dishes that will add spice and pizzazz to any dining experience. Owned and operated by the father and son team of Javier and Javier Ornelas, it has become a community favorite since opening in 1997. The elegant Hispanic-influenced décor turns the dining area into a welcoming and relaxing place to enjoy a quiet meal with friends and family. On the first Sunday of each month, Mi Hacienda has a clown come in to entertain the younger diners. Mi Hacienda is the ideal place to host special events such as Cinco De Mayo parties and quinceañeras. The Ornelas' have two area restaurants to better serve their faithful patrons. The first is located on Midlothian Turnpike and the second location, which opened in 2002, can be found on Hull Street Road. At both locations you'll find the same fabulous menu, be greeted with a warm smile, a bowl of chips and their famous spicy white ranch dipping sauce. However, if you want to spice up your night with a different kind of salsa then head for the Midlothian Turnpike location where you will also find a big dance floor where Mi Hacienda offers karaoke, salsa nights, Latin nights, lessons and many more ways to have fun. There is also a DJ booth and two bar areas. Make any night fiesta night with a visit to Mi Hacienda.

8250 Midlothian Turnpike, Midlothian VA (804) 560-6994
10827 Hull Street Road, Midlothian VA (804) 674-7790

Capital Ale House Downtown (Richmond)

The Capital Ale House Downtown, located at 623 East Main Street in Richmond, is the original. Opened to help change the beer scene in the area, its success was confirmed when it was named One of the World's Most Brilliant Beer Bars in America by All About Beer magazine. With a focus on providing only the finest ales and lagers for their customers, they have forty exceptional varieties on tap that change often to highlight seasonal and specialty brews. Capital Ale House also has an extensive selection of over two-hundred different bottled beers from America's handcrafted micro-brews to imports that bring the flavor and tradition of the world's great beers. The Ale House has a large and inviting menu with several surprising and unique offerings such as the Stuffed Pretzel featuring a Usinger's Kielbasa grilled and topped with Havarti cheese and sauerkraut stuffed in a soft pretzel with whole grain mustard, as well as other great sandwiches. Each dish is masterfully crafted to be enjoyed with the full selection of beers available and many include beer as one of the ingredients such as the sixteen ounce rack of lamb, seasoned and perfectly grilled, then finished with a Belhaven Scotch Ale sauce. The Capital Ale House is found inside a one hundred plus year old building and features an "ice rail" in the stately upstairs bar while downstairs patrons can enjoy the pool tables, darts and other games available. Visit the Capital Ale House Downtown and enjoy superb libations and cuisine in an elegant and warming atmosphere.

623 E Main Street, Richmond VA (804) 643-ALES (2537) *www.capitalalehouse.com*

Virginia Diner

The family owned and operated Virginia Diner has been serving up down-home style cooking and providing good old Southern hospitality since 1929. Originally housed in a refurbished railroad dining car, this gourmet business has grown to include a mail order and Internet catalog. Virginia Diner currently has over 24 varieties of gourmet nuts and confections available, along with the fantastic and flavorful meals for which it is famous. The popular diner has been tagged as being The Peanut Capital of the World™ and is truly A Legend in a Nutshell™, even though the original dining car has been relegated to a fond memory. Popular menu favorites at the diner include old fashioned Brunswick stew, baked Virginia ham biscuits and their phenomenal southern fried chicken. You will also want to be sure to sample their incredible homemade soups and salads and have them wrap up a few of their tasty sandwiches for the trip home. Of course no visit to the Virginia Diner would be complete without a slice of their world famous peanut pie, or another delicious and decadent dessert. Their catalog offers not only the Virginia Diner's wonderful selection of peanuts but also mixed nuts, sweet and smoky Virginia hams and tantalizing snacks like seasoned and chocolate-coated nuts. Savor the flavors of Virginia at the Virginia Diner on route 460 in Wakefield.

322 W Main Street, Wakefield VA
(757) 899-3106 or (888) VA DINER *www.vadiner.com*

Meriwether Godsey & Meriwether's Restaurant Group

Meriwether Godsey is an employee-owned business with a top-end catering service, two restaurants and a complete set of dining management services. The company has dozens of contracts to manage dining facilities at colleges, schools, senior living and cultural arts facilities. It provides consulting services to schools and businesses on all aspects of food preparation and service. Meriwether Godsey can provide everything from nutritional analysis and menu planning to kitchen efficiency studies, cost control and computerization. The more than 400 talented owners—managers, chefs and service staff—are often delighted, but never satisfied. The proof is in the pudding. The rector emeritus of Chatham Hall has said, "We are blessed Meriwether Godsey of Lynchburg is near us. Our kitchen is heaven, not a headache." The company has been lauded in *Richmond* magazine, *Southern Living*, *Lynchburg Living*, *Bon Appetit* and *Gourmet*. Meriwether Godsey's catering operation serves thousands of events each year ranging from luncheons to black tie dinners. The caterers have served every recent Virginia governor, Senator John McCain, Archbishop Desmond Tutu, Poland's Lech Walesa, Russia's Mikhail Gorbachev and Justice Sandra Day O'Connor. The company's restaurants are Meriwether's Market Restaurant and Isabella's Italian Trattoria. Meriwether's offers casual American gourmet cuisine. Fresh, seasonal ingredients are cooked to order. Isabella's serves innovative robust cuisine in the style of the neighborhood restaurants of Italy. *Wine Spectator Magazine* has recognized both restaurants wine lists with its Award of Excellence continually since each restaurant opened. Whether you want a simple evening out, an elegant event or ongoing service for a major institution, Meriwether Godsey has something for you.

4944 Old Boonsboro Road, Lynchburg VA (catering and corporate) (434) 384-3663
4925 Boonsboro Road, Lynchburg VA (Meriwether's Market Restaurant) (434) 384-3311
3225 Old Forest Road, Lynchburg VA (Isabella's Italian Trattoria) (434) 385-1660
www.merig.com

Double T's Real Smoked Barbeque

Everyone is praising the 1999 opening of the family operated Double T's Real Smoked Barbeque Restaurant. Since its opening, Double T's has been voted the best new restaurant in Richmond and has won much acclaim internationally. When visiting Richmond, it's a must to go to Double T's Real Smoked Barbeque. The ribs, pork, chicken and beef are all smoked the old Virginia way with hickory and Shenandoah Valley applewood. The southern-style side dishes and deserts are all homemade. Throughout much of the South, oak and hickory are the woods of choice. This real wood smoke flavor makes Double T's a unique Virginia American barbeque. The real smoked meat flavor is enhanced with your choice of five regional sauces and Double T's own thick and tangy award-winning sauce. Double T's features regular size and Double T's size barbecue sandwiches. You can choose between barbeque platters of two, three or all four smoked meats and 14 different homemade side dishes. At Double T's, you can expect more than a regular barbecue place. Popular dishes include roasted corn pudding, sweet potato casserole, collard greens and Southern potato salad. Kids get their drinks in a cowboy boot and the little ones get their favorite

juice in a sippy cup. The old wood and Western décor features an open in-house hickory wood grill. Double T's has a full adult beverage bar to complement your choice of food, in pints and Double T-size mugs. You can even get souvenir T-shirts, caps, mugs and cups, making it a casual and fun place for everyone. Double T's gets its name from the nickname for Tom Taveggia, the owner and operator, who was an investment banker for 35 years. Double T's is Tom's dream to have the best real smoked Virginia barbeque you will ever have. Double T's Real Smoked Barbeque is open every day in Richmond's Carytown, across from the historic Byrd Theatre, and at the new location in the Richmond International Airport.

2907 W Cary Street, Richmond VA
(804) 353-9861
Richmond International Airport, Richmond VA

Acacia

In the Old Church Building in the quaint Carytown neighborhood of Richmond, you'll find Chef Dale Reitzer. Dale and his wife and partner Aline, own and operate Acacia, a restaurant that features daily menus focused on regional American cuisine. Dale continually searches for outstanding local and area products to incorporate into signature dishes like his scrumptious pan-roasted scallops on potato gnocchi and other fresh and flavorful vegetarian, seafood and meat entrées. This upscale bistro has a classic yet casual atmosphere and offers alfresco dining on the portico. Dale began his cooking career in 1982. Upon graduating from Johnson and Wales University in 1989, he became the chef at Alexander's in Norfolk. Over the next several years, he worked with nationally acclaimed chefs around the country, settling at Frog and the Redneck in 1993, where he met Aline. The couple and their black Labrador mix puppy Acacia moved to Atlanta in 1996. Dale finished honing his skills at the sumptuous five-star Ritz-Carlton Buckhead. There he worked with Chef Gunther Seeger. In 1998, the small family returned to Richmond and opened Acacia. A year later, Dale was listed as one of the Top Ten Best New Chefs by *Food and Wine* magazine which has also named Acacia one of the Top 100 Restaurants. A *Style Weekly* author states, "Those who enjoy good food should book a table at Acacia."

3325 W Cary Street, Richmond VA
(804) 354-6060
www.acaciarestaurant.com

The Tobacco Company Restaurant

In 1877, this corner warehouse served as a hub for the bustling tobacco and cotton trade in the South's capital city of Richmond. One hundred years later, a stunning four-story restaurant was built within these original brick walls and for 28 years it has served as The Tobacco Company Restaurant. It is designed to re-create the Victorian tobacco era of opulence which embodies the spirit of Southern hospitality and charm. When you enter through antique beveled glass doors, you'll experience the breathtaking beauty of a three-story garden atrium surrounded by fresh flowers, lush plants and unusual antiques accented by a magnificent chandelier. The brass elevator ride is just the start of a guest's journey to an exceptional dining experience. The dining floors are designed to accommodate both intimate and romantic dining with several private rooms that can handle large groups. Regional favorites highlight the extensive menu which emphasizes fresh seafood, aged Angus beef and the popular slow-roasted prime rib of beef, including seconds on the house! After dinner you can relax in the beautiful Victorian lounge and enjoy live entertainment in the spacious atrium bar, featuring the best local and regional bands. The Tobacco Company's lower level is also home to the most popular destination nightclub in the city with multiple bars, a mirrored dance floor and the hottest dance music. Visit The Tobacco Company Restaurant and Club for an unforgettable experience.

1201 E Cary Street, Richmond VA
(804) 782-9555
www.thetobaccocompany.com

Beauregard's Thai Room

For lunch or dinner in Richmond, it is hard to beat the gently spicy treats offered in Beauregard's Thai Room. The Thai Room has popular outdoor dining downstairs when weather permits and an elegant upstairs dining parlor. The outdoor courtyard was modeled after the Court of Two Sisters in New Orleans which was the stomping ground of Louisiana's General Beauregard and the place where he developed a taste for spicy foods. Gas streetlights, a fountain and the fragile beauty of the flowers make the courtyard a favorite destination. The gallery facing the courtyard features the original art of Lynn Blakemore and serigraphs by Kerry Hallum, Barbara McCan and Brett Livingston-Strong. The restaurant was voted Best Asian Restaurant and Best Thai Restaurant by *Richmond Magazine*. *Citysearch* named it Best Outdoor Dining and Best Romantic restaurant. Meals are notated with spice ratings from mild to very hot. Dinner offerings include mild green or spicy red curries and a variety of fish, meat and vegetable dishes. Lunches include items derived from other diverse regional influences as well as Thai meals. Desserts are also not strictly Thai but are delicious. An assortment of one-of-a-kind tempting ice creams or a chunk of luscious chocolate satisfies even the strongest sweet tooth. Charismatic David Roygulchareon owns Beauregard's Thai Room. David's customer service credo is, "Give the customers what they want," and Beauregard's Thai Room does exactly that.

103 E Cary Street, Richmond VA
(804) 644-2328
www.thairoom.com

Joe's Inn

Joe's Inn all began in 1952 when ex-jockey Joe Mencarini, known as Mr. Joe from Chicago, established a family restaurant that would become known as the Community Living Room. He sold the business in 1974, and it was sold again in 1977 to Nick Kafantaris. Joe's Inn has stayed in the Kafantaris family, thereby making it one of the oldest continuously family-run restaurants in the Richmond area. Nick's son, Michael, and daughter, Maria, currently own and operate the restaurant. Nick is now retired but is often found on-site visiting with patrons and enjoying his family and friends. Joe's daughter Diana still makes 120 gallons of the meat sauce from scratch each week. Several customers have continued to support Joe's Inn ever since Mr. Joe's days of running the restaurant, and families have longstanding traditions of gathering here. Joe's serves several different spaghetti dishes such as the Spaghetti a la Joe and Spaghetti a la Greek. The menu also features delicious traditional and vegetarian lasagnas, veal, chicken and eggplant parmigiana. Joe's Inn offers several fantastic breakfasts and fresh, tasty desserts, plus a fine selection of appetizers, soups and salads. As one customer said about Joe's Inn, "It's like mom's house, no matter what you do or where you go in the world, you come back and you are home."

205 N Shields Avenue, Richmond VA
(804) 355-2282
2616 Buford Road, Richmond VA
(804) 320-9700
7140 Mechanicsville Turnpike, Mechanicsville VA
(804) 569-0411
www.joesinn.com

Courthouse Café

Courthouse Café is guilty of one thing: serving fine home cooking. This small business adventure of Kathy Hughes' has turned out to be very rewarding. The focus is on making guests feel welcome by providing the best food and service for the money. This homey restaurant is famous for its chicken salad, which has been the featured item on the menu since the restaurant opened in 2004. Chicken salad is not the only delicious item on the menu. Courthouse Café's Brunswick stew and home cooked breakfasts are also crowd pleasers. The recipes have been developed by Kathy throughout her 30 years of cooking. A casual observer could walk into the restaurant on any given day and hear happy diners chorusing, "That's the best I've ever had!" Guests are treated like they are old friends or family. If you want to enjoy a home cooked meal in a relaxed atmosphere, come to the Courthouse Café.

224 W Main Street Suite A, Hopewell VA
(804) 458-3874

The Hard Shell

Does fabulous seafood make your heart beat faster? Then you'd better make sure you visit the Hard Shell Restaurant, located in downtown Richmond's historic Shockoe Slip. Locals have known it as one of the best seafood restaurants in town for the past 10 years, and word is getting out. The Hard Shell features Richmond's largest selection of fresh local and regional seafood, prepared just the way you like it. The restaurant also boasts an extensive raw seafood bar, which includes oysters, clams, shrimp, mussels, crab legs, lobster and Louisiana crawfish. The Hard Shell has been voted Richmond's Best Seafood Restaurant for five years by Richmond magazine. It also won Critic's Choice and People's Choice awards from Style magazine, no small feat in a town well versed in fine seafood. Beyond seafood, the Hard Shell offers superb beef dishes, such as filet mignon, prime rib and baby back ribs. If you can hit a *specials night*, you're in luck. Sunday specials include all-you-can-eat crab legs or ribs and a seafood combo; Monday is lobster night. Enjoy your dinners with a selection from the wine list or full bar. The Hard Shell also has private rooms and special menus for anything from wedding rehearsal dinners to corporate events. The Hard Shell combines a fun and casual atmosphere with creatively prepared food. You are invited to enjoy a dining experience that is as good as it gets.

1411 E Cary Street, Richmond VA
(804) 643-2333
www.thehardshell.com

Bill's Barbecue

On June 2, 1930, a little one-window takeout place opened in Norfolk. It was called Bill's Barbecue and 75 years and seven locations later, it's still owned and operated by the Richardson family. It is still going strong and serving up some of the best barbecue in the Old Dominion State. Bill's Barbecue features a menu that includes a broad range of moderately priced quick service items including their signature minced pork barbecue, peak-of-flavor™ pies and freshly squeezed made-to-order limeades and lemonades. Their wonderful Virginia hams are basted and oven roasted for more than 14 hours and all pies are made completely from scratch from the crust to the toppings, every day. Ms. Rhoda M. Richardson-Elliott, President and daughter of founder William Steven Richardson Sr., demands the highest quality and standards for every ingredient and product sold. Many of the vendors that Bill's

Barbecue work with have been doing business with the company for more than 20 years. While Bill's has received many accolades throughout the last seven decades, the management team feels their greatest reward is the satisfied comments from their long-time customers. One interesting aspect of the business is that while there have been a multitude of Williams in the family, including the founder, none of them went by Bill. The story is that an out of work sign painter offered to make the sign in exchange for free meals. As far as anyone knows, he actually pulled the name from thin air. Find out for yourself what many have known for more than 75 years. Visit to Bill's Barbecue, where A Trial Makes a Customer™.

927 Myers Street, Richmond VA
(804) 353-2757

Strawberry Street Café

The renowned Strawberry Street Café exudes a warm, rich intimacy that weaves a spell of relaxation and camaraderie around each guest. This charming and popular neighborhood café, located in the Fan District, is most famous for its Bathtub Salad Bar which has been a mainstay of the eatery since its opening in 1976. The tub occupies the center of the café and is filled daily with ice and loaded up with bowls of fresh fruit, vegetables and prepared salads. Both the Strawberry Street Café and its original idea gained national recognition in 1995 as a featured answer on the popular *Jeopardy!* game show. This prominent café serves more than just great salads, they also have an extensive menu of fabulous dishes created by co-owner and chef Ron Joseph. Included among the favorites are the Maryland crab cakes, chicken pot pie and a nice selection of vegetarian dishes. Both Joseph and co-owner L. Grayson Collins feel that it is important to help their community and they sponsor numerous charitable events

and fundraisers. The café attracts a diverse and multi-generational clientele that comes in not only for the great food and ambiance, but for their innovative wine program. Strawberry Street Café has been the recipient of the Gold Cluster award several times and offers an excellent selection of Virginia wines. Experience the very best in fresh food, fantastic service and fine wine with a visit to the Strawberry Street Café.

421 N Strawberry Street, Richmond VA
(804) 353-6860
www.strawberrystreetcafe.com

Manhattans

Manhattans has quickly become the destination restaurant for those in the know. In just two short years it has garnered a reputation for distinction and fine cuisine that goes far beyond the pale. Owner Nat Dance along with Executive Chef Shawn Scott focus on providing nothing but the very best, top-quality foods and services. Manhattans' personable staff offer quintessential, unobtrusive service and are dedicated to ensuring that your visit is a pleasant one each and every time. The eclectic yet romantic ambiance lends itself well to intimate dinners for two and large gatherings alike. With the restaurant's near-proximity to the nation's capitol, it has become a popular favorite for many prominent figures and entertainers including the owner's mother, Rosalyn Dance, who serves in the House of Delegates for the State of Virginia. Shawn has been recognized by the American Culinary Federation several times for his culinary skills and his incredible signature dishes. Manhattans' menu is comprised of a choice array of traditional favorites and original entrees that will make you sit up and take notice. A popular appetizer option is the sweet potato mezzaluna, which is house-made pasta stuffed with sweet potato with fresh ginger served over a walnut-brown butter sauce and topped with fresh crab meat and crème fraiche. Entrees include scrumptious strawberry barbecue glazed port porterhouse steak, boursin shrimp and scallops and sesame crusted salmon salad with ginger-lime dressing. Revel in the satisfaction that comes from an excellent and savory meal served in a decadent atmosphere by a devoted staff at Manhattans.

112 N 5th Street, Richmond VA
(804) 644-5777
www.manhattansva.com

Cockade City Grill

Chef Artis Fortineau gives a Cajun zip to his signature dishes at the popular Cockade City Grill in Petersburg. Since opening in April 2003, Owner Glenn Bailey and his personable staff have established a reputation for providing great food and great fun in Old Towne Petersburg. The restaurant is known for the best burger in the tri-cities area and a local newspaper named it Best Value and Best Place to be on a Saturday Night. Cockade City Grill is housed in a historic building that was completed in 1815 and managed to survive the fire that swept through the city later in the year. President Madison christened the town the Cockade City of the Union because the Petersburg regiment wore red plumes, or cockades, on their hats during the war of 1812. During the 1940s and 50s, it became a diner, patronized by military personnel from Camp Lee which is now the Army's Fort Lee. Glenn named the grill in honor of the town's military history and the restaurant still retains a significant amount of its historic look and feel. The kitchen is visible which adds to the intimate, family-like feeling of the grill. On Friday and Saturday nights, Cockade City Grill offers live entertainment and on Tuesdays it features karaoke. Meet the gang, relax and enjoy a terrific meal that will spice up your day at Cockade City Grill.

305 N Sycamore Street, Petersburg VA
(804) 862-2537

Extra Billy's Barbecue

Genuine hickory pit-cooked barbecue is at its best at Extra Billy's Barbecue in Richmond. For over 20 years, the Harr family has been cooking pork butts, beef brisket, ribs, sausage and chicken over the smoke and heat of hickory. The smoke-kissed meats complemented with Extra Billy's own tangy, tomato-based barbecue sauce are area favorites. To round out the menu, great coleslaw, potato salad, baked beans and hushpuppies are prepared daily. Extra Billy's Barbecue two restaurants each have a casual atmosphere and provide full service at lunch and dinner. The original store on West Broad Street features a salad bar with a great selection of fresh vegetables and fruits. Homemade soup is always available at lunch. The second location on Alverser in Midlothian features an on-site brewery with four brews on tap. Both locations are busy providing eat-in, carry-out, delivery and catering services. The Harrs chose the name Extra Billy's to attach some Virginia interest and flavor to their establishment. William Smith, a two-time Virginia Governor and a Civil War general, was given the nickname Extra Billy because of the extra efforts he put into any undertaking. The Harrs live up to these expectations. Since 1912, when Henry Harr opened a small café, the Harr family has continuously been in the restaurant business. Today, Bob, Lisa and Jason Harr are the fourth generation of operators of Extra Billy's Barbecue. For a down-home barbecue experience, stop by Extra Billy's.

5205 W Broad Street, Richmond VA (804) 282-3949
1110 Alverser Drive, Midlothian VA (804) 379-8727
www.extrabillys.com

Aunt Sarah's Pancake House

To say that Aunt Sarah's Pancake House, a Richmond favorite since 1962, is a family business would be a significant understatement. The story begins with high school sweethearts Theresa and John Dankos who worked together at John's father's restaurant. Years later, the couple decided to buy the North Glass House, owned by Host International, so that they could settle down to a business of their own. That business became known as Aunt Sarah's Pancake House. Today, Aunt Sarah's Pancake House is a popular restaurant which has expanded to include a total of 16 locations throughout the Richmond area with plans for future growth. Although Teresa has passed on, John is still active in the business along with his son Glenn and numerous other family members who are involved in varied aspects of the business. Aunt Sarah's prides itself on using local vendors for much of their foodstuff, many who have been suppliers since the restaurant first opened. Many of the employees have been with the company for better than 15 years which is a further tribute to the legacy of Aunt Sarah's in its employees. Breakfast is served all day, with a wonderful selection of lunches and dinners available at affordable prices. Bring your family and enjoy a tradition more than forty years in the making at Aunt Sarah's Pancake House.

Route 1, Richmond VA
(804) 264-9189

The Red Door

Nestled in Richmond's bustling business district, The Red Door Restaurant, owned by Joe and Shelia Folley, is a great place to enjoy a hearty business lunch or relax after work. The Red Door, purchased by the Folleys in 1991, has become a local favorite and is touted as one of Richmond's best-kept secrets by Richmond denizens. The Red Door's homemade bread, soups, spanakopita and desserts are just a few of the many items made fresh daily. The menu features a myriad of delightful choices influenced by American, Italian and Greek cuisine. For starters, patrons can choose dolmades, which are grape leaves filled with seasoned rice, or fried cheese ravioli served with marinara sauce. Sandwiches and subs are special favorites at The Red Door. Submarine sandwich varieties include Italian, meatball and cheese and steak and cheese. You'll also find barbecue sandwiches, grilled pastrami and Swiss cheese or good old-fashioned bacon, lettuce and tomato sandwiches. When you are looking for something a bit heartier, turn to the Italian Delights portion of the menu where you can choose from savory entrées such as veal parmigiana, cannelloni or The Red Door special made with pasta, meat sauce, meat balls, sausage, pepperoni and baked cheese. The Red Door brings the taste of Greece to you with its wonderful souvlaki and gyros. Additionally, The Red Door has a selection of Tex-Mex-influenced dishes, fresh seafood selections and pita pizzas. The relaxed atmosphere and friendly staff make The Red Door Restaurant the ideal lunch or supper destination on your next visit to downtown Richmond.

314 E Grace Street, Richmond VA
(804) 649-1588

Benjamin's Great Cows and Crabs

To Benjamin McGehee's credit, his restaurant, Benjamin's Great Cows and Crabs, has a lot more going for it than just the eye-catching name. Winning the hearts of local gourmands with its fresh seafood and hand-cut steaks, Benjamin's was named the Best New Restaurant in Lynchburg when it opened in 2003. It has also made the pages of *Small-Town Restaurants in Virginia* and *A Taste of Virginia History*, two books celebrating the state's culinary tradition. The theme inside the 1920s restaurant is rustic, highlighted by a wooden bar and real trees in the middle of the dining area that act as structural supports. Diners seated on the deck enjoy a panoramic view of the Blue Ridge Mountains. A graduate of Lynchburg's own Liberty University, Benjamin is proud to have launched his business in his hometown after working his way through the food service industry. A stint as a dishwasher planted the seed, while training under three different executive chefs filled him with the knowledge and confidence to strike out on his own. In addition to steaks, Benjamin's offers crab cakes, pan-seared salmon and a lovely chicken breast served with portobello mushrooms. The desserts are always tempting and creative. *Esquire* magazine bestowed a Best Name award on the restaurant, which it certainly deserves. To appreciate the fine cuisine behind the name, dine at Benjamin's Great Cows and Crabs.

14900 Forest Road, Forest VA
(434) 534-6077
www.cowsandcrabs.com

Crab Louie's Seafood Tavern

For 250 years, the beautiful manor home that houses Crab Louie's Seafood Tavern has been an oasis of hospitality for weary travelers. It all began circa 1745 when two Scottish brothers, one from East Lothian and the other from West Lothian, joined together to build the house on the family's Virginia coal mine property. In the spirit of compromise, they named the home Midlothian. The brothers were a part of the influential Wooldridge family who controlled much of Virginia's early coal mining industry. The family's mines were also named Midlothian, as was the town, which later grew around the property. The home served as a private dwelling for Abraham S. Wooldridge whose hospitality was so well known that drivers using the Lynchburg-Richmond stagecoach used the home as a refreshment stop for passengers. Later, Hancock descendants of the family inherited the home and it housed a long line of physicians. In 1875, the home was sold to the Jewett family who owned it for 100 years. The Jewetts ran a popular boarding house named The Sycamores while

raising their six children. For more than 20 years now, Crab Louie's Seafood Tavern has been maintaining the grand home's history for superior hospitality by offering fabulous cuisine in a cozy and intimate atmosphere. From their award-winning crab cakes to their exquisite Chambourd chocolate mousse, Crab Louie's Seafood Tavern has everything needed to make your meal a memorable one.

1352 Sycamore Square, Midlothian VA
(804) 275-CRAB (2722)
www.crablouies.com

1 North Belmont

To create fine French cuisine, one needs skill, plenty of time and a well-lined pocketbook. Chef Frits Huntjens makes no apologies for his expenses and with just a single visit to 1 North Belmont, you'll see that his gourmet creations are worth every penny. Huntjens got his start in the food business at the age of 12 when his parents opened a French restaurant in the Netherlands. He graduated from the National Culinary Apprentice Program in the Netherlands and went on to become an *aide*

de cuisine in Belgium where he worked under the tutelage of Paul van Vliet. In 1976, Frits was honored to be the youngest member inducted into Chaine des Rotisseurs, an international fraternity of gastronomy located in the United Kingdom. He then led The Mansion Restaurant to winning the only AAA Four-Diamond award in the state of Kentucky. From there, he moved on to Richmond to work concurrently as a consultant for the re-opening of the Richmond Convention Center and as general manager of the Marriott. Now as the owner and chef of the fabulous and popular 1 North Belmont, Frits is able to put all of his culinary and hospitality experience together to create a haven of rich ambiance and magnificent cuisine. The exemplary staff is perfectly trained and attentive without being intrusive. Utilizing fresh local produce and wondrous gourmet goods from around the globe, Frits cooks up an exquisite epicurean experience that can only be found at 1 North Belmont.

1 North Belmont Avenue, Richmond VA
(804) 358-0050
www.1northbelmont.com

The Zeus Gallery Café

The Zeus Gallery Café in the popular museum district of Richmond is the ideal eatery for those who appreciate fine art and fine food equally. Owner Ted Doll, Manager Jeanne Strong and their experienced staff put their hearts and souls into every aspect of the business to create an optimal dining experience every time. The intimate atmosphere lends itself to romantic trysts and has become a popular place to get engaged since it opened in 1990. Using engraved brass nameplates, Doll has cleverly given each of his comfortable booths its own moniker, such as the Lucky Booth, where most of those engagements take place, and the amusing Phone Booth or John Wilkes Booth. The walls are lined with frequently changed displays of artwork created by local artisans and regulars come by often to see what's new. This locally owned and operated business believes in supporting the community so Doll purchases ingredients from local growers and vendors. Chef Oscar McCrowell utilizes these fresh ingredients to provide guests with an ever-changing menu of delicious dishes such as the pan seared Mediterranean chicken breast with roasted red peppers. Other favorites include the braised rockfish filet and roasted rack of New Zealand lamb. Zeus Gallery Café stocks a choice selection of wines from around the world, a fine selection of beers and also contains a full bar. For a place where form, function and fine foods come together, visit Zeus Gallery Café.

201 N Belmont Avenue, Richmond VA
(804) 359-3219

Capital Ale House at Innsbrook

The Capital Ale House at Innsbrook on Cox Road is the second and newest location for this popular Ale House. Accolades include being named, along with its original location, Richmond's Best Bar by Richmond magazine and one of the Top Twenty Beer Bars in America by BeerAdocate.com. With the continued focus on providing only the finest ales and lagers available for their customers, the Innsbrook location has over 10,000-square feet of space to cater to the areas business professionals and families. This popular Ale House offers two dining rooms and a spacious patio situated next to a beautiful water feature complete with ducks, geese and turtles. Three bars, the largest of which is dedicated non-smoking, pour ales and lagers from 77 taps and hold 250 brands of bottled beers. Similar to the original Ale House, the bars hold their signature "ice rail" down the center to help keep your beers at optimal serving temperature and there is a separate room with pool, darts and other games. The same large Capital Ale House menu which uses the many beers as part of its recipes, pair well with the vast array of handcrafted ales and lagers available. Prince Edward Island Mussels steamed in Belgian Wit Beer are a fine example of their beer and food pairings. Relax and treat yourself to the very best at the Capital Ale House at Innsbrook.

4024-A Cox Road, Glen Allen VA
(804) 780-ALES (2537)
www.capitalalehouse.com

La Grotta Ristorante

Established in 1994 by Owner and Chef Antonio, La Grotta Ristorante utilizes rustic cooking methods to prepare fresh culinary delights on-site. Antonio couples old world Italian décor and authentic northern Italian cuisine from his Italian heritage in this fresh and exciting restaurant. Born in Potenza, Italy, he attended Impas Culinary School. After moving to the United States in 1981, Antonio went to work in the top Italian restaurants in Washington, D.C. In 1987, he opened his first establishment, Ohio Scalini, to much public praise. In 1990, Antonio packed up and brought his talent to Richmond, where he and his partner, Carlo, opened Amici in 1991. Due to popular demand and amazing success, Antonio opened La Grotta Ristorante in 1994 followed by Pronto in 1998. La Grotta offers an extensive wine cellar plus authentic homemade pastas and a pleasing array of meat and seafood dishes. Visit La Grotta Ristorante for a little slice of Italy.

1218 E Cary Street, Richmond VA
(804) 644-2466
www.lagrottaristorante.com

Millie's Diner

Rarely do phrases like exotic, gourmet and greasy spoon go together. Millie's Diner, however, is truly like no other restaurant you will find. It's hard even for devoted regulars to describe the delicious fare. Set in a brick building that used to serve Richmond tobacco plant workers, you might call Millie's a haute diner, because it's been setting trends and the standard in fabulous food ever since Lisa and Paul Keevil resurrected it in 1989. They have an ever-changing menu that fuses Asian, tropical, Cajun and Southern flavors in a glorious panoply of delicious food that has earned rave reviews from the *Los Angeles Times* to *The New York Times*. At Millie's, they do things the old-fashioned way, from scratch. Millie's Diner features the freshest ingredients available, innovative seasonings and imaginative cooking techniques from a lineup of great chefs who approach cooking like art. Their appetizers are dazzling, their main dishes are delightful, and their desserts are impressive. No matter what you select from the menu, you can't go wrong. Try the fried green tomatoes with spicy Thai shrimp or Millie's antipasti alongside *garam masala* roasted rack of lamb. Whatever you choose, Millie's has an extensive list of great wines to go with it. Not only is the food great, but the ambiance and service are terrific as well. Where else do the tabletop jukeboxes play everything from Patsy Cline to Prokofiev? Stand in line if you have to, but don't miss Millie's Diner, it's a culinary palace in disguise.

2603 E Main Street, Richmond VA
(804) 643-5512
www.milliesdiner.com

Sidewalk Cafe

In the popular and historic Fan district of Richmond, a thriving and bustling community has become a tight-knit neighborhood. This neighborhood's perfect hangout is the Sidewalk Café, a fabulous place to meet up with your friends and grab a bite and a brew. Since 1989, this popular café, owned by partners Johnny Giavos and Earnest Von Ofeinhein, has served the Fan district. The café is most commonly known for having absolutely great food and its warm, friendly atmosphere makes it an ideal place to relax. Citysearch named it the Best Cheap Eats in 2002 and 2003 and the Best Bar in the Fan District in 2001. The eclectic menu truly has something for everyone and includes tasty noshes such as Greek nachos, big submarine sandwiches and huge dishes of pasta served with thick marinara sauce. The Sidewalk Café also serves as a surrogate home for the students of nearby University of Richmond and T.C. Williams School of Law. For years, the students have flocked to the café and many of them may not have made it to graduation without the nourishing food and help of Johnny, Earnest and their friendly staff. The Sidewalk Café owners are also huge soccer fans and they promote various youth soccer teams, local leagues and adult teams. Many a night is spent hosting parties and watching the World Cup soccer matches on television. Make the Sidewalk Café a must on your next visit to the Fan district, where you can watch a game, grab a bite and meet the neighborhood.

2101 W Main Street, Richmond VA
(804) 358-0645

Penny Lane Pub

Looking for a place to watch the soccer match and enjoy some bangers 'n' mash washed down with a pint of black and tan? You've come to the right place if you find yourself in Penny Lane Pub. The second oldest restaurant in downtown Richmond, Penny Lane Pub caters to those from the United Kingdom suffering from culture shock. Boasting a bevy of British brews on draft, Penny Lane Pub has the atmosphere of an authentic British neighborhood pub, featuring soccer posters and Beatles memorabilia. Owner Terry O'Neill and his wife Rose, both from Liverpool, the home of the Beatles, opened the pub in 1978. They designed their restaurant for those who have British heritage or interests in mind, especially Beatles fans. Terry calls Penny Lane "a neighborhood bar without the neighborhood." The pub serves cottage pie, fish and chips and other traditional British food, but "not too traditional, they had to make it taste good!" quips Terry. Penny Lane Pub is family owned and operated with Rose and Terry's son Terence and daughter-in-law Lisa now helping run the pub. This cozy pub invites patrons to sit and chat by the fireplace or participate in some friendly competition in the upstairs game room. If you're looking for a pleasant way to spend an evening shooting pool, darts or bull over a pint, be sure and check out Penny Lane Pub.

421 E Franklin Street, Richmond VA
(804) 780-1682
www.pennylanepub.com

Perly's Delicatessen

A fire at Perly's Delicatessen in 1997 completely destroyed the building. What others may have considered a tragedy, Owner Gray Wyatt saw an opportunity to rebuild it the way he had always wanted it to be. The restaurant has been at its present location in downtown Richmond since 1961. When Harry and Mary Perlstein started Perly's, it was one of the first delis in Richmond, and it still has the cozy atmosphere and great service that it has always been known for. Gary believes that good food is easy when you use fresh ingredients and pay attention to what you're doing in the preparation. He is also blessed with a loyal and hardworking staff, and one of his servers, Nan McQueen, had worked as a server for 33 years before she had to leave for knee surgery. Perly's features a breakfast and lunch menu as well as take-out, and there are daily lunch specials as well as soups of the day. Getting customers their orders promptly is a priority for the Perly's staff but a fast turn-around time is not at the expense of great food. If you are looking for an excellent meal at a reasonable price served by friendly people, be sure to visit Perly's Delicatessen.

111 E Grace Street, Richmond VA
(804) 649-2779

Becky's Breakfast & Lunch

Every town has that one special restaurant, the one you went to with your parents on Saturday afternoons as a kid. This is the restaurant where the governor, police chief and a few other prominent citizens could be seen picking up their lunch on a busy day or claiming the corner booth. For Richmond, that place is Becky's Breakfast & Lunch on East Cary Street. Becky's opened in 1958 and has continued to be a popular favorite for generations of customers. It's not hard to figure out why. This neighborhood diner features a wonderful menu filled with traditional homemade favorites that are sure to please everyone. More importantly, people come back for the warm hospitality and friendly, fantastic service. Server Julia Simmons has been with Becky's for more than 30 years and always has a kind smile for her customers, many of whom she knows by name. Additionally, the diner's featured specials haven't changed in more than 20 years. Folks know they are getting the same fresh, made-from-scratch favorites that they have come to love. House specialties in the morning include a variety of combination plates with eggs, breakfast meats and breads along with omelets, breakfast sandwiches and pancakes. In the afternoon, choose from a generous assortment of sandwiches, salads and daily specials such as pot roast with all the trimmings. Becky's further offers a lighter fare menu, scrumptious homemade cakes and free delivery. For great food and great people, stop in for a bite at Becky's Breakfast & Lunch.

100 E Cary Street,
Richmond VA
(804) 643-9736
www.beckys-diner.com

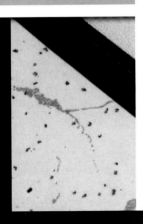

3rd Street Diner

In the heart of the bustling and historic town of Richmond you will find a piece of history that's open 24 hours a day and serves a great cup of coffee. Welcome to the 3rd Street Diner, owned by Andreas and Sophia Pyliaris and their son William. This historical landmark is considered the best diner in the state. Originally the site was the private home of a local judge who donated his house to a nurse known as Aunt Sally Tompkins for use as a hospital during the Civil War. The hospital opened 10 days after the battle of Manassas in 1861 and was one of the few private hospitals allowed to remain open through the end of the war. President Jefferson Davis took note of the nurse's efforts and awarded her the rank of Confederate Captain of the Cavalry. While the hospital was in operation it quickly became known for its cleanliness and well-prepared food.

The site first became a diner in 1926 during an era when coffee cost a nickel and schoolboys came by in knickers. Nowadays the diner is open 24 hours a day, 365 days a year. The Pyliaris family caters mostly to late night diners, college students and the downtown lunch crowd. The diner has a warm and comfortable atmosphere and serves fantastic home-style meals. Whether you're a weary traveler just passing through or a native Virginian, stop in and see why the 3rd Street Diner has earned the fond title of being an institution for the community of Richmond.

218 E Main Street, Richmond VA
(804) 788-4750

The Ironhorse Restaurant

Ashland is a delightful and charming destination town filled with elegant boutiques, terrific eateries and inspiring galleries. In the heart of this thriving community The Ironhorse Restaurant flourishes. This early 1900s historic building once housed the D.B. Cox Department Store and many of the restaurant's patrons reminisce about where the various departments used to be. Now filled with train memorabilia, this popular eatery offers delicious meals made from scratch. The Ironhorse uses only the freshest and highest quality ingredients available. Chef Todd Butler utilizes farm fresh local produce, free-range chickens and organic ingredients whenever possible to consistently present tantalizing dishes that are sure to please. The Ironhorse is open for lunch and dinner Monday through Saturday and reservations are recommended. The lunch menu offers a classic selection of salads, sandwiches and daily specials. In the evening, Chef Todd creates frequently changing and always tantalizing dishes such as wild mushroom and goat cheese ravioli or New Zealand rack of lamb with roasted red pepper demi-glace. Owner Mimi Siff and Manager David McNamara focus on providing high-quality customer service while creating a great environment in which to both work and dine. The ever-changing menu is a terrific incentive for becoming a regular patron, and the warm, friendly atmosphere makes for a comfortable place to visit with friends and smile at all the familiar faces. Make your next meal a memorable one with a visit to The Ironhorse Restaurant, where Mimi and her fabulous staff have been serving delicious meals since 1990.

**100 S Railroad Avenue, Ashland VA
(504) 752-6410**
www.ironhorserestaurant.com

Anna's Pizza

The creation of a pizza is an art. Everyone desires something different. For some it must be served on a thin, crisp crust with light sauce and lots of cheese, while others prefer thick, chewy pizza dripping with tomatoes. Take a group of friends to a pizza place and it will take 20 minutes to decide what to order. Fortunately, where to go is never an issue. If you want great pizza, go to Anna's Pizza. Owned and operated by Joe and Francine Volo, Anna's has been serving up terrific submarine sandwiches and fabulous Northern-style pizzas at great prices for more than 10 years. This family-oriented restaurant is laid-back and casual, making it the ideal place to bring the kids or hang out with friends. Anna's Pizza was honored to win the Channel 12 Hall Of Fame award for having never received health violations from the Department of Health. The Volos use homemade sauces and from-scratch dough to make their famous pizzas. Other menu items include fresh salads with salami and provolone and a nice selection of appetizers including the traditional favorite, deep-fried mushrooms. Another wonderful addition to this fun restaurant is their junior waitress Rosa. Rosa is Joe and Francine's two-year-old daughter. She can often be found tottering after the waitresses and visiting tables while they take your order. Rosa's charming smile and bubbly personality are the perfect complements to a great dining experience. Anna's was previously featured in the Under 30 restaurant section of Richmond Times and voted number one for its Northern Pizza Style. Come enjoy the friendly staff and delicious pizzas and subs at Anna's Pizza.

Midlothian: (804) 675-0002
Ashland: (804) 798-9259
Mechanicsville: (804) 730-7203
Warsaw: (804) 333-9222

Saffron Ltd.

Half of what makes a meal truly fabulous is its presentation. For a beautiful presentation, head to Saffron, Richmond's largest and most distinctive purveyor of fine china and dining accessories. Owned by Mariam Mobrem and Afagh Mohajer, this stylish shop is well known for its incredible stock, top-notch service and bridal registry. Saffron's extensive inventory includes a wide variety of both traditional and contemporary patterns that will please even the most discriminating of shoppers. According to Mohajer, Saffron's goal is to bring the best of New York, California and Europe together in one store and it does so magnificently. "Customer satisfaction matters to us. When our customers leave, we ensure they do so feeling good. We have yet to have an unhappy customer," says Mobrem. It is this dedication to excellence that has made Saffron the place to go for table settings, gifts and accessories. The store nearly overflows with opulent and stunningly beautiful place settings and accoutrements, all cleverly arranged in charming vignettes. From Waterford and Orrefors crystal to Union Street Glass stemware and Versace china, Saffron has

something to suit everyone's taste and budget. Additionally, Saffron caters to the collector in all of us with such specialties such as Goble porcelain, Jay Strongwater figurines and choice pieces from the Vera Wang collection of china and crystal. Set a table so beautiful that the meal itself will be merely an afterthought with stunning selections from Saffron.

5707 Grove Avenue, Richmond VA
(804) 673-2800
www.saffronchinaonline.com

Alexander's Fine Foods

For nearly 30 years, Spiro and Bill Georgogianis have been serving the Petersburg area some of the finest Greek and Italian foods in the state. Alexander's Fine Foods uses nothing but the freshest, top-quality ingredients in their traditional recipes. This family-oriented restaurant welcomes patrons and makes them feel as though they are all good friends. To the Georgogianis, they are. Many diners have been eating at Alexander's since the Georgogianis first opened it. Lynn Allen, a friendly and popular waitress here for 10 years, always has a cheerful smile and kind word for her

regular patrons and new guests alike. The menu is filled with a choice selection of classic favorites such as souvlaki and spicy Italian sausage dishes. You can also find a tasty assortment of cold plates and salads. House specialties include the tried and true veal parmegiana and newly created favorite, Athenian style chicken, half a chicken prepared with fresh lemon, butter and spices. The dessert menu is filled with tempting, scrumptious offerings. You'll want to order seconds of their perfect baklava, creamy rice pudding or the decadent praline cheese cake. Alexander's Fine Foods has daily specials and can provide carryout-catering for small and large groups. Enjoy the warm ambience and fantastic meals available at Alexander's Fine Foods.

101 W Bank Street, Petersburg VA
(804) 733-7134

King's Famous Barbecue

For more than 50 years, King's Famous Barbecue has been serving up some of the finest barbecue in Virginia. It all began with a trio of brothers, John, Robert and Clinton King. John was a veteran of the Battle of the Bulge campaign of World War II when he joined with his brothers to start their business. They borrowed $1,200 from a friend and opened the doors. They would buy one pork shoulder at a time, use those proceeds to buy the next one and so forth. Each shoulder was smoked for hours over a hickory and oak log fire until it was tender and perfect. The restaurant became John's life. "He was always there tending to everything," says his granddaughter Alicia Hawks Burdzel who now co-owns the restaurant with her mother Joan. Alicia and Joan are the only two Kings still involved with the restaurant, but they take pride in continuing the long tradition of great service and fantastic food. In keeping with tradition, King's Famous Barbecue is open Tuesday through Sunday. In the old days, the brothers always took Mondays off to go fishing and bring the catch back to the restaurant. Locals knew to show up on Tuesday for fresh fish dishes. This family friendly eatery offers something for everyone, including a few dishes without the famous and fabulous barbecue sauce. They have a terrific selection of sandwiches and sides along with incredible apple pie. Sink your teeth into tender pork, succulent beef and tangy chicken all barbecued to perfection at King's Famous Barbecue.

2910 S Crater Road, Petersburg VA
(804) 732-0975
www.kingsfamousbarbecue.com

Half Way House

At Half Way House, the Young family continues a tradition of gracious Southern hospitality that goes back to 1760, when the house operated as a stagecoach stop between Richmond and Petersburg. When you stop to relax and dine at Half Way House, you will be following in the footsteps of such fellow wayfarers as George Washington, Thomas Jefferson, Patrick Henry and Gen. Robert E. Lee. The house also served as headquarters for Gen. Benjamin F. Butler during the final assault on Richmond in 1864. When you enter the English basement, you go down three steps and three centuries in time. The intimate antique setting can entertain a group of up to 40 people or charm a couple in search of a romantic dining adventure. The house specialty is sure to please with its combination of a petite filet mignon grilled to your specifications and fried shrimp. Half Way House serves only the finest Angus beef and freshest Chesapeake Bay seafood. Home baked breads and desserts plus an extensive wine selection complement the traditional dishes. The service is excellent, because working at the restaurant means becoming part of the family, and turnover is low, resulting in experienced professionals who love what they do. For a dining experience to remember, step back in time and visit the historic Half Way House restaurant.

10301 Jefferson Davis Highway, Richmond VA
(804) 275-1760
www.halfwayhouserestaurant.com

Carytown Burgers and Fries

Big, fat, juicy burgers are what you'll find at Carytown Burgers and Fries. Owner Mike Barber has found that the key to a good burger is freshness and high quality ingredients. They use meat that's fresh everyday and their buns are made locally and brought in fresh every day, too. "If it's on the menu, it's the best in town," says Mike. If you're not a meat-eater, don't worry, they have a grill just for vegetarian selections where they don't allow meat to be cooked. Catering services are offered as well. They bring everything, all you have to do is supply the hungry people. There is a beautiful outdoor patio that's light and airy in the summer and enclosed and heated in the winter. If you prefer, there's a bright and cozy non-smoking room inside and upstairs for smaller parties. Each burger is grilled using a special process developed by Mike that sears the meat inside and outside, giving it a delicious flavor throughout. Mike also knows that good food alone is not enough for success. It takes an outstanding, cheerful and skilled wait staff to prepare and deliver your food right to your table. Be sure to stop in, relax and try one of their delicious burgers. Mike will see to it that you have the best burger in town.

3500 ½ W Cary Street, Richmond VA
(804) 358-5225
www.carytownburgersandfries.com

Davis & Main

At the intersection of Davis Avenue and Main Street, in the historic Fan district of Richmond, is a place visitors can discover and locals have enjoyed since 1987–the popular Davis & Main Restaurant. Housed in a 1910 Victoria-style building which was once home to an illegal gambling parlor with slot machines in the garage, this charming restaurant has been voted most romantic restaurant in the Fan. This simple, yet elegant, restaurant prides itself on being supportive of its community by utilizing local vendors and being friendly to the environment by recycling all bottles, cans and cardboard. The restaurant is an advocate of local arts and theatre, and is a pre- and post-show favorite destination, serving dinner until midnight every day. Owner Robert Noland, who has worked in all aspects of the restaurant business for the past 15 years, became manager in 1999 and full owner in 2005. The talented kitchen staff maintains signature dishes and adds new items to keep the menu as fresh and exciting as the food itself. Davis & Main features Virginia wines, specialty sodas and local beer. The menu includes smoked trout and pork tenderloin appetizer; spinach, sweet potato and portabella salad; rosemary garlic marinated beef medallions, and its popular half-pound Angus beef burger. On your next trip to Richmond, support classic dining and the community with a visit to Davis & Main.

2501 W Main Street, Richmond VA
(804) 353-6641
www.davisandmain.com

Honey Whyte's All-American Café

Located in historic Shockoe Bottom, Honey Whyte's All-American Café provides patrons with a Cheers-like environment. At this cozy café, it will only take a couple of visits before you become a loyal regular and everyone knows your name. Here you'll find an enticing traditional American menu offering all your old favorites. Additionally, you can find unique, delicious favorites like fried olives, fried pickles and sausage dip. This neighborhood café and bar also offers live entertainment on Thursdays, Fridays and Saturdays. You can enjoy acoustic bluegrass, blues and folk all weekend long with low or no covers. Owned by Leslie and John Jingloski since 2003, Honey Whyte's has quickly made a name for itself as a favorite among locals for delicious entrées and talented local and touring bands. For a cozy and classy environment and a real taste of local flavor, head to Honey Whyte's All-American Café on Tobacco Row.

2116 E Main Street, Richmond VA
(804) 643-6022

Hyperlink Café

State Senator Benjamin J. Lambert III is no doubt an inspiration to his children, but equally inspirational was their grandmother, a gourmet cook who operated a catering business in Henrico County for 30 years. This background provided the catalyst for the launching of Hyperlink Café, a venture completely designed and executed by three of Benjamin's children. Charles, David and Ann Frances used their combined degrees and expertise to develop an innovative, updated version of the café concept. Located around the corner from the Virginia Commonwealth University Munroe Park campus, the Hyperlink is situated in a large, renovated theater which provides the space for three different turfs. In the first area, tables for two line the windows. Upstairs are four Internet stations, 16 Ethernet ports

and an unlimited capacity for wireless Internet use. Downstairs, a fully stocked bar and a sleek dance floor make this the main party room. Artwork by talented local college students decorates the tall walls. In the corner, an oxygen bar sells oxygen laced with a single or blended aroma, furnishing a quick drug-free revitalization. The café offers music, fund-raisers, special events and great food, striving for a diverse variety of activities and entertainment. There is even an aroma to cure boredom, but you won't need it. As good as its motto, Hyperlink Café specializes in "linking one great time to the next."

814 W Grace Street, Richmond VA
(804) 254-1942
www.hyperlinkva.com

Kobe: Japanese Steaks & Sushi

Just step inside Kobe: Japanese Steaks & Sushi and you'll see what makes it so popular. Owner Sam Yamaguchi wants you to experience a night in Japan with a romantic atmosphere and an exciting restaurant all in one place. You may have a hard time choosing between the two forms of authentic Japanese cuisine. There is the vast array of traditional Japanese sushi and sashimi and the wonderful hibachi-style meals prepared for you by skillful teriyaki chefs right at your table. Sam and his wonderful employees are dedicated to providing exceptional and friendly service and they will be happy to help you decide. With two beautifully decorated floors and upbeat music playing in the background, each member of your party is sure to find the perfect dish to savor. You'll find a full bar and an excellent wine list along with Japanese and domestic beers and *sake*. And if you should happen to come in on a special occasion, like a birthday, the staff will gather around your table and sing the Happy Song as they serve you a lovely dessert, take your picture and present it to you in your own take-home portfolio. At Kobe: Japanese Steaks and Sushi, expect great food, great service and an unforgettable dining experience.

19 S 13th Street, Richmond VA
(804) 643-8080
www.kobesteakandsushi.com

Spinnaker's Restaurant

After nearly 20 years of owning the popular family restaurant called Spinnaker's, Gregg Gregory has earned the right to reflect upon his success. "The secret is hiring only nice people and exceeding the expectations of our guests," he says. Certainly the menu would exceed anyone's expectations for variety. The appetizers alone present such an abundance of choices that you might just order a bunch for your table, pass them around and call it a meal. The crab dip, cheese quesadilla and onion rings are a few highlights. If you make it as far as the entrée selections, you'll have fun choosing between a half-pound burger and the Maryland-style crab cakes or between one of the many steaks or pasta dishes. You will want to sample the restaurant's signature Flower Pot Bread, a yummy wheat bread cooked in a clay flower pot. Many places call themselves kid friendly, but Spinnaker's delivers on its claim with its Kids Eat Free policy on Monday through Thursday. If the name of the restaurant sounds familiar, you might be remembering that Spinnaker's was once a corporation with many locations on the Southeast coast. Gregg bought the business and made it into this one location in Richmond's Chesterfield Towne Center, where the feel is definitely local rather than corporate. Bring the whole family to Spinnaker's soon.

11500 Midlothian Turnpike, Richmond VA
(804) 794-0045
www.spinnakersrichmond.com

Millstone Tea Room

In 2001, Jared and Melanie Srsic took a weathered, old building sitting in front of a vintage 1939 mill and transformed it into Millstone Tea Room, a restaurant evocative of tea rooms that dotted the South in times gone by. The 40-seat dining room is a gem nestled into the foothills of the Blue Ridge Mountains. You can sit at a copper topped table and sip wine from an extensive wine list, while you take in a view of the rolling hills. Jared's kitchen staff creates signature meals, featuring steamed mussels, steaks and jumbo crab cakes. Melanie's pastries, including the profiteroles filled with Tahitian vanilla bean ice cream, are perfect tea accompaniments. All ingredients are fresh and local, and the menu changes with the seasons, reflecting Jared and Melanie's belief that local organic food makes the most exciting menu. All of the dinners are served in several courses by a staff that has been on hand since Millstone Tea Room opened. The five-star service brings in patrons from all over Virginia. In the summer, patio dining is an added treat. The friendly, yesteryear atmosphere makes Millstone a one-of-a-kind traveler's delight. Only 20 minutes from Lynchburg, and open Wednesday through Saturday for dinner and Sundays for brunch, Millstone Tea Room invites you to enjoy its country setting and delightful offerings.

9058 Big Island Highway, Bedford VA
(540) 587-7100
www.millstonetearoom1939.com

Yoho's American Diner

When most people think of a diner, they conjure up a cross between Hollywood's gleaming art deco creations of the 1950s and Arnold's Place from Happy Days. They also remember the comfortable booths, kitschy knick-knacks and down-home style food served by friendly waitresses named Flo and Alice. Luckily for the residents of Richmond, Yoho's American Diner still serves up generous portions of fantastic homemade favorites at a great low price. With a focus on keeping it simple, Owner Guy Yoho can usually deliver whatever the customer requests. Yoho's American Diner is well known for its delicious fresh seafood dishes and their hearty homemade soups. The diner's diverse clientele ranges from folks on their lunch breaks, students and families to local prominent businessmen and politicians. Just about everyone loves the great food at the American Diner. The inviting atmosphere is relaxed and informal, which makes it ideal for everything from quick business lunches to dinner with the gang after soccer practice. The décor of the American Diner is almost as big a draw as the food. Yoho has used the diner as the backdrop for a wonderful collection of antiques and well-displayed oddities that he fi gures is worth more than the diner itself. At the very least the collection is suitable for providing some entertaining dining conversation. On your next visit to Richmond stop in at the American Diner for some great food served by those friendly waitresses who remember what service really means.

11001 Midlothian Turnpike, Richmond VA
(804) 378-5145

Old Original Bookbinders Restaurant

In the 1950s and 60s, everyone from Bob Hope and Richard Nixon to Frank Sinatra and his Rat Pack stopped in for one of the famous 5-pound lobsters this legendary restaurant is known for. Samuel Bookbinder opened the Old Original Bookbinders Restaurant on Philadelphia's waterfront in 1865, and it's been Philadelphia's dining destination and social mecca ever since. Elizabeth Taylor, David Bowie, Mohammed Ali, and yes, Madonna, have all dined alongside locals here and are drawn by the superlative seafood, service, and rich sense of history. John Taxin bought the restaurant from the Bookbinder's in the 1940s, and now his grandson John E. Taxin has opened the first offshoot of this 140-year-old tradition right here in Richmond. True to form, John found the renovated 1901 American cigar company building near the James River to open Bookbinders and the food matches the outstanding quality that John and his family have built their reputation on. But Bookbinders has made its own name for itself, winning the Wine Spectator Award of Excellence for four years. Like the first Bookbinders, they have a large live lobster tank and the signature snapper soup, plus an extensive seafood menu featuring a raw bar and entrees that include shellfish cioppino, crabcades, USDA prime steaks, and of course, the must-have, Live Maine lobster. Executive Chef Roger Murphy spent a year at the Philadelphia location to ensure the food meets the standard of excellence the Bookbinder name is known for. Richmond is indeed lucky to have this wonderful restaurant, and the Old Original Bookbinders Restaurant is proud to carry on its legacy.

2306 E Cary Street, Richmond VA (804) 643-6900
125 Walnut Street, Philadelphia VA (215) 925-7027
www.bookbinders.biz

Shopping & Antiques

Gameboard Antiques

Sometimes a hobby grows into something more. This is exactly what happened for Mary and Bob Game. From Mary's hobby of collecting primitive antiques for her 1741 home and her last name, Gameboard Antiques was born in 1986. She realized her passion as a collector had grown into an exciting business she knows and loves. Mary has been selling antiques for 20 years and she is known for locating items that her customers are searching for. Her antique shop is full of old farm tables, country cupboards and, of course, gameboards. Located in the historic Hallsborough Tavern building, built in 1800, this fabulous shop has more than just old stuff in it. The building was an early tavern and country store, as well as an overnight stagecoach stop between Richmond and Lynchburg. It still retains all the country charm of its past years. Gameboard Antiques also specializes in reproduction Windsor chairs, handmade candles and folk art accessories. Come into Gameboard Antiques and take home a special treasure from the past—it's a tradition.

**16300 Midlothian Turnpike,
Midlothian VA
(804) 794-9200**

Jermie's Needlework Boutique

In 1976, two friends with similar interests, Jerry Crute and Hermie Powell, combined their skills and names to open Jermie's Needlework Boutique, an old-fashioned ladies boutique. Today, this elegant and charming shop is owned by Liz Patton and Sonya Heath. Jermie's is managed by Page Rayner along with employees Mary Beth and Betty. They have all been with the company for more than 10 years. Additionally, staff members Sonya, Cookie, Jackie and Liz have worked at Jermie's for more than 20 years. Combined, this makes for over 110 years of needlework experience and knowledge, all of which is available to the patrons of this one-of-a-kind shop. Jermie's carries an exquisite collection of needlepoint canvases along with supplies and instructional material. A table in the shop offers a well-lit, comfortable environment where customers and the staff can interact and work on projects. For those who are interested in learning needlepoint, the ladies of the staff are happy to offer informal lessons any time of day. Many customers become weekly regulars, so the shop is always bustling with cheery patrons that often become friends. In addition to needlepoint, the shop carries custom bedding, fine linens, men's handkerchiefs, bath towels and other accessories. Each month, the shop features a special promotion that highlights one of their lines such as linen, lingerie or particular needlework projects. Come join the fun and spend an afternoon with the ladies at Jermie's Needlework Boutique.

5701 Grove Avenue, Richmond VA
(804) 282-8021

Memories Galore, Your Scrapbooking Store

Bringing you more than 10,000 scrapbooking items, Memories Galore, Your Scrapbooking Store, is your destination for scrapbooking supplies and inspiration. Serving the tri-cities market with two locations, Memories Galore stocks everything you need to make beautiful memory books for your family and friends to enjoy. Mixing cutting edge scrapbooking supplies with best-selling basics, these stores have lots to offer both the beginner scrapbooker and the advanced scrapbooking artist. They are locally owned and operated and have a friendly staff to help you make your selections. Everything offered in the stores is archival safe and acid free to keep your precious photos safe for generations. For those people that have never scrapbooked but have shoe boxes filled with photos in their closets, time at Memories Galore will be well spent. The store has quick and easy scrapbooking solutions to help you get those photos organized and into albums. Memories Galore also provides journaling supplies so your photos tell a story. Visit Memories Galore for ideas and tips on everything from weddings and family to travel and holidays.

3991 Deep Rock Road, Richmond VA
(804) 565-2000
4800 Market Square Lane, Midlothian VA
(804) 744-6500
www.memoriesgalore.com

Midlothian Antiques Center

There is an antique heaven in the heart of the village of Midlothian. Midlothian Antiques Center comprises 17,000 square feet where 100 dealers display their quality antiques, collectibles and decorative accessories. Owners Ken and Sharon Blount have a low dealer turnover, but they have a fast turnover rate for merchandise. Midlothian Antiques Center is the perfect combination for patrons searching for a treasured piece of history. The mall-like antique market contains items ranging from furniture, glassware and linens to old fishing tackle. The diversity in age and type of antiques stocked in the center make Midlothian Antiques Center one of the most popular antique shopping locations in the area. The Blounts and staff know a large percentage of their repeat customers personally. They hold two open houses every year, one in spring and one for the holidays. Thousands of customers turn out for the open houses, often bringing the whole family along. The owners have five children of their own, so naturally the store is friendly to children as well as wheelchair accessible. Some of the Midlothian Antiques Center business practices are unusual in antique retail; they offer a layaway program, holds and returns. This is the ideal destination to find vintage collectibles. They are located two miles west of Chesterfield Towne Center Shopping Mall, and two miles east of the Route 288 interchange. As the Midlothian Antiques Center logo says, *Live Life in the Past Lane.*

13591 Midlothian Turnpike, Midlothian VA
(804) 897-4913

Gates Antiques Ltd.

Gates Antiques Ltd. is many things for many people. For some the antiques are merely a status symbol. For others, they are pieces of living history. For the Gates family of Midlothian, antiques are a lifestyle. Jo E. Gates grew up in a house full of antiques, with parents who greatly enjoyed purchasing and refurbishing them. After her marriage to husband and partner John Gates, Jo's father told her to go out to the barn and select whatever she wanted from his unfinished stock. Jo and John furnished their home with antiques and in 1961, a business was born. Today, Gates Antiques Ltd. has four main buildings as well as a reputation for quality and fairness. The Gates' son, Jay, began spending most of his waking time at the shop by the time he was four. At the tender age of six he was knowledgeable enough about antiques that he was able to make his first museum sale when he sold a rare, formal high chair to the Magnolia Grange museum. Gates Antiques Ltd. specializes in 18th and 19th century American and English furniture and accoutrements. They offer a full restoration workshop and have often provided period items for historical films. Their focus is to preserve history for future generations and they believe in the concept of merging the past with the present to make it livable and inviting. In addition, the Gates have written their own textbook for beginning through intermediate antique enthusiasts and provide classes for those who want to expand their knowledge and love for antiques. Make Gates Antiques Ltd. your Midlothian resource for fine antiques, accessories and gifts.

12700 Old Buckingham Road, Midlothian VA
(804) 794-8472
www.gatesantiques.com

Penniston's Alley Antiques

Located in historic Old Town Petersburg inside two circa 1814 federal townhouses, you'll find Penniston's Alley Antiques and Collectibles. These two long-lived buildings are among the few remaining structures that survived a great fire in 1815 and went on to endure the ravages of the Civil War. Owners Sid Scott and Chris Brown are flight attendants who have collected accessories and furniture from around the world as well as locally to place in their shop. Visitors are delighted when they walk into this sparkling clean establishment to find a layout with a comfortable, homelike atmosphere. Penniston's Alley specializes in artfully displayed fine 19th century American empire furniture as well as a wide selection of quality antiques and collectibles including English Staffordshire, Flow Blue and glassware. You won't be able to resist sitting down and relaxing here for a while. If you are looking for special jewelry, don't pass up the fine selection of cultured pearls, the Baltic Sea amber and costume jewelry. Penniston's Alley owners and staff are not only knowledgeable in their trade, but can provide details on the rich history of this historic Civil War town. Make Penniston's Alley a destination to enjoy, relax and shop.

102 W Old Street, Petersburg VA
(804) 722-0135
www.craterroad.com/pennistons.html

Enchanted

The owner of Enchanted, Mary Brockman, started her business after she helped with a church bazaar. The bazaar was so successful that it gave Mary the confidence she needed to open her own antique shop in downtown Lynchburg, in 1998. She has been busy searching for antique merchandise for her shop ever since. Enchanted focuses on offering 18th and 19th century English, American and Continental antiques, porcelain and art. Mary's exceptional taste has helped her develop one of the finest porcelain selections in central Virginia. She also offers Oriental rugs and antique silver at appealing prices. The inventory at Enchanted changes weekly, so you will always find something fresh when you visit. Enchanted offers gift and bridal registries to help make your gift giving decisions easier. If you are looking for quality antiques, come to Enchanted, and let Mary and her charming staff help you find appealing items to bring character to your home.

1204 Main Street, Lynchburg VA
(434) 846-5580

Virginia Born & Bred

Nestled in the Shenandoah Valley, Virginia Born & Bred is a small Lexington shop that carries items of beauty and utility, from wonderful Virginia foods to the works of contemporary artists. The staff searches diligently for the finest Virginia themed goods, which include gourmet foods and wines, gift baskets and kitchenware. You will love the Virginia peanuts, hams and local cookbooks. The pottery collection includes the distinctive hand painted pottery of Emerson Creek. You can find beautiful home accessories, garden accents and handcrafted jewelry. Much of the art on display is in the American folk tradition. This official Williamsburg shop carries many gifts related to historic Lexington, Williamsburg and Colonial Virginia. Collectibles include Mary Myers' skillfully carved wooden nutcrackers, including renditions of George Washington and Robert E. Lee. Other wares celebrate such Lexington schools as Washington & Lee University and the Virginia Military Institute. Julie Lindsey and Peggy Maass purchased Virginia Born & Bred in 1993 and in 1995 launched their first mail order catalog. In 2004, three years after Peggy's untimely death, Julie brought in Michele Hentz and Janet Beebe to further develop the mail order and Internet business. Their catalogue now goes out to 500,000 customers. These three ladies pride themselves on superior customer service and guarantee your complete satisfaction. Visit Virginia Born & Bred, where Julie and her staff add exciting discoveries each year.

16 W Washington Street, Lexington VA
(540) 463-1832 or (800) 437-2452
www.virginiabornandbred.com

The Treasure Box

The Treasure Box, in Midlothian, is a one-stop shop for the entirety of your gift-giving needs. This fabulous gift boutique specializes in the fun, funky and fabulous. Carrying a wide selection of themed gifts and accessories The Treasure Box has something for the college grad, golf fan or animal lover on your birthday and holiday lists. They carry a charming array of gifts and accessories for Red Hat Ladies, equestrians, fisherman and hunters. For the police officer, fireman or EMT in your life, The Treasure Box carries a great selection of figurines and collectables commemorating the men, women and lifestyle of the emergency services professions. Owners Carolyn C. and Russell Daugherty opened the shop in May of 2005 after Carolyn realized the area needed a gift-oriented shop. The focus has been to provide unique and special interest gifts for all ages. The Treasure Box offers wonderful collectables and décor items at affordable prices. Their business cards read "Gifts to be Treasured," and that is truly what they have awaiting customers. Displays and inventory change often to reflect the seasons and holidays, and to continually offer fresh, new items. The friendly staff excels in customer service and is always happy to help you find what you're looking for. Stop in and visit with the folks at The Treasure Box and find something that's just perfect for everyone on your gift list.

4838 Commonwealth Center
Parkway, Midlothian VA
(804) 744-0018

Precious Memories Reading and Collectibles

Bell Hooks said, "Life-transforming ideas have always come to me through books." This is a perfect description of Linda Pate's vision when she opened Precious Memories Reading and Collectibles in 2004. Precious Memories is not just a bookstore, it's an affirmation of the importance of community, connection with others and how it can be created through the influence of books. Books bring people together and by reading them and talking about them people learn and grow with and from each other. Linda's bookstore is a labor of love and her theme is that books hold the keys that help people get through life. In developing Precious Memories she's set the stage for many different community opportunities. She's partnered with the Richmond Public School system and the Let's Read Program by offering reading and activity space and guidance to children and youth. Her Trading Post offers the opportunity for those who may be financially challenged to read for free. She supports and encourages local authors, holds book signings and features an author of the month. Friday nights are poetry nights and there are many other different readings, workshops and retreats where people can come with friends and family. Of course, her invitation to just come in, relax and relate to each other is always open. So if you're in the market for a good book, come visit Linda at Precious Memories.

3229 Idlewood Avenue, Richmond VA
(804) 726-8501
www.preciousmemoriesreading.com

The Eclectic Shop

The Eclectic Shop is the largest Fenton Art Glass dealer in Virginia and one of the largest nationwide. Owned by Mike and Betty Eyler, the shop is an eclectic mix of everything you can imagine in gift wares. The Manly Room, created for the manly man, opened in 2005. The Eylers work to provide everything anyone could want or need at The Eclectic Shop. The over 5,000-square-foot area is filled with over 200 different lines of collectibles and gifts. The Christmas section has 2,000 square feet devoted to it and is stocked all year with choices from well-known brand names such as Department 56, Cow Parade, Snowbabies and Clothtique Santas. The web store allows an online perusal of Fenton, Lenox and Charming Tails. They also carry Willow

Tree and Byers' Choice. In stock items are shipped within 24 hours of your order, with free gift wrapping and shipping on orders over 50 dollars and all other orders shipped for only five dollars. Layaway and special orders are accommodated. Browse the website or for an awe-inspiring experience or swing by The Eclectic Shop showroom and spend an afternoon enjoying a Colonial Heights treasure.

26 Pickwick Shopping Center,
Colonial Heights VA
(804) 526-9165 or (877) 732-0178
www.eclecticshop.com

Silver Thistle

Since 1997, Silver Thistle has been offering unique and imaginative home accessories and fine gifts from around the world. Much of this upscale merchandise is usually only found through interior designers. Silver Thistle's large, eclectic inventory exudes quality and rarity while spanning numerous decorative styles. Brides can find tasteful wedding invitations and a bridal registry that allows a choice of over 100 patterns of fine and casual china, plus stemware and table linens. Silver Thistle is also the place to turn for lamps, mirrors, rugs and accent furniture; it carries the largest lampshade collection in the area. Classic personal stationary and desktop accessories, like clocks and frames, are always appreciated. Customers seeking to start or add to collections often find the pieces they seek at Silver Thistle, like William Wood's realistic tin and hand-cut copper floral

arrangements. Look also for enameled boxes by New York designer Jay Strongwater. These pieces are crafted like fine jewelry and inset with crystals. Majolica and silver collectors also find intriguing choices. The shop carries fine antique furniture and Oriental carpets along with many special occasion gifts, including unusual holiday ornaments, silver-plated music boxes, baby blankets and refreshing oddities, like an elegant bottle of laundry soap that smells just like the beach. With surprising diversity and items destined for heirloom status, a walk through Silver Thistle is always exciting. Join customers from Washington, D.C., Texas and California who cherish this shop. Visit Silver Thistle in Lynchburg or browse through a delightful and well-organized website.

4925 Boonsboro Road, Lynchburg VA
(434) 384-3882
www.thesilverthistle.com

Black Swan Books

Black Swan Books is a specialty bookseller that deals almost exclusively in rare, out-of-print and first edition books. A buyer is usually on-site, but it is recommended that you call prior to your visit to ensure availability. The shop accepts classic literature, scholarly works, anything having to do with Virginia or the Civil War and children's books. Black Swan also has an interest in tomes about art, religion and philosophy as well as volumes dedicated to gardening and cooking. Owners Nicholas and Ellen Cooke are also interested in leather-bound volumes and those of an antiquarian nature. Although they do not accept textbooks, paperbacks, current popular fiction or most encyclopedias, if you have a volume you feel is interesting or of value, take it to Black Swan Books for appraisal. Black Swan judges each book based on condition, content, scarcity and available store stock. Sellers are paid with either cash or store credit. If you can't make it down to the Black Swan, its buyers can come to you. Just call and make an appointment, and someone will come over to review your books. Gather up your unwanted editions and take them to Black Swan Books, the extraordinary purveyors of the rare, scarce and out-of-print books you've been searching for.

2601 W Main Street, Richmond VA
(804) 353-9476
www.blackswanbooks.com

Metro Sound & Music Co.

If you're in Richmond and need an instrument, Metro Sound & Music is likely to have what you're looking for. When you're ready to record, Metro Sound Studio is ready too. Metro supplies quality vintage and new instruments. They feature the incredible new Brubaker line of guitars with the exclusive interchangeable module pre-amp and deep bolt-through neck attachment. They carry a rare variety of vintage treasures in addition to the new inventory. Metro has every conceivable musical product from guitars and PA systems to lights and keyboards. For recording purposes, the Metro Sound Studio is second to none. Located upstairs, the 3,500-square-foot jewel boasts five arranging rooms, all air-conditioned. The main tracking room is an impressive 60 feet by 26 feet, the biggest in the region. A spacious engineering room and isolation booth round out these accommodations, along with a roomy waiting area, optional kitchen and catered meals. Downstairs, the full-line music store gives the players access to an amazing array of modern and classic instruments and effects, providing endless creative opportunities. The Metro staff is a valuable resource of skilled musicians, vocalists and recording engineers all able to assist you. Recording options range from demo packages to complete 64-track music production. Owner Mark Szafranski believes in his products and so do his customers. The store was rated as the editor's choice by *Richmond* magazine as Richmond's Best Instrument Store. One look inside Metro Sound & Music will make you a believer, too.

117 W Broad Street, Richmond VA
(804) 643-7125 or (800) 587-0033
www.metrosound.com

Accents Unlimited

Accents Unlimited in Midlothian offers customers an exciting resource for gifts, jewelry and personal accessories. Since 1985 Accents Unlimited has been offering the best in personalized service and products of fine quality and value. With a welcoming atmosphere and an uncommon selection of goods, this fabulous store is also a place where friends can meet, explore and truly enjoy their shopping experience. Accents Unlimited carries an extensive array of accessories including the Vera Bradley collection of handbags and luggage. Additionally, they feature customizable sterling jewelry from Chamilia that allows you to purchase special beads to create and change your own anklet, bracelet or necklace. Shoppers will delight in the cornucopia of Christmas decorations and ornaments, including Snowbabies and collectible Santas. Other specialties include clever tapestry throws called Zoppini that are made using a photograph provided by the customer at the time of order. Corky, a three-year-old Yorkshire terrier, is the store's official greeter who enjoys meeting and playing with other dogs when they come with their owners to tour the shop. In honor of Corky and dog lovers everywhere, the shop also carries a wide selection of dog-oriented products. The inventory here changes often, making this store a must-see on all of your trips to the Midlothian area. So stop on in, Corky is waiting for you at Accents Unlimited.

4632 Commonwealth Centre Parkway, Midlothian VA
(804) 763-1566

The Gardener's Gate

If you've grown tired of the same old floral arrangements, then check out the original and contemporary designs created by Lisa Wiggins of The Gardener's Gate in Hopewell. Lisa opened this delightful shop in 2002 with the help of her husband and partner Jud Rietdorf. They have quickly turned it into the resource for fabulous flowers, gifts and antiques. Known primarily for their party and garden arrangements, The Gardener's Gate uses unusual and interesting materials in each custom creation. Lisa truly loves what she does and it shines through in each of her original designs. Whether she is using classic red roses in a simple glass vase or exotics that overflow from a vintage basket, you are sure to have a memorable and provocative arrangement when she is done. In conjunction with the fabulous array of majestic flowers and floral arrangements that are available, The Gardener's Gate also offers patrons a wide selection of gift items including glass and stemware, soybean candles and home décor. Additionally, this whimsical florist can provide fantastic fruit baskets that feature luscious fresh fruits artfully arranged into things of beauty. The Gardener's Gate is also listed as a full service FTD Florist, which means you can order online or by phone 24 hours a day and receive incredible works of living floral art delivered right to your door. Expect and receive the very best with flowers and gifts from The Gardener's Gate.

208 N Main Street, Hopewell VA
(804) 452-4424 or (866) 452-4424
www.gardenersgate.net

Wineries

Barboursville Vineyards

Wine Spectator magazine calls Barboursville Vineyards "America's most dynamic large regional winery—and its most urbane." If you haven't tried its prize winning Cabernet Franc, the tasting room inside the northern Italian-style farmhouse is a great place to get acquainted with it or any of the other 15 wines produced here. One feels the air of urbanity not only inside the tasting room but at the winery's Palladio Restaurant, where the wines find their true complement in the classic northern Italian cuisine. Barboursville Vineyard achieved a milestone in 1997 when the Cabernet Franc won the Virginia Governor's Cup. Later vintages continue to earn praise, such as the 2004, which a critic for the *Napa Valley Register* ranked as the best he tasted at one wine show. He commended the "deep earthy-cherry aroma" and the "faint black pepper note" that added complexity. In short, this winery is living up to the dreams of the Zonin family, who established Barboursville Vineyard in 1976 to bring the great Italian winemaking tradition to Virginia. Believe it or not, the outstanding wine and food are not the only reasons to visit the vineyard. There is history to explore as well among the ruins of the Barbour mansion, designed by Thomas Jefferson to be the grandest residence in Orange County. There's also room for three couples to stay at the adjoining 1804 Inn. Venture to Barboursville Vineyards, and make a day of it.

17655 Winery Road, Barboursville VA
(540) 832-3824
www.barboursvillewine.com

James River Cellars Winery

James River Cellars Winery is a remarkable example of one of over 100 unique and charming wineries in Virginia, producing some of the countries top wines. Viticulturist and Owner Ray Lazarchic, his daughter Mitzi, and her Winemaker husband, James Batterson, work carefully to create the award-winning nectars this winery is famous for producing. The crew at James River is delighted that the Dolce Vino, an icc-style dessert wine made using the unique Chardonel grape, won the Governor's Cup, the most esteemed wine competition in Virginia. Lazarchic maintains the vineyards, whcih include nine different grape varieties on 20 acres at their farm in Montpelier, Virginia. Batterson then creates an amazing array of different wines all from 100 percent Virginia grown grapes. The winery, with its down-to-earth family oriented atmosphere, is an enjoyable place to visit. Fridays on the Patio os a monthly event which features live music, light food, and wine-tasting, where hundreds of people show up to partake in the fun. The winery is open year 'round, seven days a week for wine tasting and tours. You can also bring a picnic and enjoy their beautiful patio or sit indoors and look out over the property. The gift shop also offers special merchandise for shoppers. One visit to James River Cellars Winery and you'll want to choose several wines to bring home with you.

11008 Washington Highway, Glen Allen VA
(804) 550-7516
www.jamesrivercellars.com

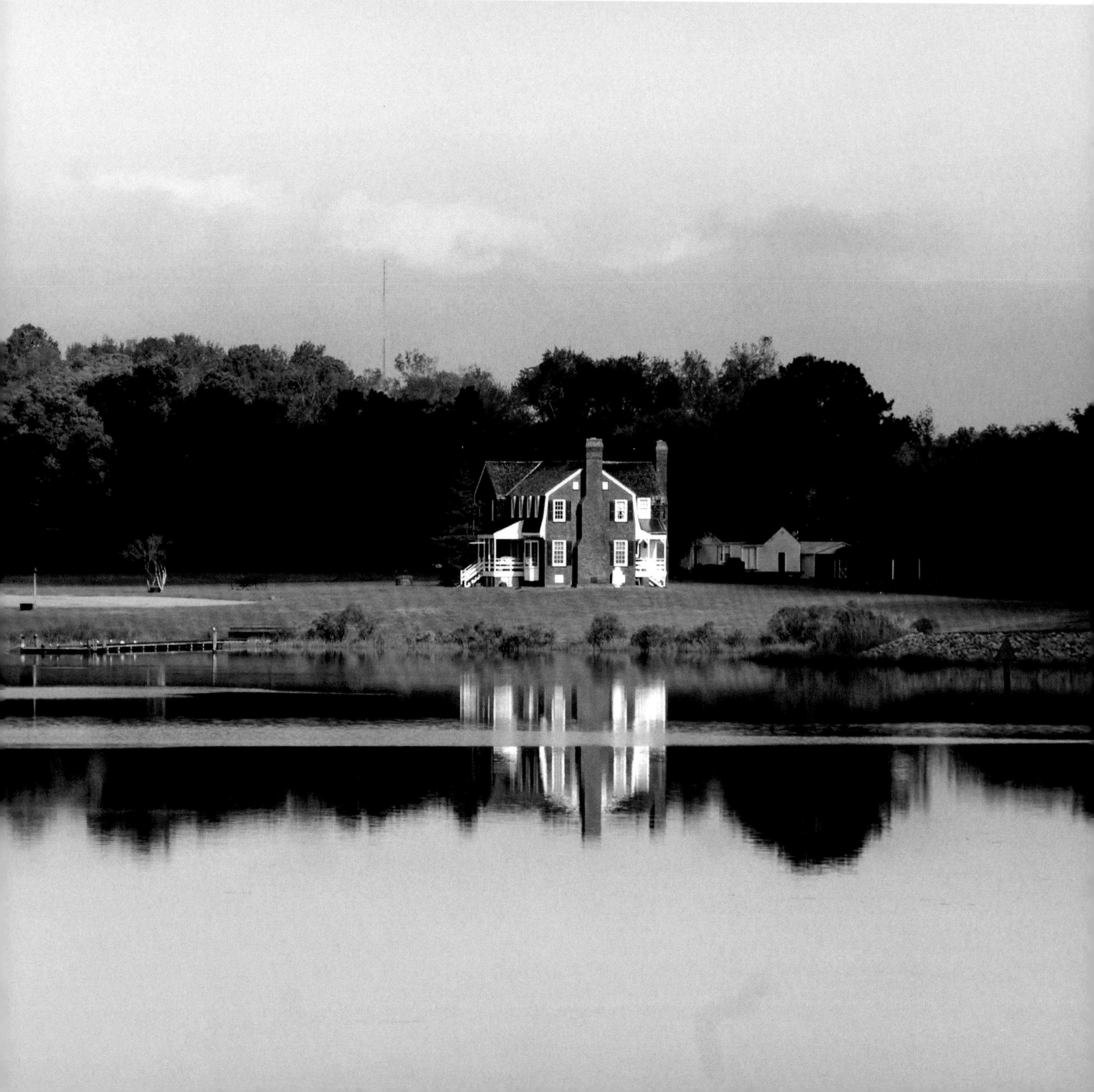

Northern Virginia

Accommodations

Alexandria & Arlington and Capital Area Bed & Breakfast Networks

You'll experience a feeling much like the one that accompanies staying with family friends when you choose your accommodations through the Alexandria & Arlington and Capital Area Bed & Breakfast Networks, or AABBN. When you ring the bell, you will feel like a distant relative expected for a visit. The network makes reservations for charming homes with one to 40 rooms at each location. All proprietors are gracious hosts with hospitality running through their veins. The network can help you secure a whole house for an extended visit or a quick overnight getaway in one cozy room. Travel-savvy customers find all of the network's homes desirably located in older neighborhoods, in or close to Old Town Alexandria and Washington DC. The network's listings also include bed and breakfasts and extended stay homes in northern Virginia, Maryland and beyond. Are you staying in the capital area for 30 days or more? Arrange a fully furnished extended stay through AABBN. The network is a complimentary service for the well traveled who seek more than a hotel room. Visit the network's useful website for suggestions personally tailored to your needs. Try the Alexandria & Arlington and Capital Area Bed & Breakfast Networks for your next stay in the capital area. The welcome mat is out for you.

4938 Hampden Lane, Bethesda MD
(703) 549-3415
www.aabbn.com

Americana Hotel

The Americana Hotel, completed in 1963, was one of the first hotels constructed in Arlington's urban village of Crystal City and is renowned for its superb guest accommodations and concierge services. This stately hotel is family owned and operated by Libby and Carole Newman and offers 102 comfortable rooms along with an extended list of amenities, including a complimentary Continental breakfast, parking and a shuttle service. The Americana underwent remodeling in 2004 and features an array of modern luxuries, such as cable television and wireless Internet access, as well as laundry and valet service, daily newspapers and air-conditioned rooms. Hotel staff members are dedicated to providing guests with personable and personalized service at every turn and are happy to assist you with anything you might need during your stay. Guests can also make arrangements with the hotel for tours of Crystal City, which is teeming with exciting metropolitan attractions, including an extensive network of underground shopping areas and connecting corridors. Americana Hotel is centrally located just one block from Crystal City Metro, which can quickly take you such attractions as Arlington Cemetery and the White House. Enjoy a relaxed stay in Arlington highlighted by impeccable service reminiscent of a bygone era at the Americana Hotel.

1400 Jefferson Davis Highway, Arlington VA
(703) 979-3772

The Inn of Rosslyn

The excitement and sights of Washington, D.C. are just five minutes away from the comfortable, quiet rooms of the Inn of Rosslyn. Father and son team John and William D. Green built the hotel in 1957, and it continues to remain in the caring hands of the family, operated now by William's daughter Carole. The cozy, 38-unit hotel is situated in a residential neighborhood just two short blocks from the Rosslyn Washington Metro subway station, where the monuments and attractions of the capital city are mere stops away. After a deluxe Continental breakfast, leave your vehicle in the inn's free parking lot and enjoy a short walk to the station in the fresh air or take advantage of the complimentary shuttle service to quickly get you to the subway and off exploring. The smiling employees clearly enjoy their work, perhaps illustrated best by longtime manager Bertha Carpenter, who recently retired after more than 40 years of service at the hotel. Staff members are quick to recommend one of the several nearby dining establishments or many area sightseeing options, such as the White House, Capitol Building and Arlington National Cemetery. For convenience and comfort, stay at the Green family's inviting hotel, the Inn of Rosslyn, on your next trip to Washington, D.C.

1601 Arlington Boulevard, Arlington VA
(703) 524-3400

Washington Suites Alexandria

Too bad Washington Suites Alexandria wasn't around in George Washington's day, because he would have enjoyed the comforts of this Alexandria hotel. No doubt it's the all-suite accommodations and ideal location that draw men of distinction to this full-service hotel. All of their suites feature a full kitchen, a newly remodeled bathroom, oversized working desk with high speed Internet and a living room. The hotel is located in a quiet residential neighborhood, just minutes away from Old Town Alexandria and nine miles from dozens of Washington, D.C. attractions. Some of the free amenities that make this hotel a great value are the continental breakfast, the shuttle to and from Van Dorn Metro Station, and ample outdoor parking. The hotel also features a business center, a fitness center and a full service restaurant. Stop by Duke's Market Café, the full service restaurant, for an order of crab cakes or a fine steak. AAA awards Washington Suites Alexandria three diamonds for such thoughtful touches as an in-room hair dryer, iron and ironing board, the daily paper delivered to your doorstep each morning, and freshly baked cookies at check in. If you are hosting a meeting you will find 5,000 square feet of meeting space to accommodate up to 100 guests. All inclusive meeting packages are available. All meeting rooms include complimentary, unlimited high-speed Internet pull-down multimedia screens. Book your next visit to D.C. at Washington Suites Alexandria—that's what George Washington would do.

100 S Reynolds Street, Alexandria VA
(703) 370-9600 or (877) 736-2500
www.washingtonsuitesalexandria.com

Bakeries, Coffee & Tea

Kingsbury Chocolates

There are some things in life you can skimp on, like coffee filters and plastic glasses; but when it comes to chocolate, only the finest quality will do. Find sumptuous handmade chocolates in a multitude of delicious flavors at Kingsbury Chocolates, where Owner and Chocolatier Rob Kingsbury uses only fresh ingredients and imported chocolates to create a distinctive array of fine specialty confections. Rob, a Vermont native, spent the spring of his youth helping his grandparents with their maple syrup farm and working in his grandmother's restaurant during the summer. His gourmet treats reflect his past culinary experiences and include such delights as Vermont maple popcorn balls, dark chocolate bourbon cherries and a variety of sugar crèmes. Kingsbury Chocolates further offers an original assortment of truffles in such flavors as cardamom blueberry and caramel coffee. An outstanding Brie truffle features triple Brie cheese and dark chocolate rolled in toasted black sesame seeds. Rob also carries a selection of premium ice creams, made by local companies like Gifford's, as well as hot chocolate mixes and chocolate fondues. Rob's chocolates, which have been featured in numerous magazines, including *Southern Living*, make ideal hostess or thank you gifts, and Rob's two or four-piece truffle boxes are perfect as party favors or place setting additions. Rob and his talented staff also specialize in creating corporate gift baskets and customized chocolates that come packaged with your company's name or logo. Indulge yourself with exquisite confections from Kingsbury Chocolates.

1017 King Street, Alexandria VA
(703) 548-2800
www.kingsburychocolates.com

Fashion

Janal Leather

Customers can always find a great fitting leather jacket or a pair of Western style boots in just the right color at Janal Leather, because the shop specializes in custom made items. Owners Alfredo Arguijo and Janice Kraus opened the store full of handmade leather goods and silver jewelry in 2004. Alfredo grew up learning about the leather industry, and his family still owns a leather manufacturing business in Mexico. Because of Alfredo's family connections, Janal is able to offer its customers very competitive prices. The store, located in historic downtown Culpeper, carries a full selection of jackets, purses, belts and boots ready for you to wear out of the store. The Trinity Flowers Western mule is hand painted with beautiful swirling flowers, and the Petite Bowler purse is sure to add a chic punch to your ensemble. Men's jacket choices range from the classic Rustic Bomber to the hip look of the Leon Racer. If your heart is set on a particular color or style not in stock, Alfredo and Janice are happy to have a piece custom made just for you. The high quality Spanish and Italian leather, regarded by many as the best leather in the world, is hand tooled and crafted in Leon, Mexico. Artisans give each item detailed attention, and one pair of boots may take 16 hours or more to create. For quality leather goods handcrafted to your specifications, visit Janal Leather.

102 E Davis Street, Culpeper VA
(540) 829-5590
www.janalleather.com

Galleries & Fine Art

My Place in Tuscany

Add vibrant, elegant and artful touches to every room of your home with a visit to My Place in Tuscany, a spectacular Italian ceramics shop and Italian art gallery in historic Old Town Alexandria. The owner travels throughout Italy several times each year to explore and meet with many artists and to personally select stunning, handmade ceramics, decorative accent pieces and original paintings that line her shop. My Place in Tuscany carries a distinctive selection of ceramics, including biscotti jars, tureens, large urns and wall plates, as well as place settings, serving dishes, platters and custom pieces that feature historic images from such places as the Cortona, Sienna, Montepulciano, the Amalfi Coast, Venice and other enchanting locations. The gallery-like shop carries original artwork and unique pieces of Italian majolica, the ceramic art form which originated during the Renaissance. The majolica selected for the shop is handmade and painted free-hand by master artisans in Tuscany, Umbria, Emiglia Romana and other regions, artists who use the same Old World ceramic crafting techniques that have been handed down through the generations. Discover the beauty of Italy at My Place in Tuscany.

1127 King Street, Alexandria VA
(703) 683-8882 or (800) 261-5407
info@myplaceintuscanycom
www.myplaceintuscany.com

Elizabeth Stone Gallery

Many of the beautiful illustrations found in children's books are visual gateways that send our imaginations to far away places. It is these vivid colors and inspiring sights that prompted Elizabeth Stone, elementary school librarian, to open the Elizabeth Stone Gallery, which specializes in original art created by children's book illustrators. This gallery features the art of more than 100 internationally known and award-winning children's book illustrators, such as Wendell Minor, Elisa Kleven, Lynn Munsinger, Emily Arnold McCully, Gennady Spirin and James Ransome. Elizabeth's love affair with children's book illustrations began during her 15-year stint as a librarian for the Brookside Cranbrook School in Bloomfield Hills, Michigan. There, she acquired a fine collection of children's book artwork for the school which has since been enjoyed by a multitude of students, faculty and parents. Elizabeth relocated her gallery from Michigan to Old Town Alexandria in 2006. She expanded her business to include the placement of children's book art in pediatric hospitals and facilities as well as in corporate and government collections. Elizabeth Stone Gallery offers a distinctive collection of original art, signed limited editions and children's books that are ideal for the young and young at heart. Whether you are new to the world of children's book illustration or an avid collector in search of new and inspiring pieces, you will thoroughly enjoy the magical world of Elizabeth Stone Gallery.

1127 King Street, Suite 201, Alexandria VA
(703) 706-0025
www.elizabethstonegallery.com

Gallery Lafayette

Gallery Lafayette in Old Town Alexandria is the studio of artist Todd Healy, a place to find antique prints, including bird's eye views of Washington, D.C. and the surrounding vicinity, and a frame shop. The handsome display space shows off Todd's well known watercolors of historic buildings in and around Alexandria. Todd's studio is home to his original art, his hand watercolored limited edition prints and gifts with Alexandria and Mount Vernon themes. A native Virginian, Todd studied art in Southern California and central Florida before moving to Alexandria in 1976. Todd and his staff truly love being here and gear the shop to serve their neighbors. In 1986, Todd started an annual tradition with his first Alexandria calendar and now sells 30,000 copies of the calendar each year. Make Gallery Lafayette part of your exploration of Old Town Alexandria.

320 King Street, Alexandria VA
(703) 548-5266
www.gallerylafayette.net

Sackville Galleries

Russell B. Niblett, a self-proclaimed history buff, began collecting paintings and other original works of art more than 15 years ago. In 1999, he opened the doors to Sackville Galleries, where Russell shares his passion for art with patrons. Collectors from around the country count on the galleries for their selection of American and European fine paintings and antiques. You may discover Italian marble statues from the 1900s, beautiful bronzes or antique French furniture on a visit to Sackville Galleries. Russell also specializes in delicate Dresden and Staffordshire porcelain figurines. Sackville Galleries exhibits the paintings of the late Washington, D.C. artist Benson Moore, a renowned landscape and wildlife artist, and Marian Heitmueller, an early 20th century artist whose subject matter often included the Blackfoot Native American Indian tribe. If you have an undiscovered treasure in your attic, the gallery is happy to recommend various local service providers, such as certified appraisers. Store manager Michelle LeFrance can also advise shoppers on how to care for their purchases to ensure they will be handed down to future generations. Visit the Sackville Galleries in Old Town Alexandria for finds both old and new.

1001 & 1009 King Street, Alexandria VA
(703) 838-5507

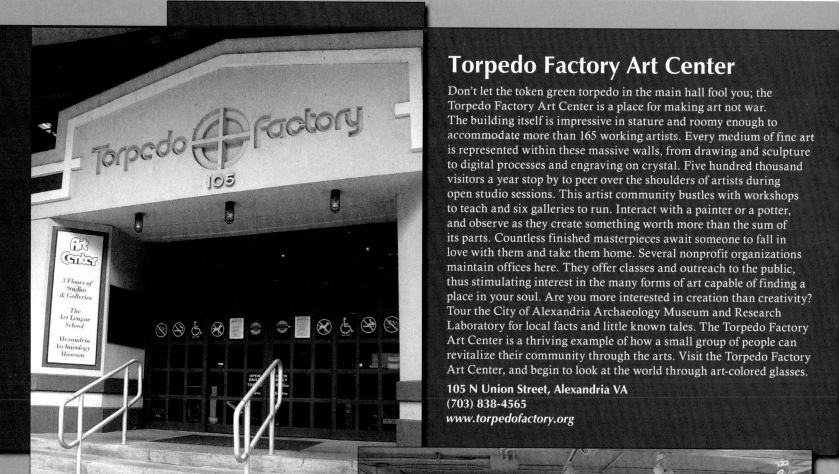

Torpedo Factory Art Center

Don't let the token green torpedo in the main hall fool you; the Torpedo Factory Art Center is a place for making art not war. The building itself is impressive in stature and roomy enough to accommodate more than 165 working artists. Every medium of fine art is represented within these massive walls, from drawing and sculpture to digital processes and engraving on crystal. Five hundred thousand visitors a year stop by to peer over the shoulders of artists during open studio sessions. This artist community bustles with workshops to teach and six galleries to run. Interact with a painter or a potter, and observe as they create something worth more than the sum of its parts. Countless finished masterpieces await someone to fall in love with them and take them home. Several nonprofit organizations maintain offices here. They offer classes and outreach to the public, thus stimulating interest in the many forms of art capable of finding a place in your soul. Are you more interested in creation than creativity? Tour the City of Alexandria Archaeology Museum and Research Laboratory for local facts and little known tales. The Torpedo Factory Art Center is a thriving example of how a small group of people can revitalize their community through the arts. Visit the Torpedo Factory Art Center, and begin to look at the world through art-colored glasses.

105 N Union Street, Alexandria VA
(703) 838-4565
www.torpedofactory.org

Art & Framing by Valentino

Visitors to Art & Framing by Valentino quickly discover that the gallery's dedication to up-and-coming local artists extends beyond simply exhibiting their works. Through online features, plus shows and receptions held at the gallery, customers learn about the painters themselves and may even get to meet the artists in person. Paintings often take on a deeper meaning when accompanied by knowledge of a person's history, such as the works of retired firefighter Michael McGurk, who fought dangerous blazes and served his community for many years, including participating in recovery efforts after September 11th. Owner Rose Valentino, who opened the store in 1986, also offers original and limited edition artwork by nationally known artists as well as custom framing. As members of the Professional Picture Framing Association, or PPFA, the gallery's qualified staff members provide top quality conservation framing of your precious works. Valentino's framers can preserve small mementos and other keepsakes that do not fit in standard frames in three-dimensional shadow boxes. Come to Art & Framing by Valentino in the Hollin Hall Shopping Center or visit their website for an in-depth look at Washington metro artists and an opportunity to meet all your framing needs.

7916 Fort Hunt Road, Alexandria VA
(703) 768-9300
www.art-and-framing.com

Health & Beauty

Salon Guenet

Salon Guenet creates techniques based on individual lifestyles. This vision is derived from current fashions, art and music, as they collaborate with numerous professionals in their field of work. Inspired by their vocation, the staff members constantly advance their knowledge in order to offer the latest styles and trends during consultation. The team at Salon Guenet is educated by Vidal Sassoon in London and hold over 23 years of experience in the field. As creative hair designers and color specialists, their goal is to make every guest look and feel their best. Salon Guenet also offers Ultimate Spa manicures and pedicures using therapeutic ingredients. Whether you want to look special for a wedding, anniversary or just a fun night out on the town, Salon Guenet will help you flaunt your absolute best.

312 S Washington Street, Suite 6C, Alexandria VA
(703) 299-8878
www.salonguenet.com

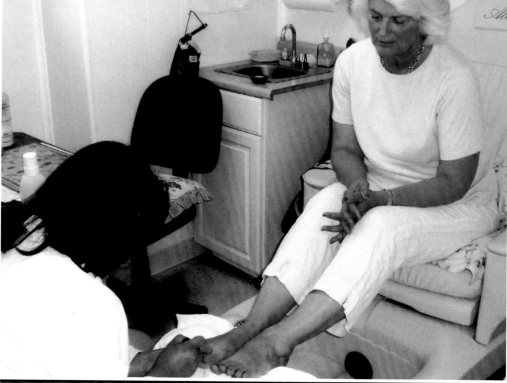

Sugar House Day Spa and Salon

Sugar House Day Spa and Salon is a sweet place to visit. The freestanding 1795 townhouse has been lovingly restored to its original grandeur, taking full advantage of 12-foot ceilings, handsome period moldings and solid brass chandeliers. Guests stepping into the Sugar House for the first time find themselves awed by the grand mahogany staircase and original pine floors. The spa gets its name from the Old Town sugar refinery that the 10,000-square-foot building was built over. Three stories of hair, nail and body treatments assure discriminating clients will feel nurtured. Geared to the needs of the urban client who doesn't have time to travel to an overnight spa, the Sugar House is ideally located a short distance from the King Street Metro and Washington, D.C. Owners Erika and Nandor Szuprics and Robert and Mary Steidl have created an environment of relaxation in a high-tech world. Luxurious chaises support your body while you retreat. Guests appreciate private dressing rooms, house lockers and treatment rooms that feature Vichy showers. Enjoy your facial or massage in a large suite with a fireplace. The Sugar House focuses on preventive health care and positive wellness treatments that will boost your energy and self-confidence. Find your sweet spot at Sugar House Day Spa and Salon.

111 N Alfred Street, Alexandria VA
(703) 549-9940
www.sugarhousedayspa.com

Spa Zen

Escape to a peaceful haven; indulge in a new level of comfort; revitalize your body, mind and spirit; and be totally pampered at Spa Zen, a full-service day spa in the heart of downtown Culpeper, where the staff is attuned to your every need. Try out the signature spa package, known as Zen Tranquility, which spoils you with an herbal body wrap, an hour long hot stone massage, a hydrating stress relief facial, and a spa manicure and pedicure. Spa Zen is the Shangri-la style creation of Janev Yucel, who owned a successful spa in Los Angeles and moved to Culpeper to retire and be close to her family. Janev, an aesthetician for more than 25 years, hails from Cyprus, then Turkey and London, before settling in California. When she saw the need for a high-end spa in Culpeper, she came out of retirement to provide beauty care and stress relief to men and women of all ages. She loves helping people stay youthful with products that keep you looking and feeling great. Her specialties are European facials, microdermabrasion and aromatherapy with essential oils she mixes herself. The shop exudes peace and tranquility with an Asian Zen theme. You will want to start unwinding and relaxing by arriving early and turning off the cell phone in preparation for luxurious pampering by the expert staff at Spa Zen.

302 E Davis Street, Suite 100, Culpeper VA
(540) 727-0327
www.spazenspa.com

Home & Garden

Decorium Gift & Home

Decorium Gift & Home is a King Street classic that attracts locals from Northern Virginia, the District of Columbia and Maryland. The store has also become a tourist attraction. Decorium was started by Jeff Albert, who grew up with a mother who was an interior designer and a father who owned a retail furniture establishment. It was only time before Jeff would have his own furniture shop. After 25 years in the corporate retail environment, Jeff made his entry into opening his own business, now called Decorium Gift & Home. Decorium marries classic designs with today's artfully and whimsical home and gift items in an air that is just as brilliant as it is fantastic. Decorium is not just a place to buy furniture or a great gift, but can draw from a library with over 500 books to find that perfect piece for your home. The store also offers in-home consultations with a team of people that have over 27 years of design experience. Don't miss Decorium Gift & Home to find a fun gift or to put some personality into your dwelling.

116 King Street, Alexandria VA
(703) 739-4662
www.decoriumhome.com

Buon Fresco & the Academy of Wall Artistry

Buon Fresco & the Academy of Wall Artistry is an innovative, award-winning and trend-setting decorative art studio. Its work has been featured in magazines such as *Better Homes & Gardens* and the *Washingtonian,* and in newspapers such as the *Washington Post* and the *Wall Street Journal.* It has been featured two times on Home & Garden Television and in the Dreamworks film, *Head of State.* Recent awards include the Best of 2005 Excellence in Design award from *Walls & Ceilings Magazine.* The studio has won the Elizabeth Warnock Prize for Decorative Painting Excellence twice. The Academy of Wall Artistry is Buon Fresco's school, founded to pass the studio's artistic excellence on to students. The curriculum of the Academy features Buon Fresco's exclusive designs and techniques, and teaches studio specialties such as Venetian plaster, gold and metal leafing, decorative painting and focal wall design. Another useful topic is marketing and business instruction for artists. Courses are designed for students ranging from beginner to advanced. The Academy conducts its classes in Alexandria, minutes from the nation's capitol. Private and group instruction is available at your location. Buon Fresco & the Academy of Wall Artistry are directed by Victoria Bingham. Andre Kouznetsov is the principal muralist for Buon Fresco. For more information, contact the studio at its website or through its toll-free telephone number.

6442 Overlook Drive, Alexandria VA
(703) 914-5606 or
(888) N-FRESCO (637-3726)
www.bfresco.com

The Fine Art of André N. Kouznetsov

André N. Kouznetsov is well known in Washington D.C. for such striking murals as the Art Deco jazz mural at BET restaurant. Kouznetsov's full-length portrait of Plàcido Domingo dominates a wall at Café Milano and a textured map mural of Provencal, France, sets the mood at Le Lavandou. His stunning mural of an intricately detailed Baroque Italian cupola appears to be multi-dimensional, though it is painted over a flat as a board ceiling in a Maryland residence. André began to win an audience for his art in 1981 during mandatory military service in the Soviet army. Rather than being stationed in a frozen outpost, André painted murals for the army in St. Petersburg not far from the tiny hamlet of Siverskaya, where he grew up. Today, he is a citizen of the United States with a loyal following in the nation's capital city. Depending on the theme, Kouznetsov's paintings can use light and color for brilliant or restrained drama. His pieces have consistently sold out at art shows, including the National Symphony Orchestra Show Houses. In one such show house, his mural of the Dordogne France can be seen to this day in a Dreamworks film, *Head of State*, whose committee chose the house after reviewing Kouznetsov's mural and wall designs for the space. A selection of available paintings and murals are viewable on André's website. He is also available for portrait commissions on a limited basis. To learn more about André Kouznetsov's painting and mural art, visit the website or call the studio.

6442 Overlook Drive, Alexandria VA
(888) 637-3726 (Studio) or (202) 437-5426 (Cell)
www.Andre-K.com

Photos by Bob Lennox

J. Brown & Co.

J. Brown & Co. offers home décor and accessories, along with floral and garden accents, in an exceptional setting. Only top-quality items make it into J. Brown's inventory. At this shop, you'll discover rare painted armoires and furniture to complement your décor. Stroll through the rooms and you'll see Anna Weatherley china, Jay Strongwater pieces and MacKenzie-Childs' extraordinary tableware. You'll find striking objects from the Faberge, Victoria and Richard collections. Chandeliers, lamps and porcelain's from Chelsea House adorn the shop. Oil paintings line the walls. J. Brown stocks a fabulous collection of permanent floral products you can choose from to create your own custom arrangement. Outdoor garden furnishings such as Faux Bois benches, containers, and French pots are here for the discerning landscaper. John Brown, the proprietor, is frequently off on a quest to find more wonders for his great clients and friends to decorate with. John's philosophy is, "Get in touch with your senses. Surround yourself with furnishings and accessories that you feel comfortable with. Use your beautiful pieces daily." Light a candle for a wonderful scent, sit in a chair with a comfy down pillow or enjoy a beverage in an attractive vessel. Let J. Brown & Co. help make your surroundings beautiful—your style.

1119 King Street, Alexandria VA
(703) 548-9010

My Place in Tuscany

Add vibrant, elegant and artful touches to every room of your home with a visit to My Place in Tuscany, a spectacular Italian ceramics shop and Italian art gallery in historic Old Town Alexandria. The owner travels throughout Italy several times each year to explore and meet with many artists and to personally select stunning, handmade ceramics, decorative accent pieces and original paintings that line her shop. My Place in Tuscany carries a distinctive selection of ceramics, including biscotti jars, tureens, large urns and wall plates, as well as place settings, serving dishes, platters and custom pieces that feature historic images from such places as the Cortona, Sienna, Montepulciano, the Amalfi Coast, Venice and other enchanting locations. The gallery-like shop carries original artwork and unique pieces of Italian majolica, the ceramic art form which originated during the Renaissance. The majolica selected for the shop is handmade and painted free-hand by master artisans in Tuscany, Umbria, Emiglia Romana and other regions, artists who use the same Old World ceramic crafting techniques that have been handed down through the generations. Discover the beauty of Italy at My Place in Tuscany.

1127 King Street, Alexandria VA
(703) 683-8882 or (800) 261-5407
info@myplaceintuscanycom
www.myplaceintuscany.com

Markets

The Virginia Shop

Tradition is the foundation of the Virginia Shop. The shop, which specializes in Virginia food gifts, was built as a warehouse in 1765 by John Fitzgerald, who worked as George Washington's aide-de-camp during the Revolution and later became Alexandria's mayor. The interior proudly displays an array of hospitality pineapples. The pineapples stem from the tradition of returning ship's captains who used to impale the expensive fruit on their front gates as an announcement of a successful return. Owner Bob Lorenson takes pride in the Virginia Shop's status among locals as the old town country store, where customers can buy jumbo gourmet Virginia peanuts and other unusual food items. Food is not the only thing available in this American treasure, decorated in the Colonial home tradition. You can pick up Virginia wines and gift baskets, too. Take advantage of the opportunity to snoop around this treasure trove from the past, and you will find unusual books and gift baskets tucked away in nooks and crannies throughout the store. Strolling into the Virginia Shop is like taking a walk through the portals of time. Be sure to say hello to Bob and helpers Jessica and Sally while you are there.

104 S Union Street, Alexandria, VA
(703) 836-3160 or (888) 297-8288
www.thevirginiashop.com

Restaurants & Cafés

Landini Brothers Restaurant

Many restaurants claim to have an extensive wine list, but how many have over 6,000 bottles in their cellar? Landini Brothers Restaurant, by the river in Old Town Alexandria, not only houses that impressive collection of varietals, but each plate that emerges from its kitchen contains carefully blended flavors to please your palate and artistic design. The Tuscan chefs powering this display of good taste are the Landini brothers, Franco and Piero, who continue the tradition of fine Italian dining that their father, Francesco, began in 1976. Today the restaurant, which can seat 300 diners, frequently hosts celebrities and politicians who seek a fresh and simple Tuscan meal. Start the engines of your appetite with thinly sliced prosciutto wrapped around honeydew melon and melting on your tongue. For your pasta course, try the *tortellini alla panna*, freshly made pasta filled with veal, shaped into rings and sautéed in a light cream sauce. The seafood selections of soft shell crab, mussels and clams travel the shortest distance possible to arrive on your plate with all their natural flavor intact. Landini Brothers Restaurant offers many preparations of veal, chicken and lamb. Their cuts of meat are all certified, prime Black Angus, dry-aged for the steak connoisseur. Follow the lead of Landini Brothers' many loyal customers, and call Franco and Piero today to reserve your table at Landini Brothers Restaurant.

115 King Street, Alexandria VA
(703) 836-8404
www.landinibrothers.com

Gadsby's Tavern

Few places can say they offer fine dining dating back to 1770, but the one-of-a-kind Gadsby's Tavern in Alexandria offers a journey back to the 18th century when some of our founding fathers dined and slept here. Gadsby's Tavern and the attached Gadsby's Tavern Museum consist of two late 18th century buildings named for Englishman John Gadsby who was once the proprietor here. The three dining rooms and the bar look much as they might have looked 200 years ago with their restored pine floors and hurricane lamps on polished wood tables and chairs. Servers in period dress offer period dishes that continue to appeal to modern palates. Look for pork chops, broiled ham steak or half a duckling. Other favorites include peanut soup and a puff pastry stuffed with Virginia ham, Scottish smoked salmon and Chesapeake Bay crabmeat. The tavern, which operated as a center of political, commercial, and social life in early Alexandria, served such notables as George Washington, John Adams and Thomas Jefferson along with lesser known local figures. The American Legion saved the building from being demolished in the early 20th century. Today, it is a historic landmark and offers the largest scenic patio in Alexandria. Experience the taste of another time with a visit to Gadsby's Tavern.

138 N Royal Street, Alexandria VA
(703) 548-1288
www.gadsbystavern.org

Las Tapas and Le Gaulois Restaurants

Said Oudghiri, owner of Old Town Alexandria's Las Tapas and Le Gaulois Restaurants, began his culinary career in the romantic city of Casablanca in the late 1920s, where he worked in his father's premier bakery, La Princiere Patisserie. Later he trained with Marriott hotels, where he qualified as a food and beverage manager, and from there he fulfilled his dream of becoming a restaurateur by opening his first dining house, Dar Essalam, meaning House of Peace, in Washington, D.C. Several of his loyal patrons felt that Alexandria needed his culinary touch, and in 2000, he made their dreams come true by purchasing Las Tapas and Le Gaulois, both located on historic King Street. Las Tapas offers more than 70 different tapas, or little portions, featuring vegetables, beef, fish and poultry, as well as fruits, nuts and cheeses. The restaurant also offers full dinners, along with hearty homemade breads and delightful wines. Le Gaulois, a *Zagat Survey* award winning eatery, features a distinguished menu and a graceful, welcoming atmosphere that is equally ideal for intimate dinners or corporate affairs. Here, diners enjoy a classic French menu with such favorites as *coquilles St Jacques Marsalle* and *moules marinières*. Le Gaulois is also famous for its tempting desserts, like raspberry mango mousse cake and scrumptious crème brûlée. Enjoy a repast of dainty and delicious tapas or a hearty entrée created from Old World recipes by dining at Said Oudghiri's fine Alexandria establishments, Las Tapas and Le Gaulois.

Las Tapas: 710 King Street, Alexandria VA (703) 836-4000
Le Gaulois: 1106 King Street, Alexandria VA (703) 739-9494

Murphy's Grand Irish Pub

Murphy's Grand Irish Pub offers patrons a warm and welcoming atmosphere that embraces a weary soul and revives it with spirits, merriment and good food. Proprietors Tom and Melinda Mooney opened the popular gathering spot in 1979 and quickly gained a large and diverse following of loyal clientele. Murphy's offers open fireside dining complemented by a varied menu of freshly prepared culinary delights. Menu favorites include tender corned beef and traditional fish and chips, along with Irish meat and potato pie. Harp, Guinness and Mooney's Irish stout are among the draft beers of choice and they also serve a variety of bottled beers such as New Castle and Rolling Rock. Murphy's Grand Irish Pub is also well-known for its Sunday brunch. Further highlights of Murphy's include the fabulous and friendly staff and the traditional, live Irish entertainment, which is preformed nightly. Treat yourself to a night out with the gang and head to Murphy's Grand Irish Pub, where good fun and great food make for grand memories.

713 King Street, Alexandria VA
(703) 548-1717
2914 Pacific Avenue, Virginia Beach VA
(757) 417-7701
www.murphyspub.com

Pat Troy's Ireland's Own Restaurant & Pub

Every night of the week, the sounds of lively Irish music waft across the square that stands adjacent to Pat Troy's Ireland's Own Restaurant & Pub. It's not uncommon to hear the voices of regulars and visitors join together in laughter and song, regardless of who the night's featured performer might be. If you're fortunate, you'll be here at a time when owner Pat Troy demonstrates his unique rendition of the Unicorn Song, something you're sure to find memorable. Many years back, Pat left his native Ireland and journeyed to the United States. In 1974, he opened the Irish Walk, a gift shop, and in 1980, he started his first restaurant, Ireland's Own. In 2000, Pat opened his current facility in the heart of Old Town Alexandria, quickly becoming a focus of the Irish community in the Washington, D.C. area. Pat isn't just a restaurateur either, as his work with the Project Children program and his service as chairman and founder of the annual St. Patrick's Day Parade demonstrates. As if that wasn't enough, Pat also hosts a radio show focusing on news from Ireland every Sunday morning with his daughter Kathleen Molloy. For fine Irish food and cheer, or to try former President Reagan's favorite corned beef and cabbage, stop by Pat Troy's Ireland's Own Restaurant & Pub.

111 N Pitt Street, Alexandria VA
(703) 549-4535
www.pattroysirishpub.com

Tempo Restaurant

When you picture an elegant dining establishment that offers inventive Italian cuisine and fancy French cooking, you are probably not picturing a place that once served as a gas station. Tempo Restaurant in Alexandria's West End manages the transition flawlessly with a fanciful combination of exquisite French and northern Italian dishes served in a charming setting that attracts a loyal local crowd. The brainchild of owners Wendy and Serge Albert, the restaurant offers a beautiful dining room with high ceilings and track lighting to enhance dining ambience. Tempo benefits from Serge's training at the culinary school of Toulouse in southwest France and his experience as a chef at several of Washington's higher-priced Italian restaurants. Wendy's affinity for New American cuisine and Southwestern flavors along with a moderately priced menu make Tempo a first choice for many diners in the Strawberry Hill district. *Prix fixe* menus are available, and an intimate banquet room welcomes private parties of up to 25 people. Start your meal with such fine choices as carpaccio or the calamari salad, then go on to such delights as the Italian *linguine con broccoli rabe e granchio*, *medaillon de boeuf au Roquefort* or the *Poisson de Golfe*. For French, Italian and Southwestern fare with neighborhood appeal, visit Tempo Restaurant.

4231 Duke Street, Alexandria VA
(703) 370-7900
www.temporestaurant.com

Union Street Public House

Step into Union Street Public House, and you will feel the welcoming atmosphere of a true neighborhood gathering place. Bruce the bartender has been behind the bar since the doors opened two decades ago. He passes on the personality of the community with local tales of *back in the old days*, told and retold for 20 years. The Tap Room is lively on weekends as the community gathers for the ongoing party that makes the pub a nighttime hotspot in Old Town Alexandria. Union Street Public House has an international following and also serves many faithful regulars. With its display of fresh oysters on a bed of ice behind the bar, the Raw Bar shows the mellower side of this busy public house and is a respite from the continuous activity of the Tap Room. Take in the red brick walls, homey nautical theme and smoke-free air as the full-service bar pours your favorite classic cocktail or a beer, perhaps a Starr Hill brew from nearby Charlottesville. You can enjoy the full menu, which includes a selection of classic steaks, in both the Tap Room and Raw Bar. Looking for a place to dine and drink where you can feel like a regular? Welcome to Union Street Public House.

121 S Union Street, Alexandria VA
(703) 548-1785
www.unionstreetpublichouse.com

The Wharf

Sit back, relax and soak up some of Alexandria's majestic history while enjoying delicious, perfectly prepared steaks, seafood and chops at The Wharf. This exceptional Old Town gathering spot was first renovated and opened as a restaurant in 1971, but boasts many features from its construction in the 1790s. The renovators who updated the building made every effort to retain the structure's inherent charm by preserving original beams and columns, some of which still bear the char marks left by a Civil War-era fire. This careful attention to detail gives The Wharf an authentic atmosphere that could never be replicated with clever paint or accoutrements. The Wharf is currently owned and operated by restaurateur Ralph Davis, who owns several area restaurants, including RT's Restaurant, Polo Grill and the Warehouse Bar & Grill. Known as Old Town Alexandria's seafood restaurant, The Wharf's distinguished menu includes contemporary and traditional Chesapeake Bay creations that are sure to please, such as local seashell crabs, Maryland fried oysters, their famous Jumbo Lump Crabcakes and whole Maine lobsters. The Wharf also offers a full range of spirits, including premium vodkas and single barrel bourbons. Over the past three decades The Wharf has earned numerous accolades for its exceptional service and distinctive cuisine, including a vote from *Washington Magazine* for the best crab cakes in the Washington, D.C. area. Gather with friends and family to eat, drink and revel in Virginia's dynamic history at The Wharf.

119 King Street, Alexandria VA
(703) 836-2836
www.wharfrestaurant.com

Mango Mike's

Imagine stepping off a Caribbean cruise ship and hearing a party going on in a place up the street. You follow the music to find a hideaway festooned with beach décor, where the DJ has everyone dancing, and the bartender is serving drinks in coconut shells. The good news is that you don't have to travel outside of the D.C. area to enjoy good times in the Caribbean, because you will find all of this, plus sensational food, at Mango Mike's in Alexandria. That drink in the coconut shell is called a Coconut Colada, and it's just one of the many fun concoctions served here. There's the rum drink that comes flaming in a volcano-shaped bowl. The house cocktail, the Mangorita, is a frozen margarita topped with fresh mango and lime juice. As for the food, island salads, fresh seafood and chicken with jerk spices are a few of the crowd pleasers. With some of the dishes, half the fun is what you put on top of them, such as the fire-roasted tomato salsa that comes with the Caribbean Crab Quesadilla or the peach ketchup that sweetens the Trinidad CocoLocoNut Shrimp. Owner Mike Anderson says that his outdoor patio is the largest in Virginia. Join the castaways from the dance floor there in whiling away a pleasant Caribbean night. For cool drinks, exotic eats and Caribbean beats, head to Mango Mike's.

4580 Duke Street, Alexandria VA
(703) 370-3800
www.mangomikes.com

Foti's Restaurant

Husband and wife team Frank and Sue Maragos showcase fresh, seasonal flavors in the Mediterranean influenced cuisine at Foti's Restaurant. Sue manages the restaurant, and welcomes guests with a friendly smile. With its exposed brick walls, hardwood floors and crisp white linens, Foti's feels at once upscale and comfortable. Opened in 2005, the restaurant quickly gained respect from food critics and patrons alike, and *Washingtonian* readers voted Foti's one of the Top 100 Restaurants. Frank, who is also the head chef, enjoys updating classic favorites. He reinvents the standard fried egg and cheese sandwich using garlic toasted ciabatta bread with baby arugula, Virginia ham and Parmesan cheese. Another popular dish is the vanilla roasted Maine lobster with Johnny cakes and a Chardonnay butter sauce. The menu changes to emphasize local foods at the peak of their season. Sommelier Tyler Packwood's wine selections deftly highlight the flavors of each meal, and he is happy to make recommendations. The wines come from a dozen countries around the world, and all are rigorously tested to meet Tyler's high standards. Check out Foti's website for a closer look at the restaurant, menu and reviews, or contact Foti's directly by phone. Visit Frank and Sue Maragos at Foti's Restaurant for fresh, innovative cuisine paired with superb wine in a relaxing atmosphere.

219 E Davis Street, Suite 110, Culpeper VA
(540) 829-8400
www.fotisrestaurant.com

Shooter McGee's

Shooter McGee's aims for a relaxed community feel, and after 24 years as a neighborhood restaurant and tavern in western Alexandria, owner Steve Mann and his staff know a lot of folks by name. Newcomers get comfortable immediately upon walking in the doors and sense the *Cheers*-style atmosphere, that combined with all-American food has made this restaurant such a longstanding hit. Baby back ribs and Jack Daniels strip steak, both at bargain prices, headline the menu here. The gourmet Angus burgers have been a hit since the restaurant opened in 1979. Mediterranean salads and a mixed bag of Southern specialties, including hearty soups, specialty sandwiches and entrées, assure everyone in your party will be pleased. You can slide on up to the bar and take in your favorite game from one of seven televisions or choose the dining room. A weekly football contest and live entertainment on some nights give plenty of excuses for regularly including Shooter McGee's in your schedule. The Sunday brunch here is legendary, with everything from a Belgian waffle bar to the signature creamed chipped corned beef. Shooter advertises Delectables and Cure-alls, and that's just what you can expect—a fix for whatever you need, from camaraderie to a hearty meal. Take your tip from the locals and aim for Shooter McGee's.

5239 Duke Street, Alexandria VA
(703) 751-9266
www.shootermcgees.com

San Antonio Bar & Grill

Apart from the food, prepared with meticulous attention to detail, the San Antonio Bar & Grill satisfies customers with two locations—in Arlington and Alexandria. Owner Jaime Vargas attended the Oaxaca School of Culinary Art and the Culinary School of Susana Trilling at Rancho Aurora. He creates all of the menu items from scratch. Some of his creations include ceviche, chimichangas and fajitas that almost make his customers swoon. Consider trying his Tex-Mex style fajitas with chicken or shrimp or with quail marinated in olive oil, garlic and cilantro. Jaime acquired his passion for excellence as a boy in Bolivia and brought it with him when he moved to the United States in the 1970s. He evidences that passion by surrounding himself with talent. José

is the head chef, and Mauricio has been his sous chef since Jaime's first day in business in 1993. Both locations boast a full-service bar and a lively happy hour crowd. Takeout is available. Try the San Antonio Bar & Grill, and you will face such tough choices as which delicious dish to choose. You can simplify your dilemma by going to both locations and trying a different entrée at each one.

1664 Crystal Square Arcade, Arlington VA
(703) 415-0126
200 Swamp Fox Road, Alexandria, VA
(703) 329-6400

Daniel O'Connell's Restaurant

Billed as a modern Irish restaurant in an ancient Irish setting, Daniel O'Connell's Restaurant offers patrons an authentic Irish dining experience highlighted by exceptional service and a welcoming atmosphere. This popular Alexandria dining destination is located in a King Street dwelling originally commissioned by George Washington's Aide de Camp Colonel. Fitzgerald, who went on to become mayor of this historically rich city. Daniel O'Connell's Restaurant, named for the famous mid 19th century Irish politician, belongs to a trio of friends—Mark Kirwan, John Brennan and Billy O'Sullivan—who who are dedicated to educating Americans about Ireland's

New Age. The restaurant features four separate bars, three with the last names of the owners and a fourth named after Colonel Fitzgerald. The menu, a triumph of tantalizing taste sensations, includes beef tenderloin, cedar grilled salmon and traditional fish-and-chips, as well as such decadent desserts as warm blueberry bread pudding and Molten Bittersweet chocolate cake. The restaurant serves exceptional cuisine, perfectly prepared from recipes created by Irish chefs who have traveled the world honing their skills. The four bars serve house-brewed beers, made from a special recipe that Mark gleaned from Dublin's Phoenix Brewing Company. Gather with friends and family while embracing Ireland's emerging culinary culture at Daniel O'Connell's Restaurant, where Old World ambience and New Age flavors unite.

112 King Street, Alexandria VA
(703) 739-1124
www.danieloconnells.com

Shopping & Antiques

Van Bommel Antiek Haus

Have you ever been on a trip to the Continent and found yourself in a shop full of antiquities, where you could rifle through hundreds of Delft tiles looking to personalize your collection, a canopy of baskets and wooden dough bowls hanging above your head? Steve Young of Van Bommel Antiek Haus sees to it that you have an Old World experience at his shop in Old Town Alexandria. Steve's best friend and partner, Reijer Van Bommel, lives in the Netherlands, where he scours Europe for distinctive items from Holland, Belgium and France. Each year Reijer sends a gigantic shipment of his finds to Steve, who lovingly cares for each one-of-a-kind item. The walls of Van Bommel Antiek Haus are hung with oil portraits and landscapes from the 17th, 18th and 19th centuries. Collectors delight in work by James Hamilton, W.S. Stone, Frank S. Blake and contemporary Russian artists at Van Bommel's. Something awaits every treasure hunter in the shop's collection of French bronzes, 19th century Biedermeier furniture and 18th century chandeliers. With four rooms of art and antiques, you will find the bookend or rare icon that will make a mark on your living space and remain unduplicated in your neighbor's décor with a visit to Van Bommel Antiek Haus.

1007 King Street, Alexandria VA
(703) 683-4141

Barkley Square Gourmet Dog Bakery & Boutique

The Barkley Square Gourmet Dog Bakery & Boutique is staffed by an unusual partnership. The human owner, Kristina Robertson, appointed Cocoa to be her canine vice president, and they run the place together. Cocoa has a firm philosophy that he must greet every visitor with a wuff or an arf. He supervises day-to-day activities inside the store and insists it's his duty to follow kiddie customers carrying ice cream. The bakery specializes in baked dog treats made with local ingredients and birthday cakes for discriminating canine clientele. Not to worry though, Cocoa and Kristina insist that all the ingredients are people friendly and natural. Don't miss the doggy happy hour in the alley. It centers on the doggy swimming pool, and Kristina has prevailed upon Cocoa to feature treats for any human accompanied by their dog. Cocoa insists on catering to dogs with special needs, so people and dogs receive the highest level of service. Don't skip the Barkley Square custom line of dog bling and jewelry either. Barkley Square is the perfect place to buy dog treats and pick up a collar that best fits your dog's personality. Treat yourself and your pooch to a visit at Barkley Square Gourmet Dog Bakery & Boutique.

1 Wales Alley, Alexandria VA
(703) 519-7565
www.barkleysquarebakery.com

Embellishments A' La Maison

On your visit to Old Town Alexandria you may wonder if you have been transported through time back to your last trip abroad. Embellishments A' La Maison is as French as a kiss atop the Eiffel Tower. Owners Nick Somers and Victoria Birkett purvey more than home décor in their boutique. All of their items help you create a lifestyle of European ease and quality. At Embellishments A' La Maison the focus is not on housekeeping, but on keeping a home with joie de vivre. In the bath and body section enjoy the natural emollients of Vie Luxe, Malie and Archipelago. Discover the Lampe Berger fragrance system for enhancing your home environment. Developed over a century ago, Lampe Berger actually eliminates the odors in your environment with an elegant porcelain or glass lamp design. Feeling a little Parisian today? Pick up the signature of all mademoiselles—the Longchamp handbag, or Kate Spade and Brighton fashion accessories. Scents by Agraria, Anthousa and Trapp are also available here. The gourmet section features favorites such as Bella Cucina, The Barefoot Contessa and Paula Deen. Shop at Embellishments A' La Maison and walk away with the timeless secrets of a French woman.

1303 King Street, Alexandria VA
(703) 299-6262
www.emaison.net

My Place in Tuscany

Add vibrant, elegant and artful touches to every room of your home with a visit to My Place in Tuscany, a spectacular Italian ceramics shop and Italian art gallery in historic Old Town Alexandria. The owner travels throughout Italy several times each year to explore and meet with many artists and to personally select stunning, handmade ceramics, decorative accent pieces and original paintings that line her shop. My Place in Tuscany carries a distinctive selection of ceramics, including biscotti jars, tureens, large urns and wall plates, as well as place settings, serving dishes, platters and custom pieces that feature historic images from such places as the Cortona, Sienna, Montepulciano, the Amalfi Coast, Venice and other enchanting locations. The gallery-like shop carries original artwork and unique pieces of Italian majolica, the ceramic art form which originated during the Renaissance. The majolica selected for the shop is handmade and painted free-hand by master artisans in Tuscany, Umbria, Emiglia Romana and other regions, artists who use the same Old World ceramic crafting techniques that have been handed down through the generations. Discover the beauty of Italy at My Place in Tuscany.

1127 King Street, Alexandria VA
(703) 683-8882 or (800) 261-5407
info@myplaceintuscanycom
www.myplaceintuscany.com

Why Not?

Bring your children to Why Not? in the heart of Old Town Alexandria, and they will find a giant playpen full of toys ready to entertain them while you shop. Why Not? has been in operation since 1964. Owner Jeanne Graef taught co-owner Kate Schlabach everything she knew about creating a shop that children and parents would both find simply wondrous. Originally Why Not? was a tiny shop. It grew as quickly as children do to its current 4,800 square feet of joys and toys on two floors. One floor is dedicated exclusively to infants and toddlers; the other, to older tots ages four and older. The items on display are a visual delight for kids of all ages. Many hard to find imported and European toys fill the shelves on both floors. You may find a special item that reminds you of your own childhood and pass it on to your next generation. Your pleasure is sure to last beyond your initial find, when you bring that special toy home and get to revel in the joy of a child ripping open the box in a fever. Visit this one-of-a-kind toy store—Why Not?

200 King Street, Alexandria VA
(703) 548-4420

House in the Country and The Christmas Attic

Have you ever wished Christmas came more than once a year? You can enjoy the holiday feeling of good cheer any day of the year at The Christmas Attic and The House in the Country, two shops bursting with visions of sugarplums and seasonal treasures. Your Christmas list will write itself as you wander among the aisles of gifts and collectibles from popular makers The knowledgeable staff at these family-run shops will help you with your selections and even ship them to your home if needed. The Christmas Attic makes its home in a 1785 storehouse bordered by a cobblestone street in Old Town Alexandria. They specialize in Christopher Radko ornaments and gifts and have a large selection of German nutcrackers, smokers, pyramids and ornaments. They also offer an impressive selection of gifts for your pets. The House in the Country, located next to the Visitors Center, is the perfect place for the Department 56 collector, from the original Snow Village to an extensive Halloween section. They can help you select a special gift from Valentines Day all the way to New Years. They even offer free pictures with the jolly old elf himself, on weekends during the holiday season. If you can't visit us in person, then visit and shop through our web site and online catalog.

House in the Country
107 N Fairfax Street, Alexandria VA
(703) 548-4267
The Christmas Attic
125 S Union Street, Alexandria VA
(703) 548-2829
www.christmasattic.com

Chesapeake Bay

Accommodations

Marl Inn
Bed and Breakfast

Bed and breakfasts, which make comfortable and intimate alternatives to hotels, are scarce in Yorktown. The scarcity only adds to the allure of the Marl Inn Bed and Breakfast, located a half block from the restored Village of Yorktown. The inn is located on a picket-fenced half-acre lot that was originally surveyed in 1691. It is named for the hard clay called marl that was used as a building material by early colonists. Marl's strength comes from Chesapeake Bay crustacean shells. Seldon and Marcia Plumley are your hosts at their 1978 Colonial style house, the last house built in Yorktown's Colonial district. In 2001, the home underwent a renovation. All rooms have private baths and all except one are suites. All of the suites have kitchens. Guests enjoy private sitting rooms for relaxation and movies from the inn's film library. Mornings begin with full breakfasts, served in either the dining room or on the patio. Seldon's gourmet feasts often include crab quiche or Crab Cake Benedict. The Marl Inn is ideal for family travel, peaceful getaways or romantic escapes. Tourists are close to shopping, historic settlements, plantations and battlefields. You can schedule wedding receptions or group events here. Make Marl Inn Bed and Breakfast your base while you explore Yorktown and its surroundings.

220 Church Street, Yorktown VA
(757) 898-3859 or (800) 799-6207
www.marlinnbandb.com

The North River Inn

The North River Inn occupies 100 acres of Virginia fields surrounded on three sides by salt water. Here in the historic Tidewater region off the Chesapeake Bay, Toddsbury, the estate's original residence, serves as the private residence of Breck and Mary Montague, owners and innkeepers. Established as the 17th century estate of sea captain Thomas Todd, the sweeping fields have been continuously farmed for more than 350 years. Three separate buildings make up the bed-and-breakfast, and all feature water views. Toddsbury Cottage, a former tenant farmer's home, showcases original heart pine floors and 18th century artwork. The Guest House, built around

1960, carefully replicates colonial Virginia architecture and treats guests to exquisite North River views on two sides. Creek House, designed in British West Indies style, is the largest of the inn buildings and features handsome interior woodwork crafted from 18th century cypress. The gentle patina of 18th and 19th century English and American antiques contribute to the inn's air of grace and gentility. Weekday guests enjoy a Continental breakfast, served in their quarters, while the inn's professional chef prepares a generous Virginia country breakfast on weekends. Conveniently close to Williamsburg, Yorktown and Jamestown, the breathtakingly beautiful grounds offer a peaceful retreat and a peek at Virginia life as it once was. The Montagues invite you to get away to the North River Inn.

Gloucester VA
(804) 693-1616 or (877) 248-3030
www.northriverinn.com

Duke of York Hotel

The Duke of York Hotel enjoys an attractive location overlooking the York River in Yorktown's historic area. Every room in the hotel has a view of the river and the sandy beach that lies immediately across Water Street. Even the hotel pool has a river view. Soak up the sun by the pool or on the beach. Take a free trolley to local attractions, and stroll through town to see such historical sights as the Yorktown Victory Monument that commemorates the great Revolutionary War victory at Yorktown or the restored mansion of Thomas Nelson, Jr., a signer of the Declaration of Independence and Governor of Virginia. The Duke of York, owned and operated for generations by the Crockett family, has a charm all its own. The Crocketts proudly display their collection of 1960s memorabilia throughout the hotel. The décor of the rooms is reminiscent of the era, while featuring many modern conveniences. Along with their premium rooms, the hotel features deluxe and Jacuzzi suites. The Duke of York Hotel is part of Yorktown's Riverwalk Landing. Hurricane Isabel battered much of the beachfront area in 2004, but the Riverwalk Landing is a triumphant reconstruction effort. The famous Nick's Seafood Pavilion was a casualty of the hurricane, but the long time manager and chef of Nick's is now the dinner

chef at the Duke of York's River Room Restaurant. Let the Duke of York Hotel be the host on your next getaway.

508 Water Street, Yorktown VA
(757) 898-3232
www.dukeofyorkmotel.com

Inn at Warner Hall

One of Gloucester's true historic treasures, the Inn at Warner Hall, may be the only place in the world that claims George Washington, Meriwether Lewis, General Robert E. Lee and Queen Elizabeth II as direct descendents of its founder, Augustine Warner. Originally established as a plantation in 1642 by George Washington's great, great grandfather, today Warner Hall is open to the public as a full service country inn. This spectacular property resonates with a grace and elegance of centuries gone by. Set amidst 500 acres of riverfront, forests and farmland, Warner Hall offers a rare opportunity to relax and enjoy the tranquility and beauty of Colonial plantation life. A massive renovation in 1999 restored the beautiful Colonial Greek Revival to its original grandeur, combining old world charm with new world amenities. Three and a half centuries of architectural development co-exist with an extensive collection of antiques and art. Sumptuous designer fabrics grace the Inn's eleven gorgeous guest rooms which contain private baths, whirlpools, fireplaces and steam showers. The Inn offers delicious fine dining menus prepared by Executive Chef Eric Garcia on Friday and Saturday evenings. Gourmet breakfasts are included in guest lodging rates, along with use of the Inn's bicycles and kayaks. For accommodations that are nothing short of monumental, stay at the Inn at Warner Hall.

4750 Warner Hall Road, Gloucester VA
(804) 695-9565 or (800) 331-2720
www.warnerhall.com

Bethpage Camp-Resort

Bethpage Camp-Resort was named Park of the Year for 2005-2006 by the National Association of RV Parks and Campgrounds. Located on the southern reach of the Rappahannock River near Chesapeake Bay, Bethpage Camp-Resort is a treasure waiting to be discovered. The Hurley family has owned this land for 200 years. It had been the Bethpage Dairy Farm when Walter Boyd Hurley Sr. decided to turn the family dairy into a clean, well managed resort with numerous amenities. There are more than 1,000 full RV hookups. Their marina offers 400 slips. You can launch your boat there, rent a boat, or hop aboard the Bethpager, Bethpage's own newly restored 48-foot Chesapeake Deadrise. You can rent a cottage or bring the RV. There's fishing, crabbing, biking and tennis. Feel like going for a swim? There's a freshwater lake complete with a water trampoline in the center, or try one of their sparkling pools. Bethpage is a great place to catch breathtaking sunsets and enjoy quiet evenings around the fire. For group events, the Hurleys converted the old dairy barn into a group and rally center with a capacity to seat 935 people. A 500-square-foot stage includes a state-of-the-art sound and audio-visual system, and they operate a gourmet kitchen with a very professional staff. Bethpage Camp-Resort has something for everyone. Reservations are strongly encouraged.

5370A Old Virginia Street, Urbanna VA
(804) 758-4349
www.bethpagecamp.com

Heaven Scent B&B at Chick Cove Manor

Nestled among southern magnolias, English boxwood and ivy, Heaven Scent B&B at Chick Cove Manor offers a relaxing countryside respite just three miles from the beach and the Deltaville marinas. The farmhouse, on ten acres and completely redone in 2003, is filled with fine art, rich colors, flowers from the ever-expanding scent gardens, classical music, and the aroma of fresh scones. Owner Pat Patterson, who uses the product of her own gardens as much as possible, is a passionate cook and long-time favorite of friends worldwide. Guests declare everything here just melts in your mouth. She takes pleasure in spoiling her guests and sharing the comfort she has created. Guests remark, "What a blessing it's been to share your home," or, "Your hospitality could not have been more wonderful." Artichoke or tomato bruschette are typical cocktail-hour snacks served on the large screened porch facing the fountain garden. Breakfast on the porch includes fresh fruit and perhaps cheese souffle, tender omelets, eggy French toast or fresh fruit crepes. Take morning coffee or tea to the front deck facing the gambrel-roof barn, and enjoy birdsong and butterflies. Take pleasure in the gardens from a swing or the patio. Children over four years old delight in the friendly dog and cat, Pat's care, and the wildlife in this poison-free habitat. Heaven Scent B&B features three guestrooms, a family suite, one wonderful window seat, excellent king or queen beds, highspeed internet and an extensive library of books and DVDs. Genealogists are particularly welcome.

14180 General Puller Highway, Hardyville VA
(804) 832-6200
http://heavenscentbnb.com

The Essex Inn

The stately structure has stood at the intersection of Duke Street and Water Lane for more than 150 years. In 1851, Dr. Lawrence Roane built the largest building in town in a Greek revival style later to be named The Essex Inn. The Inn has seen a colorful history. White flags have been hoisted on its roof more than once. It now sits at the beginning of a historic walking tour through Tappahannock. Meticulously restored, it was known for years as the Roane-Wright-Trible house, referring to the first three owners,. It was then the Ash-Trible house, The Essex house and now The Essex Inn. The grand proportions and Old World elegance will keep you in awe. The ceilings are 20 feet high throughout. There are four chimneys supporting the 12 fireplaces, one for each room. The Inn features eight guestrooms, four in the main house and four suites in the "quarters," a separate two-story brick structure built in the 1840s behind the main house. A Butler's Pantry is located in the main house so guests may have access to a fridge, microwave, snacks, sodas and beer on tap. Innkeepers Reeves and Melodie Pogue will treat you to a full three-course gourmet breakfast every morning. Melodie is now working on publishing the second edition of her cookbook *Breakfast at Melodie's*, which includes her crabs and grits specialty, a favorite among guests at the Essex Inn. Reeves was recently published in *Gourmet Magazine*. Voted the Best Bed and Breakfast In The Northern Neck and Middle Peninsula, the Essex Inn prides itself in offering "Rivah', Romance, and Revival."

203 Duke Street, Tappahannock VA
(804) 443-9900 or (866) Essex-VA
www.EssexInnVa.com

The Tides Inn

This 106 room waterfront resort has a friendly staff who invites you to partake in a host of special touches for the whole family. Located on Carters Creek at the mouth of the Chesapeake Bay, The Tides Inn is known for its fine cuisine, golf course, spa, shopping, sailing school, marina and its historic yacht, Miss Ann. The Tides Inn sits quietly on its own 24-acre peninsula. Originally a well-kept secret among discriminating friends and travelers, today the Tides enjoys a reputation as one of the finest hotels in the mid-Atlantic. A full service Spa offers a range of classic spa treatments and soothing spa products. The Golden Eagle 18-hole championship golf course carved out of the beautiful wooded landscape around a 50-acre lake, is a challenge with its many elevation changes and is bunkered by more the 90 traps. Nine statute miles from Windmill Point and the Inter Coastal Waterway, the Tides Marina offers a full service 60 slip transient marina able to accommodate vessels up to 125 feet. After you dock, come ashore to enjoy complimentary amenities like a beautiful creek-side pool, croquet, bike riding, tennis, watercrafts of various kinds, several dining experiences and Crab Net Kids (a children's program). Celebrate special occasions at the signature restaurant, The Chesapeake Club, which overlooks the Tides Marina and Carters Creek. Take a cruise on Miss Ann, a 127-foot National Historic Landmark Yacht. Several varieties of luncheon, dinner, cocktail and full moon cruises onto the Rappahannock River and Chesapeake Bay are featured. Or be your own Captain and take a picnic basket lunch on one of the resorts electric boats (up to 6 passengers) and explore Carters Creek with your entire crew. A member of The Leading Hotels of the World, the Tides Inn is just an hour's drive from the Richmond International Airport, two and a half hours from Washington D.C. and less than one and a half hours from Norfolk.

480 King Carter Drive, Irvington VA
(800) 843-3746
www.tidesinn.com

York River Inn
Bed and Breakfast

A cozy inn with authentic Colonial charm, the York River Inn Bed and Breakfast has an envious vantage point as the only waterfront bed and breakfast in the area. It sits on a bluff overlooking the river and adjacent to the Colonial village of Yorktown. Beyond the breathtaking view, guests discover an accommodation with authentic, Virginia-crafted, period furniture and a charming innkeeper who will treat you like a treasured old friend. Innkeeper William Cole was a director at nearby Waterman's Museum for several years. His love of the area's history has imbued the York

River Inn with authenticity, and has given him a chance to share his stories about the region with his guests. The breakfasts are works of art, prepared with local ingredients and delicacies like shrimp and shad roe. The inn has three guest rooms with thoughtful amenities, including four different types of pillows in every room, so you can choose the variety that gives you the best rest. With its convenient location adjacent to a charming riverfront shopping area and the Waterman's Museum, visitors here find plenty of ways to deepen their appreciation of Virginia during their stay. Let William Cole's love of Yorktown enchant you during your stay at the York River Inn Bed and Breakfast. It will keep Virginia on your vacation map for years to come.

209 Ambler Street, Yorktown VA
(757) 887-8800 or (800) 884-7003
www.yorkriverinn.com

Buckley Hall Inn

Escape to the simple elegance of the Buckley Hall Inn in Mathews when you are ready to slow your life down. This bed-and-breakfast is located in a rural community, where you hardly ever hear anyone say that they had a hectic day. This is good news to the stressed. Imagine a day when the most important thing you do is ride a bike to the beach, observe some of the 200 species of birds at the Bethel Beach Nature Sanctuary or snap pictures of the two lighthouses. Canoeing, kayaking and fishing are just minutes away. Built more than 150 years ago, Buckley Hall feels suspended in

time, thanks to the lace fineries in the guest rooms and such antique furnishings as a Windsor chair, a four-poster bed and a Queen Anne-style writing desk and highboy. However, the whirlpool in the romantic New Point Comfort room is definitely a modern addition. Beth and Gerald Lewis opened the doors to Buckley Hall in 2000. If Gerald is jealous that Beth has gained local fame for the eggs Florentine that she often serves their guests for breakfast, he certainly doesn't show it. They are happy to team up in making their inn a quiet place for relaxation and rejuvenation. When you need a break from life in the fast lane, try the Buckley Hall Inn.

11293 Buckley Hall Road, Mathews VA
(804) 725-1900 or (888) 450-9145
www.buckleyhall.com

Edentide Inn

Relax in luxurious surroundings while enjoying the sweeping beauty of the Commonwealth of Virginia and historic Middlesex County, home to our nation's humble beginnings, with a stay at Edentide Inn Bed & Breakfast. Owner and innkeeper Tricia Wynne opened the getaway in 2000 and since that time have developed a cadre of loyal guests who return time and time again to celebrate the special moments in their lives. Edentide Inn was built in 1883 and boasts several elegant features, such as a large sitting room with a cozy fireplace, a veranda, screened porch and wide lawns. Enjoy fishing from a slip at the deep-water pier or relax on the private sandy beach. In addition to offering picturesque views and three elegantly appointed guest suites, Edentide is home to a charming basset hound and an array of miniature horses and pigs. Tricia and her skilled staff specialize in making your every wish come true, which makes Edentide the ideal place to host weddings, reunions and other special events. Two packages are available for structuring your event, and custom elements can be added to either package. The staff also assists with all the small details of event planning, such as floral arrangements, catering and beverage service. Experience a vacation where romance, relaxation and Old World elegance come together at Edentide Inn.

204 Bland Point Road, Deltaville VA
(804) 776-6915
www.edentide.com

Atherston Hall
Bed & Breakfast

Every time a guest pulls up to Atherston Hall Bed & Breakfast, Judith Dickinson recalls something that she learned when she worked as an accommodation inspector at the English Tourist Board: The first 30 seconds of a guest's arrival are critical. Therefore, she and her husband, William, strive for a fine first impression with lovely grounds that include copper fountains, hand-hewn fences and benches. The handsome two-story house, built in 1880 for a Chesapeake schooner captain and his family, is itself a welcoming sight. If all of this, along with the Dickinsons' immediate hospitality, isn't enough to win you over, there are the two resident Labradors, Abbey and Savana, who start getting to know guests right away, inviting them to play Frisbee. Atherston Hall is run on the principles of an English inn, meaning you should expect tasteful, uncluttered rooms and afternoon tea with scones, strawberry jam and Devonshire cream. The rooms are named after England's southwest counties—Somerset, Devon and Cornwall—and feature art and literature from these places. Breakfast is a festive affair with such treats as crepes, French toast with seasonal berries and waffles with caramelized bananas. William, an obsessive sailor, is ready to talk currents and winds with guests who have come to set sail on the Chesapeake. Allow him and Judith to keep you impressed throughout your stay at Atherston Hall Bed & Breakfast.

250 Prince George Street, Urbanna VA
(804) 758-2809
www.atherstonhall.com

Inn at Urbanna Creek

Guests rave about breakfast at the Inn at Urbanna Creek. In reference to the shrimp and cream cheese omelette, an English lady wrote in the guest book, "The breakfast was better than on the Queen Mary II." Another guest left this compliment: "The best Eggs Benedict anywhere!" The star in the kitchen is Lee Chewning, who has been a chef at some first-rate restaurants on the East Coast. The strategy sessions with his wife, Suzanne, before they opened the inn in 2005 must have been simple. "You'll charm the guests," Lee probably said, "and I'll handle their appetites." So far the plan has been working perfectly. Suzanne is a true ambassador for the town of Urbanna, always willing to advise guests on how best to use their time while visiting this pleasant place by the Chesapeake Bay. She loves to fill folks in on the colorful history of her classic 1870s house, which was once a boarding house run by a woman who ignored the temperance movement that prevailed at the time and made her own wine in the basement. The Inn at Urbanna Creek offers a spacious king suite, rooms with private baths and a separate cottage for maximum privacy. For your next getaway, stay at the Inn at Urbanna Creek, and don't be late for breakfast.

210 Watling Street, Urbanna VA
(804) 758-4661
www.innaturbannacreek.com

The Gables Victorian Mansion
Bed and Breakfast Inn

Set sail for the bed and breakfast experience of a lifetime at the Gables Victorian Mansion Bed and Breakfast Inn. This house was built with pieces from Captain James Clark Fisher's beloved schooner, the John B. Adams. Named one of Chesapeake Bay's top inns by Chesapeake Bay Magazine, the Queen Anne style house was completed in 1914 after eight years of construction. The wooden mast of the schooner runs through the top two stories of the home. The slate roof is

hung from the mizzenmast, and Fisher used his compass to align it with the four cardinal points of a compass rose. The ribs of the schooner form the curves of the bell-shaped gables on the third floor. The ship's munitions cabinet was transformed into a curio cabinet for Mrs. Fisher. The inn's owners, Dr. and Mrs. Norman Clark, are delighted to give tours of the historic property. The Gables main building features two delightful guest suites. The adjacent Coach House, built in 1880, was once inhabited by carriages and then by automobiles. It contains four lovely rooms. At the Coach House, you can enjoy a scoop of ice cream in the parlor near the dining room and gift shop. Stay at the Gables Victorian Mansion Bed and Breakfast Inn and see why the Washington Post called it one of the most interesting houses on Chesapeake Bay.

859 Main Street, Reedville VA
(804) 453-5209
www.thegablesbb.com

Attractions

Town of Urbanna

The town of Urbanna, Urb of Anne, named for England's Queen Anne, has often been called the most beautiful waterfront town in Virginia. Located just a few miles up the Rappahannock River from the Chesapeake Bay, Urbanna is rich in history. It was established in 1680 by the Act of Assembly as a port through which tobacco was shipped. At the time, tobacco was the currency of the colony. The Old Tobacco Warehouse, built in 1766, where the tobacco was exchanged for cash or credit, now serves as the Town of Urbanna Visitors Center. It is not the oldest building, as there are seven buildings in historic Urbanna that have been in continuous use for 300 years. The centermost portion of Urbanna has been listed on the National Register of Historic Places. Lined with exquisitely restored plantation estates, Virginia Street leads through the town's most historic area and on down to the harbor. Located in a protected deepwater environment, Urbanna's Harbor allows boaters to berth within three blocks of shops and restaurants. Urbanna is the place to enjoy the bounty of seafood that Chesapeake Bay is famous for. Whatever your palate is craving, you'll find restaurants to please you in this charming harbor community. Bed and breakfast inns are plentiful, or you can book a room at one of the plantation estates. There is even waterfront camping available. Join the folks in Urbanna on the first weekend in November to celebrate the Oyster Festival, or visit throughout the year for the finest in Southern hospitality.

45 Cross Street, Urbanna VA
(804) 758-2613
www.visiturbanna.com

Urbanna Oyster Festival

Urbanna's warmth and charm attracts thousands of visitors each year. Located on the Rappahannock River, Urbanna is traditionally known for its supply of Rappahannock River oysters, and come the first weekend in November the entire town and about 75,000 visitors gather to celebrate. It's time for the Urbanna Oyster Festival. It all started back in 1958 when some town *fathers* and merchants got together and created Urbanna Days as a way to promote the town and its economy. By 1961, the name was officially changed to the Urbanna Oyster Festival, recognizing just how much that little succulent bivalve fed the economy. There's the crowning of the Oyster Queen and Little Miss Spat (a *spat* is a baby oyster). In 1988, the General Assembly of Virginia designated the festival as the official Oyster Festival of the Commonwealth. On Friday night, the Fireman's Parade is one you won't soon forget as fire and rescue units from across Virginia come to participate. The Grand Parade is on Saturday. Highlighting the festival is the annual Virginia Oyster Shucking Championship. Winners from this event go on to St. Mary's, Maryland to represent Virginia in the United States competition. From there it's on to Galaway, Ireland, to represent the United States in the World Championship. The celebration is non-stop with several bands playing throughout the town. There's Crafters Row, an Art Show, and more than 50 different vendors to soothe your appetite. Of course, The Oyster is available in every form imaginable: raw, roasted, fried, smoked, in fritters, or in stew. Come join the festivities at the Urbanna Oyster Festival. You don't know what you've been missing.

45 Cross Street, Urbanna VA
(804) 758-0368
www.urbannaoysterfestival.com

Historic Gloucester Courthouse Circle

From the stately Colonial courthouse with its columned entrance to the simple one-room debtor's prison, the buildings of the Historic Gloucester Courthouse Circle entice visitors with their history and architecture. Incarcerated debtors were allowed out of their cells during the day but were prohibited from entering a building that had a billiard table. You will learn colorful facts such as this during your visit to this historic district, which boasts one of the oldest courthouses in the country still in use. Built in 1766, the courthouse serves today as a meeting place for the county government and the community. Other buildings clustered around this venerable structure

include the aforementioned debtor's prison as well as a multi-room jail and Clerk of the Courts offices. Just outside the Courthouse Circle stands Botetourt Masonic Lodge No. 7, one of the oldest Masonic lodges in the nation. Across Main Street from the courthouse is the pre-Revolutionary brick ordinary, the Colonial version of a bed-and-breakfast. Visitors touring these buildings will notice that the folks of Gloucester love congregating in the circle. The locals sit and read under the grand oak trees. Families plan picnics and weddings here, and the town sponsors a number of events here throughout the year. For the place in Gloucester where American history blends with everyday American life, visit Historic Gloucester Courthouse Circle.

6467 Main Street, Gloucester VA
(804) 693-0014
www.co.gloucester.va.us/court1.htm

Mathews Memorial Library

If you are passing through Mathews, you may drop by the Mathews Memorial Library if only to read your hometown newspaper or use the computers. The longer you stay in town, the more you will realize what an excellent facility this is. In fact, this community gem won a National Award for Library Service in 2005, the nation's highest honor for a library. How do you know when a library is doing a good job? One way to measure is by the amount of community support and involvement. Approximately 10,000 people live in Mathews, and more than half of them have library cards. That statistic alone speaks for how well the Mathews Memorial Library is performing its traditional role of fostering literacy. What's more, Mathews has become a popular retirement community, attracting people with extraordinary skills who have donated time and resources to the library. This shows in the array of enrichment programs that the library offers in everything from computer skills and nature studies to genealogy and history. It has also acquired an outstanding collection of recordings and compositions from which it has developed a music program that many big city libraries would envy. Visit the Mathews Memorial Library, the pride of this flourishing small town.

251 Main Street, Mathews VA
(804) 725-5747
www.mathewslibrary.org

Gloucester Museum of History

The Gloucester Museum of History is everything a history museum needs to be. It tells the story of Gloucester's past with artifacts and relics that preserve the past as a mirror to hold up to the future. It houses a replica of a country store and an old-time post office. The second floor depicts six periods of Gloucester's history, dating from millions of years ago right through to the Civil War. The museum building dates to the late 18th century and began as an inn, where travelers could get a room and a meal for a fair price. The Gloucester Historical Committee administers the museum, and the county board of supervisors appoints members. Admission is free, courtesy of the county, but donations are appreciated. Expect a different focus and some changing exhibits throughout the year. February is set aside to honor the many contributions of African-Americans to the evolving fabric of the Gloucester tapestry. April celebrates the daffodil, a flower with a rich Gloucester history. October and November are devoted to local archaeology, and May is military appreciation month. For a museum that finds many ways to investigate Gloucester's past, visit the Gloucester Museum of History.

6539 Main Street, White Marsh VA
(804) 693-1234
www.co.gloucester.va.us/museum/
historyhome.htm

Steamboat Era Museum

On June 20, 2004, Irvington's newest attraction opened its doors. The Steamboat Era Museum has embarked on a vision that will take us back in time to the 1800s. The Chesapeake Bay is rich in Steamboat history that spans over 100 years. More than 300 steamboats plied the waters of the Chesapeake Bay and its tributaries, carrying passengers and freight. It was a lifeline for social and economic connections with the rest of the world. Every Steamboat had its own unique whistle so one could identify it miles away. The Steamboat Era Museum has been gathering oral histories from local people recounting personal adventures of the era. The cameras kept rolling as colorful stories unfolded of times gone by. You can see and hear their stories on the Museum website and at kiosk stations in the museum. Keep your eyes open for the planned research and educational center as well as the restoration of the pilothouse of the Potomac, the largest relic left of any Chesapeake Bay steamboat. View miniature models, meet the captains through photos and stories, glimpse scenes from the past with dioramas, look at artifacts from the grand steamers and learn the romance of an era that occurred not so long ago. This is one stop you won't want to miss.

156 King Carter Drive, Irvington VA
(804) 438-6888
www.steamboateramuseum.org

The Bay School—A Community Arts Center

Places such as the Bay School are what make Mathews the vibrant and livable rural community that it is. This community arts center sponsors classes, workshops and events that foster an appreciation of the arts and encourage people to explore their own creativity. As one would expect, the school offers instruction in the fine arts of painting and sculpture. However, its all-inclusive approach to art makes room for classes in everything from traditional crafts, such as blacksmithing and basket weaving, to contemporary interests, such as wine tasting and partners massage. There is no typical student, as ages range from one to 89. The common threads are curiosity and enthusiasm. Something special goes on every month at the Bay School's own Art Speaks Gallery. The school's annual events are much anticipated. These include Family Art Day

Painting by Jane Stouffer

in March, the National Arts Program in April and several combined shows and sales throughout the year. One of these, the Rustic Art Show & Sale in May, gathers work from some of Virginia's best carvers, basket makers and potters. Whether you are just beginning a love affair with the arts or are seeking to sustain a passion of many years, you will find others of your kind at the Bay School—A Community Arts Center.

279 Main Street, Mathews VA
(804) 725-1278
www.bayschool-arts.com

Essex County Museum

Historic preservation comes naturally at the Essex County Museum. Europeans first settled here in the early 1600s. Tappahannock, where the museum is located, is older than Richmond, Fredericksburg and even Williamsburg. The museum displays tribal and Colonial-era artifacts related to the area's very first inhabitants, the Rappahannock and Portabago peoples. Essex County's connection to our nation's conflicts is detailed in a cavalryman's saber from the War of 1812, items from the Confederacy and memorabilia from World War I and II veterans. Personal

items of the Port Royal doctor who treated John Wilkes Booth, assassin of President Lincoln, recall a dark chapter in American history. Everyday life from bygone eras comes alive in pictures and artifacts from the Rappahannock River steamboat days as well as from home and personal items from the 19th and early 20th centuries. The museum is also a repository for county and private records, making it the first place where many people conducting research go. Copies of the popular book, *Essex County Virginia Historic Homes*, are available in the gift shop, which also stocks many other books by local authors as well as souvenirs. For exhibits that span centuries of Virginia's history, visit the Essex County Museum.

218 S Water Lane, Tappahannock VA
(804) 443-4690
www.ecmhs.org

Photo by Worth Haile

Belmont Pumpkin Farm

At Belmont Pumpkin Farm, the Gustafson family blends educational entertainment with old-fashioned family fun. From haunted hayrides to pumpkin carving contests, lively events pack every weekend from the end of September to the first weekend in November. Choose the perfect jack-o'-lantern candidate from the pumpkin patch, then build your own scarecrow with old clothes from home. Visit the friendly farm animals in the barnyard or thread your way through the corn, sorghum and sunflower mazes. After working up an appetite, you'll be ready to sample hot dogs or barbecue and an array of mouthwatering pumpkin desserts. The farm café and market offers jams and jellies, crafts, t-shirts and the ever-popular pumpkin and apple butters to take home. The pumpkin farm schedules school tours on weekdays, with educational activities that correlate with the Virginia Standard of Learning. Each year the farm's learning stations focus on different subjects that reinforce math, science, social studies, literature and fitness skills. Kids also enjoy a meal and play time during their visit and take home their very own pumpkin. Check the website to see what's scheduled and plan to enjoy a crisp fall day at Belmont Pumpkin Farm.

Route 617 at North River Road, North VA
(804) 725-7151
www.belmontpumpkinfarm.com

Deltaville Yacht Charters

Deltaville Yacht Charters, a subsidiary of East Coast Yacht Management, provides access to the Chesapeake Bay with its fleet of sail and powerboats. Sailboats in the 33 to 40-foot range are the specialty. These yachts are available as crewed or bareboat charters. Navigating the Chesapeake can be a challenge, so Willard and Bonnie Vest and their experienced staff are ready to offer advice. They can even help you plan an itinerary. You can navigate such waterways as the Rappahannock and York Rivers to arrive at quiet coves, secluded anchorages and quaint island villages. If you enjoy fine dining, the folks at Deltaville Yacht Charters will mark the location of all the four-star restaurants in this stretch of the Chesapeake Bay. If your hobby is wildlife photography, they can tell you where to find nesting families of osprey. Deltaville Yacht Charters keeps its vessels in pristinely maintained condition. Imagine dropping anchor in one of these fine boats to watch the sunset and then to admire the lights of Norfolk. For adventure, discovery and fun on the Chesapeake Bay, call Deltaville Yacht Charters for a reservation today.

16134 General Puller Highway, Deltaville VA
(804) 776-0800
www.ecym.org

Bakeries, Coffee & Tea

Mark's Coffee Café

Are you just not yourself until you've had your first cup o' joe each morning? Mark's Coffee Café can help you wake up and get going. The café's quality eye-openers are brewed from Costa Rican, Sumatran, Kenyan and Colombian beans, which were roasted at nearby Lexington Coffee Roasting Company. The laid-back atmosphere and hearty sandwiches at Mark's will inspire you to linger with your cup of coffee. A family-oriented community hot spot, Mark's breathes an eclectic atmosphere into the surrounding small town of Gloucester Point. Do you prefer your coffee a little dressed up? Take your iced, blended or hot latte with one or two of over 20 flavors. Perhaps your favorite is a mint mocha or a rich amaretto latte with tons of foam. Mark's Coffee Café also serves up a wicked chai and simmering pots of tea. Bring a friend and spend less than $20 sharing a grilled chicken sandwich, potato salad, pickle and salmon salad. Need some time alone? Bring your laptop on Friday nights and enjoy the wireless Internet connection along with live music. It's time to smell the coffee at Mark's Coffee Café.

1755 George Washington Memorial Highway, Gloucester Point VA
(804) 642-5009

Java Jacks Coffeehouse

Tappahannock is a great little town on the Rappahannock River, and there is no better way to experience it than to pay a visit to Java Jacks Coffeehouse. Located on the corner of Church Lane and Virginia Street is a 100-year-old cottage where owners Mimi and Bruce McComb have fulfilled a 20-year dream and created an exceptional café. Java Jacks takes the role of a coffeehouse to whole new level. It is here that one can experience a bistro, a bar, and teahouse, as well. The food is fabulous and everything is made from scratch. They are known for their Zeppole, Java Jack's signature bread, which comes with every breakfast. Zeppole is a light Italian fritter that comes to us from Naples, or in this case from Mimi's old family recipe that was handed down from her Italian grandmother. At

Java Jacks you can sip some joe, nibble on a Zeppole, and listen to the sounds of acoustic guitars, or maybe some jazz, or a poetry reading. There's a wide assortment of coffees to choose from and the baristas here are top notch. Gather for High Tea in the gracefully decorated tearoom. Then wander through the cottage and take a close look at the works of Gigi Vranian and other local artists. Take some coffee and tea home with you and reminisce about the next time you'll be back to Java Jacks Coffeehouse. It's a place you'll want to experience time and time again.

504 S. Church Lane, Tappahannock VA
(804) 443-JACK (5225)
www.java-jacks.com

Jessica's Sweet Shop and Bakery

You could say that the cinnamon rolls at Jessica's Sweet Shop and Bakery play an important role in the community. At no time was this more evident that when Hurricane Isabel battered Gloucester in 2003. When the radio station mentioned that Jessica's was still open, powered by a generator, the locals poured in to find comfort and to commiserate. Since opening in 2002, Jessica's had gained a reputation for being a community coffeehouse without that chain feeling. After the hurricane, it became a place where people came to heal. Even before 2002, Jessica's had a loyal following for its catering business, with its especially popular cinnamon rolls and breads.

Today, with its 25-seat dining area, Jessica's is a cozy place to enjoy a sweet breakfast or a soup, salad or sandwich for lunch. Everything is made from scratch, and the coffee is freshly roasted. Located along Main Street, Jessica's is easy to find. If you should somehow get off track, just ask any of the locals for directions. It's one of those community businesses that everyone in town knows and cherishes. To be part of the local scene, try a roll, scone or muffin at Jessica's Sweet Shop and Bakery.

6558 Main Street, Gloucester VA
(804) 693-5235

Fashion

The Dandelion

The Dandelion offers a unique shopping experience in a charming turn-of-the-century village on Carter's Creek in Lancaster County. Owners Sheila Brown and Jeannie Ward-Smith have been here for more than 30 years, and for most of that time they were only one of two stores in Irvington. Times have since changed and The Dandelion has kept that transition smooth as they continue to order fine women's clothing and accessories from more than 500 vendors. Garfield and Marks, Eileen Fisher, Sigrid Olson, Karen Kane, ISDA and David Brooks are a small sampling of the lines they carry. The options seem endless. The staff at The Dandelion is first rate with some having stayed more than 20 years. They'll help you find that perfect bit of spice you've been wanting to add to your wardrobe. Sign up for The Dandelion newsletter to receive special discounts and find out about upcoming events. Visit The Dandelion in Irvington, where they bring Old World charm together with the latest fashions.

4372 Irvington Road, Irvington VA
(804) 438-5194
www.thedandelion.com

Cyndy's Bynn

From its origins as a paperback bookstore, Cyndy's Bynn has moved into high fashion clothing, accessories and gifts. Owner Betsy Bristow opened the doors of her Urbanna shop in 1984 and since then it has become Virginia's Best Kept Secret at the Rivah. You'll find a glorious array of jackets, skirts, pants and tops for any season. Jeans and glamorous sweaters will prepare you to meet your day with confidence and pizzazz. If it's a complete outfit you're looking for, you'll be pleased with the attractive accessories and jewelry found here, including a lively selection of jeweled and painted eyeglasses for reading or sun protection. Colorful, sassy handbags will match your mood and your outfit, while cute shoes will bring a smile to your lips and a spring to your step. It's just a small step from accessorizing yourself to accessorizing your home. Cyndy's Bynn makes that step by providing creative accents for your home. Consider a monogrammed plate, an arrangement of life-like silk flowers or something distinct and beautiful, right down to the wrapping. Cyndy's Bynn stages fashion shows for special events and offers personal shopping services for apparel and gifts. Perk up your wardrobe and your home with merchandise from Cyndy's Bynn. It will be an experience you will never forget.

311 Virginia Street, Urbanna VA
(804) 758-3756
www.cyndysbynn.com

Galleries & Fine Art

Mathews Art Gallery

The small town of Mathews is a haven for crafters and artists, as you will clearly see when you visit the Mathews Art Gallery. The gallery is run as a cooperative, so about 50 local artists share space here and donate their time to daily operations. When you drop by, you might meet the talented carver who creates the wood ducks, the jewelry maker or the sculptor who works in metal. A study in variety, the gallery displays examples of everything from crafts with a long tradition, such as scrimshaw and doll making, to the modern form of painting known as abstract expressionism. Artists have moved to Mathews from all over, so trying to find a common thread in their work is really beside the point. The abstract expressionist, for example, is a retired professor who taught at Harvard. The bird carver is a retired barber. The wood carver worked on a tugboat for 20 years. Still, if you are seeking art devoted to the area's particular landscape, you won't be disappointed. You will find many paintings and prints that capture images of the local marshes and wildlife. For an encounter with the thriving arts of Mathews, go to the Mathews Art Gallery.

206 Main Street, Mathews VA
(804) 725-3326
www.mathewsartgallery.org

Nancy Thomas Gallery

Paintings by Nancy Thomas make people happy, which may be one of the reasons a Yorktown study revealed that the Nancy Thomas Gallery is one of the town's most popular destinations. Nancy's fresh, contemporary pieces evoke smiles, portray celebrations and exude wit and whimsy. And who wouldn't smile at an angel in plaid pants, draped over a watermelon clutching a bottle of wine, or a child hugging a chicken? The colorful, contemporary paintings appear in thousands of personal collections, in magazines, books and at such institutions as the Museum of American Folk Art. Her art appears on the sets of movies and television shows. It's been to the White House, as part of President Ronald Reagan's White House Christmas tree and as the theme for the Virginia state trees on the White House lawn for five years running. Nancy has given one-woman shows across America and abroad and has received countless commissions. She has lived and painted in historic Yorktown for the past 30 years. Many of Nancy's pieces are available in her Yorktown and Williamsburg galleries along with the prints, allowing everyone to find joy among Nancy's art. The galleries also sell Nancy Thomas ceramics, ornaments and jewelry.

145 Ballard Street, Yorktown VA
(877) 645-0601
402 W Duke of Gloucester Street,
Williamsburg VA
(757) 259-1938
www.nancythomas.com

The Gallery at York Hall

The Gallery at York Hall is a venue for Yorktown artists to display their creations, for visitors to learn about the area and for locals to keep in touch with community events. The gallery is part of the Celebrate Yorktown Committee, a nonprofit organization dedicated to promoting area events and educating visitors about Yorktown's rich history. Manager and volunteer Sharon Owen started the gallery in 2002 with only a little bit of money and a whole lot of resourcefulness. With a background in art and interior design, Sharon put her creativity to use in designing the gallery, which was once a clerk's office in this old courthouse building. A volunteer staff dedicated to improving the community mans the gallery, and all proceeds from the gallery further opportunities for community activities and concerts, like the Virginia Symphony, the York River Concert Band and the Yorktown Christmas celebration and boat parade. Exhibits inside the gallery change every six weeks and include just about anything a Yorktown resident might dream up, from jewelry and handmade miniatures to paintings, pottery and quilts. The helpful volunteers serve refreshments to visitors and, if you happen to be exploring the area with Fido, say they are happy to give your pooch a drink. Visit the Gallery at York Hall with its charming Colonial style architecture to keep up-to-date on the latest Yorktown happenings and creations.

301 Main Street, Yorktown VA
(757) 890-4490
www.yorkcounty.gov/cyc/gallery.html

Yates House Fine Art & Craft Gallery

Len and Blanche Scharf, of the Yates House Fine Art and Craft Gallery, practice an all-encompassing appreciation of art, which they are spreading throughout the Middle Peninsula and Northern Neck regions of Virginia. The gallery, which opened in 2004, is a showcase for more than 30 local artists who exhibit a wide range of paintings, photography, pottery, stained glass and turned wood. Blanche is an award-winning artist herself, specializing in fine silver jewelry and woven neckpieces made from fiber and beads. Len provides custom framing on-site. To capitalize on exciting future opportunities, Yates House Fine Art and Craft Gallery became a non-profit corporation in 2006. The Board of Directors is planning the means to expand on class and workshop offerings, exhibits and performing and literary arts events. Yates House, a picturesque, white-frame, 1870 Deltaville landmark, has already hosted exciting events such as a reception for member Carolyn Kreiter-Foronda, Virginia's Poet Laureate, and the regularly scheduled *Salons on the Lawn*, where dancers, musicians, artists and writers come together and share their talents with the public. On Saturday nights throughout the summer, visitors and local residents bring chairs and picnics to the *Groovin' at the Gallery* series featuring bluegrass, folk and jazz. Yates House is also the scene of the Deltaville Farmers' Market on the fourth Saturday of every month from April through November. To connect with the arts in Middlesex County, go to Yates House Fine Art and Craft Gallery.

17466 General Puller Highway, Deltaville VA
(804) 776-8505
www.yateshousegallery.com

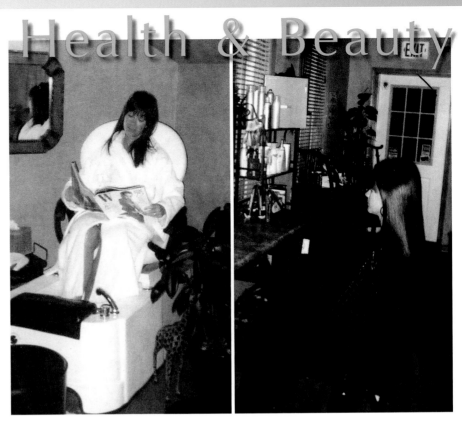

Health & Beauty

Split Enz Salon and Spa

Stylist and entrepreneur Symone Reisner brings more than 30 years experience to her vogue establishment, Split Enz Salon and Spa, which she opened in 2003. Symone underwent her initial training in her native London, moved on to Paris, and has worked with some of the world's top artists in the television, film and modeling industries. The warm, welcoming spa is reminiscent of Hemmingway's Key West and is staffed by a delightful group of professionals who take pride in offering sophisticated services and up-to-the-minute hairstyles and styling techniques. Split Enz offers a full spectrum of pampering salon and spa services for men and women, such as full body massage, nail treatments, facials and body wraps. The spa further offers a special Valentine's Day chocolate pedicure with champagne as well as a wedding package featuring a champagne breakfast and a full array of services for the bride and bridal party. A visit here includes complimentary beverages ranging from various local wines to tropical fruit juices. In addition to running Split Enz, Symone is also a platform artist who travels the country plying her trade at hair and fashion shows. Treat yourself to a day of pampering, from head to toe, at Split Enz Salon and Spa.

6616 Main Street, Gloucester VA
(804) 693-5343

Katybugs

Katybugs attracts customers looking for an escape from everyday stress and is a place to relax and purchase holistic elixirs, teas, and essential oil products designed to enhance health and well being. Spa rooms are available for massage therapy, Reiki, European facials, and holistic classes including tai chi and yoga. All of this is available in a historic home built in 1747 that resonates character, strength and enduring charm. It is said that both Thomas Jefferson and Andrew Jackson have been hosted here. Katy and her husband, Tom, seek to do more than provide a relaxing environment and freedom from stress; they want you to be able to transport your acquired tranquility home with you. They achieve their goal by providing holistic products to enhance mind, body and spirit. If the inherent stresses of modern living begin to overwhelm you, make your way to Katybugs, where Katy will greet you and assist with a healing plan to address your individual needs.

290 Virginia Street, Urbanna VA
(804) 758-8880 or (800) 403-5740
www.katybugs.com

Home & Garden

Brent and Becky's Bulbs

Brent and Becky Heath's motto is Plant Bulbs and Harvest Smiles, and their passion for daffodils runs in the family. The enterprise began in 1900 when Brent's grandfather, Charles Heath, bought 600 acres near Gloucester, Virginia and began the daffodil business that became Brent and Becky's Bulbs. Brent's father, George, helped the daffodil, the poor man's rose, gain popularity. Since Brent and Becky began hybridizing daffodils in the 1970s, they have introduced more than 20 of their own new varieties, and each year they add new hybrids to their catalogue offerings. In 2005, their new catalogue business filled more than 14,000 orders, and the Wall Street Journal calls it the #1 Bulb Company. Bulb production takes place in several locations, including the Heath's farm, other farms in the USA, Holland, Israel, Thailand and China, and their catalogue lists all types of bulbs. They credit much of their success to their dedicated staff, which includes their son, Jay, and his wife, Denise Hutchins. Brent and Becky educate gardeners about effectively integrating bulbs into the landscape and how to choose the best varieties for your climate. They've authored two award-winning books and have been inducted into the Garden Writers Hall of Fame. The Bulb Shoppe at Brent and Becky's Bulbs, which opened in 2003, offers tools, gifts, fertilizers and bulbs and fresh flowers in season. It also features gardens planted with the bulbs that are for sale here. Visit Brent and Becky's Bulbs, either online or in person, and be inspired to plant a little sunshine in your garden.

7900 Daffodil Lane, Gloucester VA (804) 693-3966 *www.brentandbeckysbulbs.com*

Chesapeake & Crescent Home

"Just walking through the store is a feast for the eyes," says Abagail Smith of Arlington, Virginia. Paula Thomasson established Chesapeake & Crescent Home of Kilmarnock in 2004 to offer eclectic options for interior design and furnishings. "Helping our customers attain a warm and inviting home is first and foremost," says Paula. Not only does the store have custom options such as kitchens and baths, but it also carries unique French and English country antiques and vintage items. New and upholstered furniture, linens, lamps and rugs can be found in this beautiful place. Copper mirrors, gorgeous clocks, frames and leather goods are also available. From design to delivery, Chesapeake & Crescent Home provides customers the opportunity to build a home that defines each person, welcomes their guests, and creates an environment of beauty, comfort and joy.

24 N Main Street, Kilmarnock VA
(804) 435-8800
www.chesapeakecrescent.com

Time to Cook

"Cooking shouldn't be work," says Hatley Bright from the kitchen of Time to Cook in Irvington. "It should be fun." To prove her point, she offers entertaining cooking classes and interactive demonstrations spiced with lots of background on cooking traditions, history and styles. As Hatley prepares a dish in front of you, she reiterates her point that you should treat cooking as something enjoyable and challenging, not as a chore. As with anything you truly enjoy doing, you can develop skills and then refine them with practice. Of course, proper equipment makes learning easier. That's why Time to Cook carries a carefully selected array of high quality knives, utensils, and pots and pans. You will find cookbooks and magazines here as well. Because half the fun of cooking is sharing what you make with others, Hatley loves getting people to try dishes or foods they don't usually eat. "I don't think I would like that," said one young lady when invited to sample a recipe featuring mushrooms, but moments later, after a tentative bite, she exclaimed, "These are delicious," proving that Time to Cook is also a place where food prejudices can be put to rest. For classes and demonstrations in the fun art of cooking, consider Time to Cook.

4349 Irvington Road, Irvington VA
(804) 438-6691
www.timetocook.net

The Wild Bunch

Trained in London, England by one of the country's top Court florists, Cynthia Naylor, proprietress of The Wild Bunch, uses her inherent talent and remarkable skills to create divine floral arrangements that are a testament to nature's grandeur. Cynthia has enjoyed a lifelong love affair with flowers, which began in childhood in her native England, where she grew and arranged flowers from her own garden. The Wild Bunch carries flowers from across the globe as well as a few from Cynthia's own garden. It offers lovely containers and vases along with floral arranging supplies, like scissors and the kenzan vases used in Japanese ikebana. Cynthia specializes in weddings and feels it is important to meet with a bride several times prior to creating arrangements in order to get a real grasp of her client's vision, which she then brings to vivid life. She has created floral masterpieces for some of the area's most prominent institutions, including the Virginia Museum of Fine Arts and the Chrysler Museum. Much of the work that Cynthia does reflects the English garden style, which generally features a wilder, more natural look as opposed to precise, manicured pieces. Bring the charm of an English garden to your home or special event with floral masterpieces from The Wild Bunch.

260 Virginia Street, Urbanna VA
(804) 758-5445
www.thewildbunchflowers.com

Cattails

As soon as you enter Cattails, a fine gifts and home décor store in Mathews, you will understand what is meant by Chesapeake Bay style. Perhaps you have heard the term, but you weren't sure how it translates into an actual look for the home. Owners Carol Joyce and Julie Tyler define it in every item that they select for Cattails. Here you will find everything from pottery, dishes and tablecloths to wood wall art, garden statuaries and fountains. These are not mass-produced souvenirs to be put on a shelf when you get home, but items for everyday living that evoke a certain sense of place. You really feel that Cattails is an extension of what you have experienced while visiting the coastal community of Mathews. You will love the very pretty gift wrapping, too, which is free. Carol and Julie became shop owners in 2005, before they had even acquired inventory. They always knew what they wanted for their store. They just didn't anticipate that the perfect building would become available so quickly. What did they want? The answer is nothing less than a showcase for what it means to stylishly live in harmony with the beautiful Chesapeake area. Go to Cattails and see what we mean.

291 Main Street, Mathews VA
(804) 725-2886

Markets

Photos by Shelley Gill

Something Different Country Store & Deli

Exceptional and hearty food can be more difficult to find than you might think. Something Different is a specialty food, wine and cheese shop that does the job particularly well, thanks to Owner Dan Gill's vision and knowledge. Not only is the food good, the casual atmosphere and attentive staff makes visitors feel welcomed and comfortable. Deli sandwiches and seasonal delicacies, such as soft crabs and local oysters are prepared to order while customers watch and interact. A local farmer and food historian, Dan purchased a 1920s country store in 1999 with the purpose of running it as a convenience store. He soon found that he needed to carve out a niche to set his business apart, and began cultivating a following for his traditional barbecue, smoked meats, homemade soups and deli sandwiches. Dan then needed chewy bread that held up to his substantial, juicy sandwiches, so he resurrected the ancient technique of substituting whey for water in the dough. Unusual in many respects, Something Different features freshly roasted coffees from around the world and Virginia peanuts. Holding a masters degree in poultry science, Dan has the intellect to know how to touch the taste buds. His unique creation of smoked turkey and country ham salad, termed THE Virginia Sandwich, has even made it into Becky Mercuri's *American Sandwich Book: Great Eats from All 50 States*. His focus on the category he calls *specialty heritage foods* has allowed him, to build his business by creating a new take on an old food genre. Take the short trip from Urbanna to what locals somewhat jovially refer to as downtown Pinetree, and experience Something Different.

3617 Old Virginia Street, Urbanna VA
(804) 758-8004
www.pine3.info

The Schooner Alliance

Whether you set the sail, take the helm or simply relax and enjoy the wind in your hair, a voyage on the Schooner Alliance will be an experience to remember. Captains Greg and Laura Lohse met at sea as part of a teaching crew and have been sailing tall ships together since 1988. Today they take day-trippers and overnight visitors to sea on their 105-foot, three-masted schooner, Alliance. Landlubbers with a fondness for sea adventures from another age are sure to feel invigorated standing on the deck of a tall ship during a day or sunset cruise. Students of all ages can learn seamanship aboard the schooner as it plies the waters of the York River and Chesapeake Bay. Try a three-night cruise, and fall asleep in your stateroom to the rhythm of the sea. You will wake to a fresh breakfast as the day breaks over the horizon. The Alliance sails out of Yorktown from the beginning of May thru the end of October, then spends the winter in the Virgin Islands. Love the tranquility of the water? Set off on the Lohse's other schooner, the restored 65-foot Serenity, for a day sail out of Cape Charles. From its deck, watch for dolphins playing and osprey hunting as the sun sets and you enjoy a glass of wine and a bite to eat. Give in to the call of the sea and set sail on the Schooner Alliance.

Riverwalk Landing, Yorktown VA
(757) 639-1233
www.schooneralliance.com

Restaurants & Cafés

Trick Dog Café

Everybody who eats at the Trick Dog Café in Irvington has probably dreamed of owning a cool place like this. The superb food and well loved home for casual fine dining has given rise to a subculture of loyal followers. They wear their Trick Dog t-shirts around town and feel a keen sense of belonging when they drop by. Robert McRaney was, in fact, a fan before he became the owner. He would cruise over to Irvington specifically to have a drink and a bite at the Trick Dog. When he found the café closed one winter, he turned his disappointment into a plan to retrieve the soul of the Trick Dog Café. These days, *Frommer's* calls the Trick Dog "the Northern Neck's best and most sophisticated restaurant—a cross between SoHo and South Beach." Executive Chef Jeffrey Johnson runs the kitchen, maintaining a menu that features fresh fish, crab cakes and steaks. The café is named for the statue of a little black dog that survived the Great Irvington Fire of 1917. Robert keeps the statue by the front door to greet guests, who pet it for good luck. For dining with a vibe, Maître d' Robert McRaney will be there to greet you and celebrate life at the Trick Dog Café.

4357 Irvington Road, Irvington VA
(804) 438-1055
www.trickdogcafe.com

White Stone Wine & Cheese

Close your eyes for just a moment and imagine you inhabit a perfect world. Would you prefer to dine in a café, a wine shop or a French bistro? White Stone Wine & Cheese is the place to go if you prefer one more than the other. It's absolutely the perfect destination if you love all three. The food is French and served at tables surrounded by racks of wine. The ambience is relaxed and quiet. It's a place for intimate dining, yet customers who have never met are comfortable starting conversations across their tables. Lunch specializes in gourmet sandwiches, and dinners combine outstanding fare with impressive value that includes being able to select your wine from the vast selection on the racks

and enjoy it at your table with no additional markups. This full-service French restaurant used to be a wine and cheese shop and retains some of charms of those early days. French music is played at night as the lights dim, and Saturday night features a four-course dinner complemented by different wines specifically chosen to match the foods. Owner Bruce Watson left his position as a hospital administrator to follow his dream, and the results at White Stone Wine & Cheese are nothing short of spectacular. Next time you are looking for a perfect world, visit White Stone Wine & Cheese.

**572 Rappahannock Drive, White Stone VA
(804) 435-2000**

Lowery's Seafood Restaurant

Generation after generation has been fed at Lowery's Seafood Restaurant in Tappahannock. A Virginia staple since 1938, Lowery's was founded by Lorelle and Wesley Lowery and continues to belong to the Lowery family. It started as a tiny restaurant with one goal—to serve the best seafood in the Tidewater. Seventy years later, a dedication to excellent seafood and impeccable service has created a 350-seat restaurant with a stellar regional reputation. Simple, traditional seafood preparation showcases the flavor of the fish here. Fried local oysters and the jumbo lump crab cakes are customer favorites. The menu also offers steak, chicken and sandwiches. All fried food here is free of trans fats. You'll find a different special each day and a kids' menu. Lowery's reputation could put a celebrity at the table next to yours. Elizabeth Taylor once enjoyed a meal here. The customers are loyal, and so are the employees. General Manager Arlene Watkins started

out as a waitress, and several employees have been with the restaurant for more than 40 years. For the last 50 years, customers have stopped to talk to the mynah. Children can fish for plastic fish in the fishing well and earn prizes for their catch. You'll find private rooms for meetings and take-out service. Experience a Tidewater tradition at Lowery's Seafood Restaurant.

**528 S Church Lane, Tappahannock VA
(804) 443-4314**
www.lowerysrestaurant.com

Sutton's Restaurant

Legions of loyal customers, most greeted by their first names, make their way to the legendary Sutton's Restaurant in Gloucester, where succulent crab cakes draw rave reviews and patrons include politicians, political candidates and a former governor. Sutton's Restaurant began in 1945 when Mary "Mamie" Sutton and her husband, Marion, started a soup and sandwich shop in an old grocery-gasoline store that had belonged to Mary's parents. In 1948, after an addition to the building, the restaurant started serving full meals, and in 1961, the restaurant moved to a new one-room building. Mrs. Sutton took over sole management of Sutton's when her husband died in 1965 and continued greeting her customers as she always had until 1989, when she semi-retired at the age of 85. After she passed away in 1993, ownership of Sutton's Restaurant passed to her son Allen, who leased management of the restaurant to Susie Robins in 2004. Deservedly famous for its homemade pies, Sutton's also serves bread pudding to die for. Daily menu specials, available only on their special day, include the popular baked chicken, served off the bone with white and dark meat separated. Fresh vegetables and local seafood round out the menu, and nearly everything is made from scratch. Sit down to dinner at Sutton's Restaurant, where the food and friendly family atmosphere have been drawing fans for more than 60 years.

**6690 Sutton Road, Gloucester VA
(804) 693-9565**

Southwind Pizza

You can learn some local geography while eating at Southwind Pizza in the town of Mathews, because all of the specialty pizzas are named after nearby islands. What's more, you may never look at pizza the same way again. Indeed, an island seems a fitting metaphor for a pizza, which certainly could be described as a little round island of comfort food. At Southwind, the landscape of the Rigby Island pizza is topped with spinach, fresh herbs and three kinds of cheese. The terrain of the Big Island includes pepperoni, Italian sausage and green peppers. The air on the Gwynn's Island entices with the aroma of tomatoes, bacon and smoked Gouda cheese. Share these pizzas and a couple more with your friends and family. Island hopping never tasted so good. Around Mathews, the locals talk of needing a Southwind Fix, meaning that if you are having a stressful day, it's time to head to Southwind Pizza to make everything better. "People consider this place an oasis," says owner Ned Lawless, who arrives at work before six every morning to start the dough. For delicious island exploration, set your sail for Southwind Pizza.

44 Church Street, Mathews VA
(804) 725-2766

Alley Café

Even at a young age Jae Kammeter, part owner and operator of Kilmarnock's popular Alley Café, knew that she wanted to be a restaurateur. Jae purchased her first restaurant, one she had worked in during high school, in 1989 and opened this second restaurant with family members George and Kurtis in 2004. Alley Café offers a relaxing ambience and a soothing nautical motif that puts customers at ease and acts as a colorful backdrop to the friendly service and tasty cuisine. Jae's son Gary is a distinctive artist whose work is featured on the eatery's walls, and her husband, David, a Menhaden fish boat captain, often pitches in to help out, making the Alley Café a true family affair. In addition to providing friendly down-home service, the Alley Café also features an extensive menu filled with classic dishes that are prepared to order using quality ingredients and

old family recipes. Specialties of the house include crab cakes and barbecue dishes, along with tender and delicious Delmonico steaks, which are available in three sizes. Another popular favorite is Captain David's Platter, a seafood lover's dream with flounder, crab cake, shrimp, clam strips and a choice of two side dishes. Alley Café is open for breakfast, lunch and dinner. Special menus for seniors and children assure the entire family will be pleased. What little one could resist the Wyatt Earp Burger? Enjoy the homemade cuisine and family atmosphere at the Alley Café.

53 Cralle Court, Kilmarnock VA
(804) 436-1100

Town Bistro

Just walking through the door of Town Bistro is a delight to the senses. Your eyes are drawn almost immediately to the open kitchen, where you can watch chef and co-owner Cristal Jett prepare scrumptious dishes using fresh, locally grown produce and native Virginia products. Delightful scents lure you deeper into the dining room, which is designed to give every table a view of the kitchen. Here, Nancy Bennett, Cristal's mom and head server, is on hand to greet you. Cristal and her partner, Kate Messner, opened the business in early 2006 and gained almost instant

acclaim by winning first prize for the best She Crab Soup at the annual Kilmarnock crab festival. Town Bistro's menu changes regularly to take advantage of seasonal goods and features primarily healthy options, prepared with olive oil and an array of fresh and dried herbs. The kitchen eschews freezers, microwaves and deep fryers. Cristal often incorporates fresh fruits into her salads and entrées and is happy to grant her customers' culinary requests, when it is within her power. Town Bistro carries a choice selection of fine Virginia wines, and Cristal, who has an uncanny knack for matching wine to cuisine, is always happy to act as sommelier. Cristal, Kate and Nancy invite you to experience old-fashioned excellence at Town Bistro.

62 Irvington Road, Kilmarnock VA
(804) 435-0070

Bartlett's Café

You're invited to stick around awhile at Bartlett's Café, where the mood is unhurried. Enjoy breakfast, lunch or dinner at a table, and then take a specialty coffee or tea to the couch, stretch out and peruse the magazines. Nobody will try to rush you out the door. "I only want employees that have a 'welcome to my house' attitude," says owner Denise Bartlett. She gets equal satisfaction from how much people feel at home here and how much they enjoy her cooking. She takes every opportunity to be innovative in the kitchen, even turning common side dishes into something special. All sandwiches come with a choice of sides, including three kinds of Denise's homemade potato salad—cheddar bacon, mustard and blue cheese.

Highlights from the generous menu include pancakes and omelettes for breakfast, 15 different sandwiches for lunch with seafood and salads for dinner. Denise makes it easy to eat healthfully at her restaurant with vegetable dishes and an emphasis on grilling rather than frying.

For dining at your own pace, try Bartlett's Café.

296 Main Street, Mathews VA
(804) 725-4900

Sandpiper Reef Restaurant

Sandpiper Reef Restaurant offers an elegant dining experience reminiscent of Europe's dinner houses, where service is always just-so, and meals are never rushed. Located five miles from Mathews in Hallieford, this popular Misti Cove eatery served as a church camp during the late 1970s and early 1980s. The restaurant itself inhabits the former camp's meeting hall, which overlooks the Piankatank River and offers diners exquisite natural views. This nonsmoking restaurant features both dining room and *al fresco* dining, as weather permits, and provides a relaxing atmosphere that is ideal for a long, lingering meal with friends, family or business associates. The friendly, welcoming staff is dedicated to providing you with gracious, perfectly executed service and welcomes large private parties and business meetings. Specialties of the house include the tender prime rib and fresh sea scallops. The eatery also offers a vegetarian platter and a full line of classic desserts, such as bread pudding and apple caramel cheesecake. In the bar you can choose from an array of cocktails or select one of the restaurant's fine wines or beers. Enjoy river views and unparalleled cuisine at the Sandpiper Reef Restaurant.

1176 Pine Hall Road, Mathews VA
(804) 725-3331
www.visitmathews.com

Shopping & Antiques

Green Gates Gifts

Green Gates Gifts is a girl's shop that men love. Wander in on a Saturday afternoon, and you may be greeted with a glass of wine or small dessert to enjoy while you shop among the store's eclectic accessories. With its entrance heralded by red and white striped awnings and twin topiaries, Green Gates reflects the mood of a beach on the French Riviera. French hen figurines peck among toile fabrics and handmade jewelry. The shop is a modern girl's haven, exhibiting big city taste with a touch of vintage thrown in for good measure. Green Gates is the kind of store that you would find if you transplanted a trendy neighborhood in Los Angeles to the small town of Gloucester Point. When the men are done shopping the knife and nautical collection, they easily settle in front of the plasma television, while their modern girls explore the Green Gates goodies at their leisure. The store sees plenty of return business, thanks to a lively mix of items to serve many needs. Such gifts as Harvey's original seatbelt handbags and Rembrandt charms are always appreciated. The designer upholstered furniture might be just what you need to perk up a room. For the sleek style of your favorite big city store, stop into Green Gates and experience flair at its best.

1467 George Washington Memorial Highway, Gloucester Point VA
(804) 642-5618
www.greengatesgifts.com

Period Designs Inc

Period Designs carries antiques as well as high quality, historically accurate reproductions of ceramics, picture frames, floor coverings and other household items from the Colonial era. Partners Michelle Erickson, Rob Hunter and Ginny Lascara maximize authenticity by creating objects using the same techniques that were used in the Colonial period. Each partner runs his or her own business under the Period Designs umbrella. Ginny and her brother Joe create period-style, painted canvas floorcloths and picture frames. They also stock any array of 18th-century natural history prints and maps. Michelle is a nationally renowned potter who specializes in museum-quality English delft and slipware. Rob is an American ceramics specialist and archaeologist. He provides the select antique ceramics carried by the partnership. Period Designs has been featured in many magazines, including *The Magazine Antiques*, *Colonial Homes* and *Early American Life*. Its products have provided authentic backgrounds for movies, such as *The Patriot*, *The New World* and *National Treasure*. If you are interested in Colonial life and art, treat yourself to a visit to Period Designs.

401 Main Street, Yorktown VA (757) 886-9482 *www.perioddesigns.com*

Yorktown Shoppe

The history of Virginia comes to life at Yorktown Shoppe. Burcher Cottage, home to Yorktown Shoppe, was built in 1881 and has been a retail store since the early 1900s. Many of the items found in the store today are replicas of things early customers might have found here. Displays of local artistry fill the shelves, including three lines of pewter, one made in Virginia. Look for woodcarvings and wooden folk items, including replicas of historical Yorktown and Williamsburg houses. Some of the most popular items in the store are the Old World balance toys, with a back and forth motion that remains as entertaining to watch today as it was more than a century ago. Colonial era dresses, Jefferson shirts and tricornered hats are in stock. Yorktown is a close-knit community, and area businesses take pride in their town. Owners George and Kathryn Sage and George and Linda Bennett are involved with local organizations that promote Yorktown's individual character and hope that visitors love the quaint village as much as they do. For friendly service and treasures reminiscent of times gone by, come to Yorktown Shoppe.

402 Main Street, Yorktown VA
(757) 898-2984
www.yorktownshoppe.com

Gloucester Emporium

Jeff Whitt keeps the mood light at his Gloucester Emporium, where customers drop by for a few laughs while shopping for a little bit of everything. Just about everybody knows the boss as Cheap Jeff, the name he goes by in his local television commercials, and they know to come to him for bargains on home furnishings, gifts and tools. Outside, the store also offers a half acre of concrete lawn products. A big part of Jeff's job is finding new merchandise from well known manufacturers. Through special arrangements with these companies, he can keep his prices competitive. His other main responsibility is to keep everybody, from his loyal customers to his staff, smiling. One member of his crew, Wardell Whiting, is in his 70s and has been with Jeff since 1994; Wardell is every bit as popular as the boss/television star himself. Not even the flooding at Gloucester Emporium from Hurricane Floyd in 1999 could dampen Jeff's spirits. He cleaned up, had a great Floyd Sale and brought the store back better than ever. "If you don't buy from me," says Cheap Jeff in his commercials, "we both lose money." If saving money on a wide range of products makes you smile, you won't want to miss Gloucester Emporium.

8234 John Clayton Memorial Highway, Gloucester VA
(804) 693-7864

Kilmarnock Antique Gallery

Whether you are a neighbor to the store or have come a long way to get here, a stop at Kilmarnock Antique Gallery will make your day. On most days you will be greeted by owners Steve and Lynn Bonner or their Yorkshire terrier, Windsor. The 100-dealer gallery abounds with variety. Shop the impressive array of grandfather clocks, hand-knotted Persian rugs direct from Iran or other antique furnishings. If you prefer housewares, you'll appreciate the sterling silver flatware, china or candelabras. Add some pizzazz to your table with a tea set or an oyster plate from one of the largest collections around. The gallery is also home to Italian ceramics known as majolica. If the gallery doesn't have what you're looking for, just ask, and the Bonners will add it to the wish list. Steve is a native of Kilmarnock, the self-proclaimed Arts and Antiques Capital of the Northern Neck, and a fourth generation local businessman. The gallery doubles as the visitor center for Kilmarnock and shares visitor center responsibilities for all of Lancaster County. *Pleasant Living* magazine calls it the best place to antique in Northern Neck, Middle Peninsula and central Virginia. This is a pet-friendly store, too, so don't leave your dog in the car. Windsor loves the company. A visit to Kilmarnock Antique Gallery is not just a shopping trip, it's an experience. Come in and take a look around, you'll be glad you did.

144 School Street, Kilmarnock VA (804) 435-1207 or (800) 497-0083
www.virginia-antiques.com

Main Street Fine Art and Antiques

Main Street Fine Art and Antiques is an antique hunter's paradise filled with original oil paintings, 18th and 19th Century furniture and even Civil War items. This is a family business that has its roots in Auslew Gallery, which was established in Norfolk in 1952 by the family patriarch Donald Lewis Sr. and his wife Beverly. His daughter Leigh Trimble and grandson Lewis act as managers of Main Street Fine Art and Antiques. Their Gallery shows landscapes and still life by Donald S. Lewis Jr. and Leigh Trimble. They have both painted professionally for many years. They also showcase a folk art collection and art by nationally known folk artist Bradley Stephens. Christopher Trimble is considered an authority on Civil War items, 19th Century fabric and antique glass. A walk through the mall is like a walk through the history of many countries. African and oceanic art can be found along side mid-century, modern, decorative arts and English antiques. Main Street Fine Art and Antiques is much more than just an antique mall.

15 N Main Street, Kilmarnock VA
(804) 435-7771
www.msfaam.com

Swan Tavern Antiques

Swan Tavern Antiques' location in historic Yorktown is a fitting home for a store devoted to fine 18th and early 19th century English and American antiques. The original building on this site, constructed in 1720, burned down, to be replaced my a meticulous reproduction in 1935 that served as a tavern, giving rise to this store's name. Owners David and Mary Peebles bring the spirit of

the tavern to the shop, where you can almost envision gentlemen sitting in Chippendale chairs and smoking in front of the fireplace or a woman writing a letter at the walnut desk in the ladies parlor. Everything is for sale here, including the beds, the bedspreads and the portraits. The English basement, which would have been used for food storage or preparation, is now home to redware and pewter that reflects the period lifestyle. The Peebles purchased Swan Tavern in 1989, and like their original shop Lisburne Lane Antiques across the river in Ordinary, they concentrate on providing authentic period pieces prized by collectors. The Peebles' daughter, Melinda Smith, manages the shop and is always willing to provide details on the pieces. People with a keen eye for antiques have a special fondness for Swan Tavern Antiques, where the Peebles' love of antiques is apparent in such specialties as miniature furniture and cabinetmaker samples, as well as fine porcelain and accessories. The Peebles and their staff invite you to Swan Tavern Antiques, where the merchandise provides a powerful link with the past.

300 Main Street, Yorktown VA
(757) 898-3033

Penny Lane Antiques and Interiors

If you are a Baby Boomer, you probably owned a stack of 45 rpm records when you were young. Penny and Joe Latham remember the days when you could get two great songs on one disk. Their two businesses, Penny Lane, an antiques and interiors store, and Paperback Writer, a coffeehouse and bookstore, are named after Beatles songs. Consider them two sides of one great experience in White Stone, the small town where the Rappahannock River meets the Chesapeake Bay. Penny Lane is three buildings full of hip furniture, decorative accessories and just about anything else that has caught Penny Latham's eye on her travels through America and Europe. The large and

small, the new and pre-owned, the functional and frivolous all find a home at Penny Lane. The cute purple house in the back is the most visited of the three buildings, so be sure to visit there. Later, take a coffee break at Paperback Writer and browse the eclectic selection of books and CDs. The weekly coffee tastings attract a crowd here, whether the focus is the coffees of Seattle or organic Ethiopian and Tasmanian blends. Be sure to make Paperback Writer and Penny Lane Antiques and Interiors stops on your magical mystery tour of White Stone.

349 Chesapeake Drive, White Stone VA
(804) 436-1984
www.pennylaneantiques.com

Latitudes

Colorful with a touch of whimsy is the easiest way to describe Debbie Hall's Latitudes, the most intriguing shop in Deltaville, according to her many customers. Latitudes offers an eclectic mix of merchandise that stimulates the senses. It's easy to see why so many patrons come by to explore the wide array of jewelry, casual wear, home decor, baby and pet items, along with the books, food and unusual gift ideas always on hand. When Debbie found the most charming building in Deltaville, she knew a store like the one she dreamed of would be a prefect fit. The building was originally a country store back in the 1930s and people still come in to, "remember when." When Debbie opened Latitudes in 2001 she expected her primary business to come in the summer due to the influx of tourists. She was pleasantly surprised, however, to find that her store is popular year-round and that November and December are just as busy as July. Debbie didn't start out working in retail, but once she realized the opportunity to adapt her love of shopping to her quest for merchandise for her own store, she knew Latitudes was the right business for her. Debbie considers herself fortunate to have staff members who really care about the shop and enjoy working with each other and the customers. The relaxed atmosphere and Key West feel offer broad appeal. See for yourself why people come from all latitudes and longitudes to check out the funky and unexpected selection at Latitudes.

16648 General Puller Highway, Deltaville VA
(804) 776-0272

Gi Gi's Antiques

Next to the historic courthouse circle in Gloucester is an antiques shop, where each item is chosen with an artist's sensibility. Artists Traci Batalon and Janice Jones, the owners of Gi Gi's Antiques, are attracted to hand painted pieces, especially china, porcelain and glassware, along with some jewelry. Seeing objects as only artists can, they enjoy showing folks what can be done with overlooked pieces that they find at estate sales. Furthermore, they are always ready to put their artistic talents to work by hand painting pieces of furniture or antiques that customers bring to them. They can even hand paint floors or any other part of your home with designs that match your personality and style. Traci and Janice met at an antiques mall. Traci was working there, and Janice commented that she was an artist, and that her work was better than the artists being represented. The work she was disparaging happened to be Traci's. Having survived this embarrassing moment, these talented women can teach us something about the art of friendship, it seems, in addition to helping us appreciate the art of antiques. For antiques that make an artistic statement, drop by Gi Gi's Antiques.

2067 Bells Lane, Hayes VA
(804) 695-9000

Lisburne Lane Antiques

Lisburne Lane Antiques may be located in Ordinary, but its collection of 18th and early 19th century American and English furniture is anything but mundane. Owners David and Mary Peebles choose the masterpieces of fine craftsmanship found here and at Lisburne Lane's companion shop, Swan Tavern Antiques in Yorktown, with the connoisseur in mind. Since starting business in 1984, the Peebles have earned the trust of the most discriminating collectors. They take seriously their commitment to providing truly fine period antiques. Casual visitors unaware of the Peebles' reputation are astonished to find such treasures as a Welsh jointed oak chair, an English Chippendale mahogany bachelor's chest or a Roanoke River Valley walnut cupboard. People also go to the Peebles for early brass, miniature furniture and such accessories as tea caddies. As a college student, David would use his transportation money to buy antiques and then hitchhike home. No one who has visited Lisburne Lane can question his priorities or his taste. Several movies filmed in Williamsburg have used furniture from the Peebles' shops. For museum-quality period antiques, visit Lisburne Lane Antiques.

4183 George Washington Highway, Ordinary VA
(804) 642-3460

Coffman's on the Coast

Coffman's on the Coast is a celebration of coastal living. Owners Brenda and Barry Coffman believe that "life is too short not to browse." Together they have created not one, but two nautical gift and fine fashion stores. One is located in Hartfield, the other is in the heart of Tappahannock. The Hartfield store is in an old country store. The Tappahannock store is in the old Clanton House. Both buildings are from the late 1800s. These eclectic little stores are filled with every maritime item you can imagine. At Coffman's you may find a handpainted cabinet with a lighthouse on it, a tide clock or a model boat. You'll find resort wear clothing, fun shoes and great hats. There's fun seafaring jewelry in silver and gold, Caswell-Massey bath and body scents, and to top it off, Captain Rodney's Salsa. Brenda and Barry offer several promotions throughout the year that give back to the community. Coffman's on the Coast is a great place to find that extraordinary gift for you or that someone special. Make sure to visit Coffman's next time you're in the mood for a touch of surf.

10675 General Puller Highway, Hartfield VA
(804) 776-7766
202 Queen Street, Tappahannock VA
(804) 445-8300
www.coffmansonthecoast.com

The Yorktown Onion

As unique as its botanical namesake, the Yorktown Onion is an accessories boutique that blooms with excitement year round. The Yorktown Onion offers permanent silk arrangements, one-of-a-kind floral center pieces and garden statuary. Some of their silk arrangements sport replicas of actual Yorktown Onions with their striking purple flowers. The store carries original oil paintings, décor with nautical themes and antique weather vanes that are sure to catch your attention. You can find Elizabeth W bath and body products, Vera Bradley handbags and many other personal and home accessories. The inventory at the Yorktown Onion is constantly fresh and new. The shop is dedicated to customer service and will call clients to let them know if something has become available that might interest them. Owned by the Bristow family, the Yorktown Onion is located in Riverwalk Landing, a thriving new retail center along the York River. This multi-million-dollar development features shops, fine dining and performance venues. The plant known as the Yorktown Onion, from which the boutique takes its name, is native to Russia. In America it grows only in York County. The seeds may have arrived from the Old World during the Revolutionary War mixed with crop seeds or fodder. There is a legend that the flowers mark spots were soldiers fell during the Revolution. The plant is protected by county and federal law. Be sure to return home with something special from the Yorktown Onion.

319 Water Street, Yorktown VA
(757) 872-8232
www.yorkcounty.gov/riverwalk/yto.htm

Wineries

Belle Mount Vineyards

Belle Mount Vineyards is a working winery, but it's also a retreat with places to stay and outdoor activities to enjoy. Owners Catherine and Ray Petrie operate a multidimensional property, focusing on Warsaw history, nature and people. This small boutique winery is known for its Chesapeake Bay Treasures series of wines. It's also known for its hospitality, and an informal tour of the vineyards feels like friends are showing you around the property. It's also an opportunity to learn about the winemaking process and enjoy a complimentary wine tasting, featuring handcrafted Chardonnay, Merlot and Cabernet Franc. Come see why this is the perfect location to grow grapes and enjoy the rolling hills and beautiful view of the Rappahannock River. Make a day of it with fishing, hiking and swimming, then camp or rent a cottage at the on-site Heritage Park Resort. The Petries want your visit to be all it can be, and they will help you plan family and group functions as well as tours and activities. They offer catering services for wedding receptions and special events in their banquet hall. Extend your visit long enough to enjoy some of Virginia's rich history. See the birthplaces of George Washington and Robert E. Lee or explore Dancing Point, where the Rappahannock Indians held rituals on Cat Point Creek. Heighten your senses at Belle Mount Vineyards, where you will find a feast for your eyes as well as your taste buds.

2570 Newland Road, Warsaw VA
(804) 333-4700 or (800) 335-5564
www.bellemount.com

Eastern Shore

Accommodations

Channel Bass Inn

You may safely suppose that John Winder, the original owner of what now is the Channel Bass Inn, was a people person. After all, he was the mayor of Chincoteague in the 1890s. Today, David and Barbara Wiedenheft own this lovely building with its six guest rooms and fill their role as innkeepers with personal warmth that follows in the Winder tradition. David and Barbara encourage socializing, meaning that if you pride yourself on being a sour puss, then you might want to choose another place to stay in Chincoteague. They will remember your name and they enjoy bringing people together so much that they offer one more opportunity for fellowship besides the expected full breakfast in the morning. On all days but Sunday and Wednesday, they serve complimentary afternoon tea in the inn's elegant tea room. Being from Leeds, Barbara knows something about good tea as well as scones, trifle and Victoria sponge cake. Conversation among the guests usually touches upon how comfortable, quiet and beautifully furnished the inn's rooms are. She and David moved to Chincoteague in 1992, no doubt for the same reasons that you came today. They are ready to help you experience everything that this beautiful island has to offer. They have even been known to give guests a hug when they check out. For lodging for extroverts, try the Channel Bass Inn.

6228 Church Street, Chincoteague VA
(757) 336-6148 or (800) 249-0818
www.channelbassinn.com

1848 Island Manor House Bed & Breakfast

Thoughts come to you in pairs when you stay at the 1848 Manor House Bed & Breakfast on Chincoteague. Island beauty and coastal charm are but one example. In considering how you should pass the day, your mind alights upon the possibilities of kayaking on the sound in the morning and enjoying the ocean in the afternoon. Perhaps this phenomenon of thoughts arising in sets of two has something to do with the history of the Manor House. Prior to the Civil War, two young men pooled their resources and built one very large house to accommodate their future families. What they couldn't anticipate was that their wives would be sisters, who would eventually find it impossible to live together under the same roof. To preserve domestic harmony, the men split the house to create a pair of matching dwellings. Although the house was reconnected via a garden room in 1982, you must be feeling a residual effect as your mind continues on its way. Of course, this isn't a bad thing, since the warm sunshine and salty sea air are heavenly, as were the freshly baked bread and quiche that you had for breakfast. Whether you are seeking one of the best inns in North America for viewing wildlife or a romantic setting for your wedding, consider the 1848 Manor House Bed & Breakfast.

4160 Main Street, Chincoteague VA
(800) 852-1505
www.islandmanor.com

Hilda Crockett's Chesapeake House

Hilda Crockett's Chesapeake House on Tangier Island offers family style meals in its main house and comfortable lodgings in two adjacent dwellings. It was difficult for us to decide which to mention first, the restaurant or the inn, because each half of the operation is headline material. Combined, they will give folks plenty to smile about as they are ferrying home from the island, memories of a restful but diet-killing visit fresh in their minds. When you stay in one of the eight guest rooms, breakfast is included and so is either lunch or dinner. The food is local fare, and the portions are all you can eat, so indulge on crab cakes, clam fritters and Virginia ham with corn pudding on the side along with homemade pound cake for dessert. Back at the inn, you find the unofficial feline mascot, Crabcake, staring at butterflies in the beautiful garden, and you suddenly realize that nothing is stopping you from doing the same. Such is life at Hilda Crockett's place, the scene for tranquility since 1939. Hilda is no longer alive, but her family still runs the place and loves to tell old stories, like the one about the time when Nancy Reagan came by with a bunch of governors' wives. The ladies were ready to start pouring the sherry they had brought along, when the straight-laced Hilda erupted. "You're not going to have that stuff in my dining room." For peace, quiet and plentiful meals, consider Hilda Crockett's Chesapeake House.

16243 Main Ridge Road, Tangier VA
(757) 891-2331
www.esva.us

Refuge Inn

If you're the kind of person who never goes on vacation without binoculars, then you'll feel right at home at the Refuge Inn on Chincoteague Island. The inn sits nestled in pines within walking distance of the Chincoteague National Wildlife Refuge, where more than 300 species of birds have been spotted. During their annual migration, huge flocks of geese settle at Chincoteague, along with other species large and small that are attracted to the diverse habitat of this barrier island. Of course, the wildlife refuge is also the place to see the famous wild ponies that are believed to be descendents of a herd shipwrecked here in the 1500s. Tour the refuge on a bike rented from the inn. After a busy day of wildlife viewing, you'll appreciate your comfortable room with its patio or balcony. In the morning or evening, be sure to stroll the grounds, winding up at the observation deck that overlooks the marsh and Assateague Island across the way. From this point, you will enjoy a view of the handsome Assateague Lighthouse protruding above the trees. The Refuge Inn features a continental breakfast with waffles, as well as a pool and fitness room. Children of any age are welcome. If your idea of a perfect escape includes a sea breeze, white sandy beaches and wildlife, then pack your binoculars and check into the Refuge Inn.

7058 Maddox Boulevard, Chincoteague VA
(888) 973-3843
www.refugeinn.com

Charlotte Hotel & Restaurant

People come not only by car to the Charlotte Hotel & Restaurant, but by boat to the wharf to stay the weekend and dine here. Most leave believing that they have found the perfect small hotel. Many compare its simple elegance to inns in Provence, France—luxurious and earthy at the same time. The building was constructed in 1907 as the White Hotel and has served many functions since then. Today, it houses the restaurant and full-service bar, a first floor lobby and eight guest rooms as well as a gallery showing the artwork of Owner Charlotte Heath. Charlotte and Gary Cochran opened the Charlotte Hotel & Restaurant in 2003. With no training, only their artistic eyes, they completed the lovely design and finish work in the hotel themselves. Their rooms feature private baths, Egyptian cotton towels and climate control. The queen-size beds with memory-foam mattresses are so comfortable that people leave wanting to buy them. The two full-time chefs at the restaurant change the menu frequently to highlight what is available from local farmers and watermen. For a touch of Provence in downtown Onancock, try the Charlotte Hotel & Restaurant.

7 North Street, Onancock VA
(757) 787-7400
www.thecharlottehotel.com

Fisherman's Lodge

Since the 1930s, visitors to Virginia's Eastern Shore have whiled away their time crabbing, exploring and relaxing at Fisherman's Lodge, a lovely getaway located just off the beaten path in Quinby. This cozy retreat features two homey lodges with a total of 10 rooms, six of which come complete with private bathrooms. Each lodge additionally boasts its own wraparound porch, a barbecue grill and spectacular views of the Barrier Islands. The spacious, well-designed grounds feature a slip where you can tie up your boat as well as a public boat ramp for launching your vessel upon arrival. Fisherman's Lodge is owned and operated by Terris Kennedy and Nancy James and is managed by Fred and Elisha Killian, who are always on-site and happy to assist you with anything you might need. The Killians are of native Indian decent, and Fred is considered an expert on local Indian culture and is always delighted to share bits of lore and history with an interested listener. Fisherman's Lodge is an ideal place for corporate retreats, family reunions and other small get-togethers. Recreational activities here include bird watching and fishing. The lodge is also close to touring and boat rental companies. Explore the wonders of the Eastern Shore with a stay at Fisherman's Lodge, a Virginia tradition for more than 70 years.

20210 Harbor Point Road, Quinby VA
(757) 442-7109 or (888) 442-7133
www.fishermanslodge.com

Spinning Wheel Bed & Breakfast

As an alternative to reality TV, Thom and Linda Nolan offer the so-called Reality Porch at their Spinning Wheel Bed & Breakfast in Onancock. Overlooking the inn's lovely gardens, the porch is the place to get in touch with what's really important, such as time spent with someone special. Life seems a little simpler from here, as you sip your iced tea. Laughter from the volleyball, badminton and croquet area behind the house rides on the evening air. Inside, the inn's Victorian

furnishings establish an atmosphere of comfortable elegance. The Spinning Wheel offers the choice of five air-conditioned guest rooms, each with a queen-size bed and private bath. The Nolans serve a full hot breakfast, though, according to many guests, the fresh muffins and apple cake make a sweetly delicious meal in themselves. Within walking distance of the inn are the many shops and restaurants of Onancock, a charming waterfront town situated between the ocean and Chesapeake Bay. The area is popular with kayakers, boaters and fishermen. For a dose of peaceful, Chesapeake-style reality, take a seat on the porch at the Spinning Wheel Bed & Breakfast.

31 North Street, Onancock VA
(757) 787-7311
www.1890spinningwheel.com

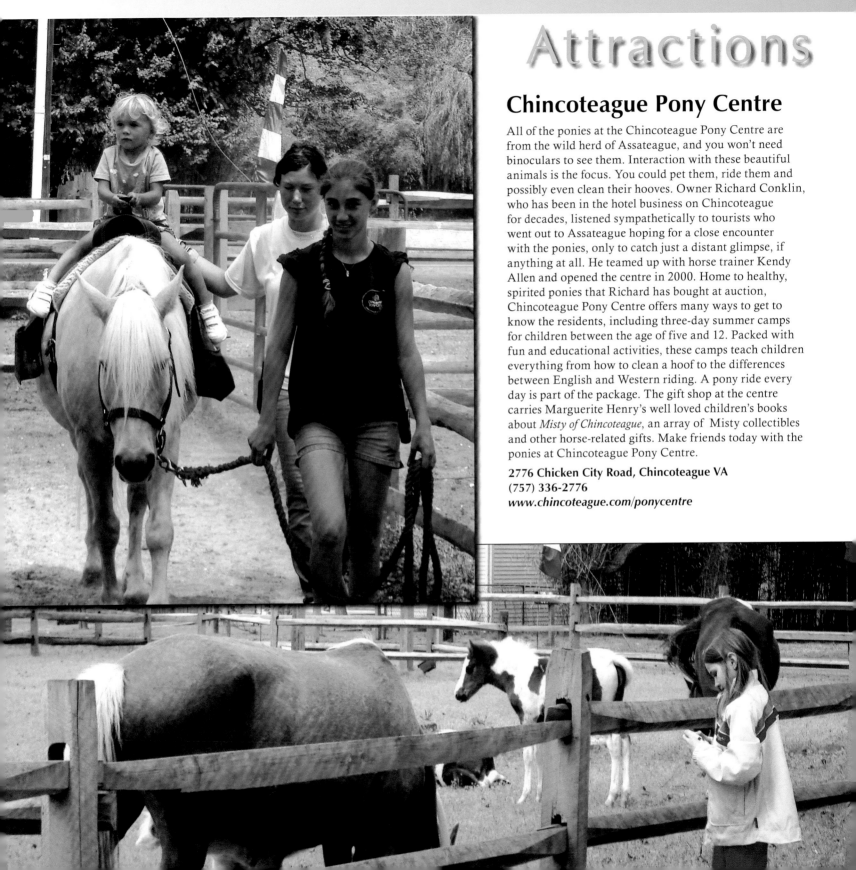

Attractions

Chincoteague Pony Centre

All of the ponies at the Chincoteague Pony Centre are from the wild herd of Assateague, and you won't need binoculars to see them. Interaction with these beautiful animals is the focus. You could pet them, ride them and possibly even clean their hooves. Owner Richard Conklin, who has been in the hotel business on Chincoteague for decades, listened sympathetically to tourists who went out to Assateague hoping for a close encounter with the ponies, only to catch just a distant glimpse, if anything at all. He teamed up with horse trainer Kendy Allen and opened the centre in 2000. Home to healthy, spirited ponies that Richard has bought at auction, Chincoteague Pony Centre offers many ways to get to know the residents, including three-day summer camps for children between the age of five and 12. Packed with fun and educational activities, these camps teach children everything from how to clean a hoof to the differences between English and Western riding. A pony ride every day is part of the package. The gift shop at the centre carries Marguerite Henry's well loved children's books about *Misty of Chincoteague*, an array of Misty collectibles and other horse-related gifts. Make friends today with the ponies at Chincoteague Pony Centre.

2776 Chicken City Road, Chincoteague VA
(757) 336-2776
www.chincoteague.com/ponycentre

Eastern Shore Railway Museum

You can almost hear the hypnotic clackety-clack as you daydream of riding the rail at the Eastern Shore Railway Museum. Among the painstakingly restored railway cars that you can enter at the museum is a 1950 Pullman Sleeper, such a perfect example of its kind that it was used as a set in a historical movie. Museum visitors are also welcome to peek inside a Pullman Observation Car, a Budd Diner and two cabooses. The museum features two non-passenger cars as well, an RF&P Baggage/Mail Car and a 1916 External Support Wooden Boxcar. History is presented without blinders in the old railway station, which appears just as it would have looked in 1920, complete with a segregated waiting area. The former Hopeton Railway Station building was moved to Parksley to serve as the centerpiece for the museum, which opened in 1988. Located midway between Norfolk, Virginia, and Pocomoke City, Maryland, Parksley was a town brought to life by the railroad, and the museum is located on the site of the train yard. The museum's maintenance shed and the crossing guard shack are original. Model train enthusiasts may arrange to view the H.O. model train layouts located inside the Mail Car, when they call at least two days in advance. For railroading history preserved in exact detail, visit the Eastern Shore Railway Museum.

18468 Dunne Avenue, Parksley VA
(757) 665-RAIL (7245)
www.parksley.org

Cape Charles Museum

In 1884, the town of Cape Charles was mapped out as the southern terminus of the newly formed New York, Philadelphia and Norfolk Railroad. This was the transfer point to Norfolk, across the Chesapeake Bay, for freight on specially constructed *carfloat* barges and for passengers on elegant bay steamers. During the next 70 years, the community enjoyed bustling growth, which is commemorated at the Cape Charles Museum, owned and operated by the Cape Charles Historical Society. This inspiring museum, founded in 1996, is dedicated to preserving and presenting the history of Cape Charles and the surrounding area. The museum is housed in a late industrial Deco building, which was constructed in 1947 and originally held two electric power generators. In 1993, Delmarva Power gave the building to the Historical Society. Today, the original 1946 Busch-Sulzer diesel engine and generator, both in working order, remain on display here. The Museum houses an extensive collection of photographs, postcards and memorabilia, along with old ship models. Just east of the main building is a reconstruction of the former Bloxom Passenger Station, and behind that lays a Richmond Fredericksburg & Potomac baggage car and a Nickel Plate Railroad caboose. Look for a tidy gift shop and numerous special events, fundraisers and traveling shows throughout the year. Learn more about area history with a visit to the Cape Charles Museum. Enjoy the town's public beach, restaurants and Victorian houses.

814 Randolph Avenue, Cape Charles VA
(757) 331-1008
www.smallmuseum.org/capechas.htm

Captain Barry's Back Bay Cruises

Since 1988, Barry Fishman has been sharing his love of Chincoteague with all who hop aboard Captain Barry's Back Bay Cruises. The boat pulls out from Landmark Plaza with a maximum of six passengers, so a good seat among a small group of adventurers is guaranteed. Even though you are on vacation, you might want to bring a notebook, because Barry's knowledge of the history, lore and wildlife of this gorgeous island is encyclopedic. The Birding and Nature Tour leaves at seven in the morning, a perfect time for spotting some of the 320 bird species that breed and feed in this rich marine environment. The half-day Coastal Encounter trip visits the coves,

channels and bays of the island, while Captain Barry spins tales of pirates, smugglers and lighthouses. You'll need to be wearing your shorts, because, as with the shorter Sea-Life Expedition, the Coastal Encounter is a hands-on adventure. Your group may dig for clams or cast nets for sea creatures. The Champagne-Sunset Cruise is a more subdued affair, an enchanting way to toast the end of a beautiful day. Personal coolers are allowed on these excursions. To discover the natural essence of Chincoteague with an enthusiastic guide, select Captain Barry's Back Bay Cruises.

8157 Sea Gull Drive, Chincoteague VA
(757) 336-6508
www.captainbarry@captainbarry.bigstep.com

Oyster & Maritime Museum

The island that the Native Americans once called Gingoteague, is known as Chincoteague today and is Virginia's only inhabited barrier island. The Oyster & Maritime Museum, built as a tribute to the islands seafaring heritage, is the depository of the island's history. The First Order Fresnel Lens from the Assateague Lighthouse is on display near the front entrance. You will also find nautical items on display, including model boats, fishing gear and tools from the oyster industry. Turn of the last century newspapers recount details of oyster wars fought over prime oyster beds. Historical maps and aerial photos document changes in Chincoteague ponies. From fossils, bones and shells to the work of master decoy carvers, the museum succeeds admirably in preserving, exhibiting and sharing the rich history of Chincoteague. The Oyster & Maritime Museum, located next to the Chincoteague National Wildlife Refuge, invites you to visit daily during the summer and on weekends in the spring and fall.

7125 Maddox Boulevard, Chincoteague VA
(757) 336-6117
www.chincoteaguechamber.com/oyster/index.html

Refuge Waterfowl Museum

The Refuge Waterfowl Museum stands at the gateway to the Chincoteague National Wildlife Refuge and Assateague National Seashore, a testament to one man's mission to preserve Virginia's coastal heritage. That man is John Maddox, who has been building the museum piece by piece since 1978. His collection of waterfowling artifacts has grown from the arrowheads he picked up as a kid to include everything from antique guns, boats and traps to a world-class flock of bird decoys. He added a wing to the museum some years ago to showcase a restored hunting carriage and another wing in 2002, where visitors find themselves surrounded by murals and carvings for a stimulating seashore experience. More than 1,000 carvings of ducks, geese and shorebirds are displayed throughout the 8,000-square-foot museum. The names of many of these old carvers have been forgotten, but such modern craftsmen as Delbert "Cigar" Daisey, the museum's resident carver, keep the painstaking tradition alive. A visitor to the museum left these poetic words: "Today all that remains of the old ways of hunting are these antique decoys, rusting gun barrels, rotting skiffs and the memories of a few aging men. The ducks and geese still come, but their numbers will never be so vast again." To glimpse a coastal way of life from the past, visit the Refuge Waterfowl Museum.

7059 Maddox Boulevard, Chincoteague VA
(757) 336-5800
www.chincoteaguechamber.com

Bakeries, Coffee & Tea

Island Creamery

The ice cream at Island Creamery on Chincoteague is made in small batches today to be eaten tomorrow. On a busy summer day, the staff could scoop as many as 150 gallons of the cold stuff, all of it made from the highest quality ingredients. That means you are getting local fruit, pure vanilla extract and excellent chocolate. By year's end, Island Creamery has usually served 35,000 waffle cones alone. Seasonal flavors, such as peach and blueberry, are especially popular. If you don't find your favorite flavor, or if you have a great idea for a flavor, be sure to tell someone at Island Creamery. It might be here the next time you drop by. The shop is open year-round, so you can defy the chill of winter with a double scoop in December, or fight the chill with a hot espresso beverage. Whether your next party is in January or July, Island Creamery has an ice cream cake that will put a smile on everyone's face. The shop also carries Chincoteague souvenirs as well as homemade fudge and distinctive gift items. For ice cream that is always fresh and rich, go to Island Creamery.

6243 Maddox Boulevard, Chincoteague VA
(757) 336-6236
www.islandcreamery.net

Muller's Ice Cream Parlour

When in Chincoteague, you could buy a quart of ice cream at a market, but then you would be missing out on the uniquely Chincoteague experience that awaits you at Muller's Ice Cream Parlour. Where else could you enjoy a single-scoop cone or a Belgian waffle smothered with ice cream, fresh fruit and whipped cream while you soak in the ambience of a building that was built in 1875 by the town's casket maker? Given the original owner's occupation, would it surprise you to know that the building is said to be haunted? Another thing that makes Muller's special is the owner, Court Lynn, who probably has ice cream for blood. He earned his spending money in college by working an ice cream truck. If anyone was ever born to his job it would have to be Court, who admits to eating ice cream everywhere he goes. Not only does he love ice cream, but he wants to make sure that he is offering the best that he can find. He has selected Coleman's Handmade Ice Cream, which is delicious on its own or as a key ingredient in one of Muller's sundaes, floats or shakes. Why settle for just ice cream? Go to Muller's Ice Cream Parlour, where you can get it in a haunted house from a genuine ice cream junkie.

4034 Main Street, Chincoteague VA
(757) 336-5894
www.chincoteaguechamber.com

Galleries & Fine Art

Turner Sculpture

If you are a collector or admirer of wildlife sculpture, you are probably familiar with the father and son team William H. and David H. Turner, whose nationally acclaimed bronze sculptures capture the beauty and motion of wild animals. William founded Turner Sculpture in 1973 and the duo established their present facility in 1983. A gallery on the premises features exquisite wildlife sculpture by both the Turners as well as pieces by other sculptors, including Guy Shover and Larry Randall. The facility also houses several studios, a welding shop and a building where the bronzes are patented. William grew up on Virginia's rural Eastern Shore and later put himself through the University of Virginia by building boats. He went on to teach school, served in the Navy and at the age of 30 put himself through dental school by making and selling ceramic wildlife figurines. William then tried his hand at porcelains and gradually went on to master the art of bronze sculpture, which he cast in a foundry that he set up in his airplane hanger. William has three sons: William II, who took over the dental practice; Robert, an attorney in nearby Accomac; and David, who began making clay models as a toddler and now oversees the company's day-to-day operations. Both David and William have received numerous awards and accolades, and their work can be viewed in public venues across the nation. Learn more about the Turners and find exceptional wildlife sculpture at Turner Sculpture.

27316 Lankford Highway, Onley VA
(757) 787-2818
www.turnersculpture.com

Osprey Nest Art Gallery

The beautiful posters that you see commemorating Pony Penning in shops and galleries around Chincoteague are the work of Kevin McBride, whose gallery you can visit while enjoying the island. It's called the Osprey Nest Art Gallery, and it's been right on Main Street since 1985. That's about the time when Kevin did his first poster for Pony Penning, though his reputation reaches far beyond Chincoteague. His watercolors and oils have been displayed at many prestigious art shows throughout the country, and his originals hang in homes and galleries as far away as Europe, Australia and Asia. He has been named the Ducks Unlimited Artist of the Year several times. Kevin's love for the natural world is evident in his work, which combines a romantic's sense with a perfectionist's skills. Kevin shows his paintings and the work of many other fine artists in his Osprey Nest Gallery, with a special emphasis on local subjects. Here is your chance to chat with Kevin and even have him sign your print. During Pony Penning, he actually has a pony at the shop. Pony Penning, the annual round up of ponies from Assateague Island, falls on the last Wednesday of July. Oh, but you already know that from seeing Kevin's posters. To meet Kevin and be swept away by his art, visit the Osprey Nest Art Gallery.

4096 S Main Street, Chincoteague Island VA
(757) 336-6042
www.ospreynestartgallery.com

Maplewood Gardens

Maplewood Gardens, located midway between Nassawadox and Exmore, offers visitors a tranquil hideaway for purchasing and enjoying landscape plants suitable for the shore. The nursery is landscaped with a bounty of shrubs, trees and perennials, along with elegant roses and fragrant herbs. This full-service garden and landscaping company also offers a charming gift cottage filled with concrete and metal statuary, arbors, benches and a myriad of gardening accessories. Owners Phil and Barbara Custis began their farming life in 1967, when they turned Phil's family homestead into a thriving 20-acre azalea farm. Over the years the couple has added many popular plants. Today the 100-year-old Victorian farmhouse is surrounded by lovely test gardens featuring plants sold at Maplewood Gardens. The grounds also house a five-field memorial baseball complex named for Phil and Barbara's deceased son, Randy, who was killed by a drunk driver at the age of nine. The complex was built from memorial gifts and donations and is free to the public as are the peaceful woodland trails, which meander past a turtle pond, over picturesque bridges and through the vibrant forest. When you arrive at Maplewood Gardens, you're likely to be greeted by Barbara's best friend and employee, Cecilia, along with Cutter, the resident border collie. A visit to the Blue Barn allows you to meet sheep, lambs and a horse named Spirit. Revel in nature's beauty and bounty with a visit to Maplewood Gardens.

6118 Seaside Road, Nassawadox VA (757) 442-9071
www.maplewoodgardens.com

Photos by BurnhamInk.com

gardenART on King St.

The very day that Joani Donohoe drove into Onancock, she knew she was home. She quickly purchased a house she loved and soon after bought the town's historic power plant and turned it into gardenART on King St., a welcoming home and garden shop dedicated to garden and home enhancement. Joani, a native of Washington, D.C., who holds degrees in botany, ornamental horticulture and landscape design, used her inherent good taste and landscaping background to turn the 1910 power plant into a whimsical garden paradise that is relaxing and pleasing to the eye. The shop offers a full range of distinctive products and services, including plants and shrubs of all kinds, professional landscape design services, soil pH testing and organic garden solutions that are earth-friendly alternatives to toxic chemicals. Joani further hand selects an exquisite array

of pots, statuary, art and furnishings for your home gardens, along with a plethora of garden necessities. The ideal place to find charming home accents, gardenArt on King St. also carries candles, cards, lotions and potions of all sorts. Joani displays a choice selection of gardening gifts throughout the year, but never is the display grander than during the Christmas holidays, when gardenART turns into a garden wonderland that gleams with holiday spirit. Indulge in your love of gardening with a tour of gardenART on King St.

44 King Street, Onancock VA
(757) 787-8818
www.gardenartonking.com

Windsor House

As you travel Route 13 through Cape Charles, you will come across a tidy Victorian home that was built in 1907 and today serves as a portal to another time and place. Windsor House, owned and operated by Kurt and Sally Lewin, is a respite from modern hustle and bustle as well as home to the Lewins' workshop, where they painstakingly handcraft exquisite Windsor style chairs using the same tools and techniques as European craftsmen did in the 1700s. The Lewins were farmers in New York State prior to starting their new venture, which began as a hobby after they were unable to locate quality Windsor chairs for their own home. They learned how to create these masterpieces of form and function from a craftsman in Canada and soon were beleaguered with requests from neighbors and friends for these chairs. The farming Lewins left their old career and home behind them and opened the Windsor House in 2003. Visitors to Windsor House can watch the Lewins at work and ask questions about the techniques and tools used to create these lovely chairs. In addition to creating Windsor style chairs, the Lewins offer a selection of blanket chests, cupboards and farm tables, as well as primitive antiques and local artwork by area potters, painters and wood carvers. For handcrafted furnishings that will become tomorrow's heirloom treasures, visit Windsor House.

4290 Capeville Road, Capeville, VA
(757) 331-4848
www.lewinwindsorhouse.com

Markets

Hot Stuff!

With more than 500 different sauces in stock, Hot Stuff! is definitely the hottest spot in Chincoteague. Enter only if you can take the heat. This is the place to shop for fiery barbecue sauces, wing sauces and salsas. If setting your mouth ablaze isn't your style, Hot Stuff! also carries mild sauces to add flavor to almost any meal or snack. In fact, the sauces here run the gamut from flaming hot to sweetly mild. Still, if you eat by the motto that zing is the thing, then you have found the right place. Hot Stuff! is the home of Wild Pony Hot Sauce, a delicious habanero sauce sold exclusively at this store. Another product with a strong local connection is the Chincoteague Crab Salsa. Would you like to try before you buy? Tasting many sauces at the sample table is part of the fun of visiting here. Hot Stuff! is very involved in the Chincoteague Oyster Festival in mid-October and the Chili Chowder Cook-off the week after that. With summer gone, the temperature on the island may have dropped by then, though Hot Stuff! makes sure that no one gets cold. How hot can you go? You'll find out when you visit Hot Stuff!

6273 Cropper Street, Chincoteague VA
(757) 336-5894
www.chincoteaguechamber.com

The Great Machipongo Clam Shack

As you travel along the Route 13 corridor, you will come across the Great Machipongo Clam Shack, a stalwart icon of all that makes the area famous. This popular fish market and eatery is owned and operated by husband and wife team Jean and Roger Mariner, whose bubbling personalities are as much of a draw as the tender and delicious fish and seafood that they sell. Touted as the home of Eat & Drive Seafood, the Great Machipongo Clam Shack offers five flavorful specials that can be munched on the go and a full menu of options for those dining in. The Clam Shack also features a fish market that sells fresh local fish and seafood, such as crab and Lil Neck clams, as well as a full selection of flash frozen delicacies from around the globe, including mahi-mahi, yellow fin tuna and sashimi-grade tilapia. Nationwide shipping is available for all products. In addition to offering a full gamut of sensational fresh, frozen and ready-to-eat fish and seafood, the clam shack stocks maps, gifts, shirts and books as well as a choice selection of local wines. You'll even find such delights as smoked alligator and pork sausage here. For local color and foods, visit the Great Machipongo Clam Shack.

6468 Lankford Highway, Route 13, Nassawadox VA
(757) 442-3800
www.greatclams.com

Recreation

Southeast Expeditions

Experience the beauty of the Eastern Shore, right up close, with a sea kayaking tour from Southeast Expeditions, where owners and kayaking experts David Burden and Bo Lusk specialize in introducing newcomers to the amazing ecosystem of this stunning area. Between them, this delightful duo has more than 20 years of kayak teaching experience. Both David and Bo studied environmental science at the University of Virginia in Charlottesville with a focus on coastal wetland ecosystems, a background that gives them a unique perspective of the area to pass on to their customers. The partners originally started Southeast Expeditions as a touring company; however, by popular demand they soon began stocking a wide selection of kayaks, gear and accessories. The company sells a full line of top name products along with rentals and classes for kayak enthusiasts of all skill levels. The company also offers kayak tours, ranging from a few hours to overnight trips, which come complete with guides and gourmet meals. In addition to spectacular kayak tours, Southeast Expeditions can also get you started on kiteboarding, an amazing new water sport that pits man against the elements for a thrilling ride across the water. View thousands of birds, explore the salt marshes, and become one with nature as you glide across the waters of the Eastern Shore with David, Bo and the gang from Southeast Expeditions.

611 Mason Avenue, Cape Charles VA
(757) 331-2680
www.sekayak.com

Photos by David Burden

Restaurants & Cafés

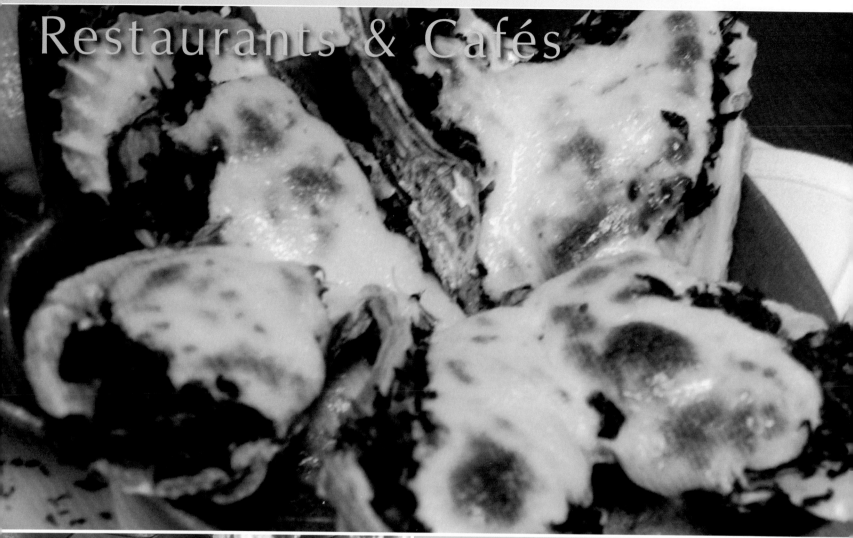

Bill's Seafood

Bill's Seafood brings together the service and quality of an upscale restaurant with the laid-back style of Chincoteague. "It's a step up without being stuffy," say owners Kevin Crome and Steven Potts, who, in 1996, took over what has been a fixture of the Chincoteague scene since 1960. Describe Bill's as you will, you certainly won't need more than a second to find the right words for the seafood, steaks and chops. *Succulent* and *delicious* will come instantly to mind. Bill's uses locally caught and grown ingredients whenever it can; its specialties are as diverse as its crab soup and its honey mustard. The Tropical Shrimp Salad, Oysters Rockefeller and Pepper-Crusted Tuna are big favorites. Virginia wines share the extensive wine list with international selections. When Bill's first opened, Chincoteague was a different, less discovered place than it is today. The clientele was mostly local, especially at breakfast, which brought in the fishermen. You can still catch an early breakfast at Bill's, which opens at 5 am. For fine dining island style, try Bill's Seafood.

4040 Main Street, Chincoteague VA
(757) 336-5831

Steamers

The folks at Steamers mean no disrespect to the many elegant restaurants on Chincoteague, but they believe that you will find the true island way of dining at their place. The fun begins when you order the all-you-can-eat steamed crabs. "We bring them out, dump them on the table, and you go at it," says co-owner Robert Bash, whose name is certainly in keeping with a restaurant at which the server hands you a knife and a mallet. All joking aside, you are in for a treat when you eat here. To assure freshness, Steamers works directly with local watermen. The crabs, which come from the Chesapeake Bay, are delivered daily. What's more, the folks at Steamers are serious when they say that dining at their place reflects the no-frills, family-oriented way of life on the island. The sounds you here at Steamers are those of families laughing and talking as they work together to conquer a mound of crabs. Spicy steamed shrimp, clam chowder and fried chicken complete the menu at Steamers. Most dinners come with hush puppies and corn on the cob. For dining that's more than a nibble and anything but dainty, head to Steamers any day of the week.

6251 Maddox Boulevard, Chincoteague VA
(757) 336-5478
www.steamersrest.com

Club Car Café

It will take you just a few minutes to drive from Onancock to the Eastern Shore Railway Museum in Parksley, and you are guaranteed a home-cooked meal at the Club Car Café when you get there. A popular spot with the locals as well as with museum visitors, the café is the place where all travelers of the BL&T Railroad Company meet. Owners Tim and Leigh Valentine came up with that clever bit. Needless to say, they would love for you to try their B.L.T. or any of their other menu items. You will find something to hit the spot no matter what time you arrive, because the café serves breakfast, lunch and dinner. Burgers and salads are popular, and dessert is well worth your while. In fact, Tim and Leigh report that a man comes from Crisfield, Maryland at least once a month for the peanut butter pie. Noteworthy beverages include the Vanilla or Chocolate Zip and the intriguing Red Neck Cappuccino. The nearby railway museum features an old station house and seven beautifully restored cars, including a Pullman Sleeper and a Pullman Observation Car. For a taste of small-town Virginia, have a bite at the Club Car Café.

18497 Dunne Avenue, Parksley VA
(757) 665-7822

Mariah's at Tower Hill Bed & Breakfast

Mariah's offers a distinguished dining experience with an exemplary staff and an alluring sense of history. This notable eatery is part of Tower Hill Bed & Breakfast, which opened in 2003 and is owned and operated by Executive Chef Tim Brown and his wife, Melanie. Tower Hill mansion was originally built in 1746 from brick imported from England. Sadly, a fire destroyed much of the dwelling's interior in 1999. In 2000, BECO, a Hampton Roads development firm, stepped in and restored the historic home and added modern touches in the process. Today, Tower Hill boasts five elegant suites in addition to Mariah's restaurant, which was named for resident ghost and former owner Mariah Saunders. Tim began working in the culinary world at age 14 and has remained there since, enjoying a career that has taken him from hotels and resorts to teaching at a top culinary university. He is also a nationally certified executive chef through the American Culinary Federation and specializes in several culinary forms, including classic French cuisine. In addition to offering sumptuous cuisine and personable service, Tower Hill features a relaxing pub, lush landscaping, incredible views and a selection of recreational activities, such as kayaking, fishing and crabbing from the private dock. Savor culinary delights and ultimate relaxation with a visit to Mariah's at Tower Hill Bed & Breakfast.

3018 Bowden Landing, Cape Charles VA
(757) 331-1700
www.towerhillbb.com

Olivia's

If your quest to find the perfect chowder has yet to include a stop at Olivia's, you have the pleasure ahead of you of sampling the Gloucester contender with a loyal following. People come from far away to buy Olivia's seafood chowder by the quart. Owners Gary and Karen Ward can spot the serious chowderhead right away, usually by his t-shirt that says something like "Will Work for a Bowl of Chowder." They are more than happy to take his order and send him merrily on his way with a take-out container, but they are equally proud of every item, more than 50 in all, on their menu. Local seafood, prime rib and Italian dishes are among their specialties. Everything at Olivia's is fresh and made to order. Gary follows a family tradition of restaurant ownership begun by his grandparents, Harry and Ella Mae Ward, who opened one of Gloucester's first restaurants in the 1950s. They taught him that the secrets to success are consistency, value and, above all, the willingness to listen to customers. That's why the Wards strive to make guests feel that they are friends of the family. They like to visit tables and invite customers to share their thoughts about their dining experience. You'll find two Olivia's locations, one in the town of Gloucester and one at Gloucester Point. Whether you are ready to enjoy a fabulous sit-down dinner or just need a chowder fix, make Olivia's your destination.

1785 George Washington Memorial Highway, Gloucester VA (804) 684-2234
6597 Main Street, Gloucester VA (804) 694-0057

The Blarney Stone Pub

What do you get when you put a culinary school graduate from San Antonio in charge of the kitchen at an Irish pub? At the Blarney Stone in Onancock, you get a corned beef quesadilla called the O'Casey-Dilla. OK, not all the food at the Blarney Stone is this funny, but thanks to Chef Alisa James, the pub fare is fresh and consistently good. The shepherd's pie and fish-and-chips get especially high marks, as does the shrimp and oyster sandwich. The McGruff just might be the biggest hot dog you've ever eaten. Picking a beer to go with your meal might take you a minute or two, because the bar keeps 12 taps flowing, with several British and Irish imports featured. If you need help in deciding, the menu takes a food and pairs it with a beer that is its perfect complement. As in a neighborhood pub back in Ireland, the emphasis at the Blarney Stone is on providing a cozy atmosphere for hanging out with friends without the blare of piped-in music and a barrage of big-screen televisions. Entertainment here is of the homemade variety and usually consists of an Irish jam session on Friday and Saturday nights. Everyone is welcome to play, sing or even dance a jig. The Blarney Stone opened in March 2005, just in time, of course, for St. Patrick's Day. For a fun place, where every day feels like a holiday, go to the Blarney Stone Pub.

10 North Street, Onancock VA
(757) 302-0300
www.blarneystonepubonancock.com

Mallards

Johnny Mo started cooking when he was 13, and by the age of 16 he had received his first cooking award. During that interview they asked him what he planned to do with his life. He told them he was going to open his own restaurant, and within 10 years he had. Mallards Restaurant opened in December 2002. It was such a hit that by April of 2005 John "Johnny Mo" Morrison went on to open two more restaurants in the Onancock area, each with its own unique twist. The original Mallards Restaurant offers fine dining in a casual environment. No need to get dressed up to experience great food. The menu changes quarterly to keep things new and exciting for both the kitchen and their guests. You may find yourself with a bowl of Mussels in a Jalapeno Broth as Johnny Mo puts down his chef's knife and picks up his guitar. He plays for a well-known Reggae band on the eastern shore. Experience the view when you head on down to Mallards on the Wharf where they offer the only waterfront dining on the bayside of Chesapeake Bay from Crisfield to Cape Charles. Mallards Sidewalk Café is over in the county seat of Accomac, where you will be able to experience the flavor of Mallards with a slight judicial twist. At any one of three Mallard locations you can pick up a bottle of one of Johnny Mo's special sauces. Three Mallards. Three experiences. It's a must to enjoy them all.

22327 Bayside Road, Onancock VA (Mallards Restaurant)
(757) 787-7333
2 Market Street, Onancock VA (Mallards at the Wharf)
(757) 787-8558
23410 Front Street, Accomac VA (Mallards Sidewalk Café)
(757) 787-7321
www.mallardsllc.com

Hampton Roads

Accommodations

Smithfield Inn

Come celebrate the genteel hospitality and graciousness of the Old South with a visit to the Smithfield Inn. This elegant inn began life as one of the first buildings to be erected in the newly chartered town of Smithfield circa the mid 1750s, later becoming a tavern in 1759, which started an innkeeping tradition that continues to thrive today. The Smithfield Inn offers patrons several stunning rooms to choose from including suites with private sitting rooms, bedrooms and private baths and two with gas fireplaces. In the Garden House, which was added to the property circa 1900, you will find additional rooms and a lovely parlor that is an ideal place to gather in the evenings. Each guest of the Smithfield Inn is treated to a full complementary breakfast in the dining room. The inn's restaurant is also open to the public for lunch and dinner, featuring delicious local cuisine. The William Rand Tavern is located on-site, opening six days a week at 4:30 p.m. and features wonderful fare consisting of favorite appetizers and sandwiches and a vast selection of foreign and domestic beer and an extensive wine list. The Smithfield Inn is also the ideal place to celebrate the special moments in your life and offers its exquisite gardens as a backdrop for weddings, reunions and other special occasions. Experience all that historic Smithfield has to offer with a stay at the centrally located and always delightful Smithfield Inn.

112 Main Street, Smithfield VA
(757) 357-1752
www.smithfieldinn.com

Williamsburg Sampler
Bed & Breakfast Inn

Although built in 1976, the Williamsburg Sampler Bed & Breakfast Inn has the gracious good looks of an 18th century plantation home and fits right into the City of Williamsburg's Architectural Protection District. The three-story, sixbedroom Colonial home has an international reputation for honeymoons, anniversaries and romantic getaways. Two of the bedrooms are private quarters, and the remaining four feature fine collections of

antique furnishings, pewter and American and English cross stitch samplers. Romance can't help but bloom in the wellappointed two-room suites with king sized four poster beds, cable televisions, refrigerators, fireplaces and access to the rooftop garden. Many celebrities choose the comforts of the Williamsburg Sampler thanks to its meticulous good looks, its great location next to Williamsburg's historic district and its many amenities, including the Carriage House Fitness Center, the Billiard Parlor and the Skip Lunch® breakfast. This renowned breakfast gets rave reviews from experts like retired Executive Chef of the Waldorf-Astoria Arno Schmidt.

In 1995, the inn was named Inn of the Year for the Commonwealth of Virginia by then-Governor George Allen. The romantic setting has inspired many engagements. Proprietor Ike Sisane even prepared an impromptu wedding here for a German couple. Expect the best of old and new at this remarkable establishment where fine details like hardwood floors, carved beds and period moldings live side by side with modern conveniences like central air conditioning. The Williamsburg Sampler Bed & Breakfast Inn invites you to sample its many charms. Make reservations well in advance because this inn is deservedly popular.

922 Jamestown Road, Williamsburg VA
(757) 253-0398 or (800) 722-1169
www.WilliamsburgSampler.com

Photos by M. Sigmon Photography

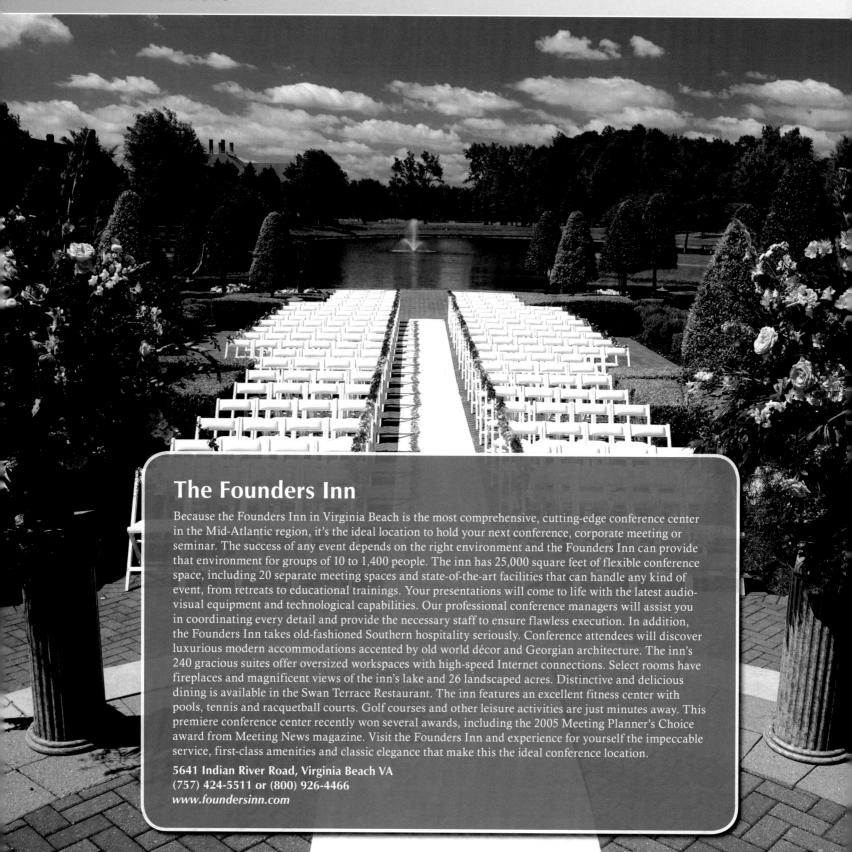

The Founders Inn

Because the Founders Inn in Virginia Beach is the most comprehensive, cutting-edge conference center in the Mid-Atlantic region, it's the ideal location to hold your next conference, corporate meeting or seminar. The success of any event depends on the right environment and the Founders Inn can provide that environment for groups of 10 to 1,400 people. The inn has 25,000 square feet of flexible conference space, including 20 separate meeting spaces and state-of-the-art facilities that can handle any kind of event, from retreats to educational trainings. Your presentations will come to life with the latest audio-visual equipment and technological capabilities. Our professional conference managers will assist you in coordinating every detail and provide the necessary staff to ensure flawless execution. In addition, the Founders Inn takes old-fashioned Southern hospitality seriously. Conference attendees will discover luxurious modern accommodations accented by old world décor and Georgian architecture. The inn's 240 gracious suites offer oversized workspaces with high-speed Internet connections. Select rooms have fireplaces and magnificent views of the inn's lake and 26 landscaped acres. Distinctive and delicious dining is available in the Swan Terrace Restaurant. The inn features an excellent fitness center with pools, tennis and racquetball courts. Golf courses and other leisure activities are just minutes away. This premiere conference center recently won several awards, including the 2005 Meeting Planner's Choice award from Meeting News magazine. Visit the Founders Inn and experience for yourself the impeccable service, first-class amenities and classic elegance that make this the ideal conference location.

5641 Indian River Road, Virginia Beach VA
(757) 424-5511 or (800) 926-4466
www.foundersinn.com

Sandbridge Realty

On your next excursion to Virginia Beach, bypass the impersonal hotels and choose instead a vacation rental from Sandbridge Realty. For more than one hundred years, visitors have spent their holidays at Sandbridge in Virginia Beach; although, the area remains a well-kept secret primarily unknown to outsiders and locals alike. With Virginia's clement temperatures remaining well into the autumn season, this is the idea destination to bring the family for a prime beach vacation while avoiding the crowds that surge the Outer Banks of the Carolina's. Sandbridge Realty has over three hundred fully stocked beach houses or condominiums for you to choose from that range in price as well as amenities. Sandbridge Realty will help you and your family find the accommodations to fit both your needs as well as your pocketbook. Whether you're looking for a King's getaway right on the water or a simpler abode with water views and a hot tub, Sandbridge Realty can make your vacation dreams a reality. They even have homes that allow pets so that the whole family can join in on the fun. Other possible amenities include private pools, Internet services, large screen televisions and game rooms with pool or ping-pong tables. Each rental is centrally located so that you can conveniently enjoy all that Virginia Beach and the surrounding areas have to offer including hiking, biking, surfing and sightseeing. Find your home away from home while enjoying the vast beauty and recreational opportunities of Virginia Beach with a vacation home from Sandbridge Realty.

581 Sandbridge Road, Virginia Beach VA
(800) 933-4800
www.sandbridge.com

Church Street Inn

When making plans for your next stay in Smithfield consider the Church Street Inn, where you can enjoy all of the comforts of home along with incredible hospitality and beautiful décor. This delightful inn has been under the ownership of Angie and Peter Lowry of Cheshire, England since 2003, when they took over the existing inn and gave it a whole new look. While this task would be daunting for most, it was a labor of love for the Lowrys, who chose to merge Angie's existing interior decorating business with their new innkeeping enterprise. Now visitors can come to the Church Street Inn and enjoy the elegant décor created by Angie and her team from Interiors by Decorating Den while luxuriating in the comfortable rooms that come complete with wireless Internet. The inn has 12 charming bedrooms, each with a private bath, plus two suites that feature fireplaces and Jacuzzi tubs. Angie uses the inn as a showcase for the design business, and much of the furniture and décor pieces are for sale. Church Street Inn strives to cater to the non-traditional traveler and those who are passing through on business or for family reunions. During the week, Angie and Peter bypass the traditional heavy breakfast and offer their guests a continental breakfast, featuring fresh coffee, juices, cereals, fruit and yogurt. Come enjoy the peaceful and elegant retreat that Peter and Angie have created at the Church Street Inn and Interiors by Decorating Den.

1607 S Church Street, Smithfield VA
(757) 357-3176
www.smithfieldchurchstreetinn.com

Mansion on Main

In 1995 Sala Clark found out that the 1889 Victorian home she was lovingly restoring, the largest house built downtown before the turn of the century, had been nicknamed the mansion on Main Street. Thus, the Mansion on Main Bed & Breakfast was christened. Attorney and town historian R.S. Thomas, who had the showcase home built to house his office, made his own discovery about its significance on the corner edge of colonial roads. As St. Luke Church's (c.1632 national shrine) recorder, Thomas learned that a vestrymen in the 1750s, Jordan Thomas, was not only his ancestor but also the county surveyor who mapped out Smithfield's first streets. Although Sala Clark did not live to see the restoration completed, her vision and efforts resurrected a place that offers the romantic beauty of a bygone era. The mansion was the first house in the Historic District to return to authentic Painted Lady splendor. The museum-like interior retains original marble finish fireplaces and heart pine floors and is resplendent with furnishings dating from the Victorian period. Extensive ornate handcarved woodwork done by European artisans is exhibited in plaster crown moldings and medallions, a grand staircase, pocket doors and wainscoting. At Mansion House Art & Antiques, the Bed & Breakfast's sister business, you are welcome to browse as well as to buy the antiques. Owner Betty Clark transformed a 1950s brick grocery store into a 4,000-square-foot gallery filled with fine antique accessories, a collection that rivals what can be found in metropolitan areas. Merchandise features oil paintings from the 1820s to the 1950s, estate jewelry that includes Victorian mourning pieces, cut glass, porcelain collectibles from Royal Doulton, Lladro, and Hummel, sterling flatware and Waterford crystal. Betty Clark specializes in oil painting restoration and a silver pattern matching service. Neither the Mansion on Main nor Mansion House Art & Antiques should be missed.

36 Main Street, Smithfield VA (757) 357-0006
www.mansion-on-main.net

120 N Church Street, Smithfield VA (757) 357-3968
www.mansiongallery.net

Edgewood Plantation

Edgewood Plantation is an inviting bed-and-breakfast and a fascinating place to learn about local history and folklore, complete with a resident ghost. The plantation gets its name from its location—on the edge of the woods of Berkeley Plantation, ancestral home of Benjamin Harrison V, a signer of the Declaration of Independence, and his grandson, William Henry Harrison, ninth president of the United States. A comfortable blend of primitive 18th century, Victorian, and Chippendale furnishings fill the home. Several guest units have fireplaces, and all have private baths. In Lizzie's Room, visitors can see the name Lizzie Roland etched into a windowpane. She was the daughter of the man who built the house and made the etching while waiting for her true love to return from the war. He never did, and legend has it that she died of a broken heart and her spirit still roams the halls. In keeping with the Victorian surroundings, Edgewood offers Victorian tea parties and lunches, where guests can try on period hats while enjoying the traditional food selections. They host a Queen's Tea on Thursdays and Fridays, a Jamestown Luncheon on Wednesdays, and an Early Settler's Breakfast on Saturdays and Sundays. In November and December, among the 18 Christmas trees in the house, they do a Candlelight Tour and Dinner, and a Somewhere in Time Christmas Tea. All of these events require at least a two day advance notice. Owners Dot and Julian Boulware seek to make each visit as enjoyable as possible. To experience the history and hospitality of Virginia firsthand, visit Edgewood Plantation.

4800 John Tyler Memorial Highway, Charles City VA
(804) 829-2962
www.edgewoodplantation.com

Colonial Capital Bed & Breakfast

Conveniently located in the heart of Williamsburg, the Colonial Capital Bed & Breakfast is only a three-block stroll from the living museum of Colonial Williamsburg, and is across the street from the campus of the College of William and Mary. Colonial Capital Bed & Breakfast offers special vacation packages that include tickets to Colonial Williamsburg, Jamestown, Yorktown, Busch Gardens, and golfing at award-winning courses. The three-story colonial revival home, tastefully decorated and furnished with antiques and period reproductions, is a recollection of the past which offers the comforts of the present. Your stay will include a gourmet breakfast in the dining room or solarium, and an afternoon tea. All bedrooms have private baths and direct telephone lines with Internet connections. Relax and enjoy a private moment or visit friends old and new in the spacious parlor, screened veranda and patio. Your hosts, Sharon and George Hollingsworth, extend genuine Southern hospitality at a fair price. Spunky, their 13-year-old miniature Schnauzer, adds a special greeting for animal lovers, but does not impose. Your hosts at the inn make sure that each guest is attended to and leaves with a smile. Children eight and older are welcome, but your pets will have to stay at home. The house has filtered water, smoke and carbon monoxide detectors, and well lit, off-street guest parking. The Colonial Capital Bed & Breakfast is your best choice for a comfortable, relaxing and trouble-free stay in historic Williamsburg.

501 Richmond Road, Williamsburg VA
(757) 229-0233 or (800) 776-0570
www.ccbb.com
ccbb@widowmaker.com

North Bend Plantation

The North Bend Plantation, circa 1801, is owned by Ridgely and George Copland. Incredibly, George is a descendent of the original owners of the house. The 850-acre plantation grows a strict rotation of corn, wheat and soybeans, attracting all manner of wildlife. An on-site pond draws ducks and nature trails lure visitors to explore the beautiful grounds punctuated by historic landmarks such as civil war trenches. North Bend Plantation is a National Registry property built for the sister of the ninth president of the United States and still contains antiques original to the house and family. Guests can also enjoy the swimming pool on the grounds and the house itself is truly outstanding with its elegant decor and comfort. Ridgely and George exude gracious southern hospitality while they freely share information about the history of the plantation and the family tree. Staying at North Bend Plantation is similar to staying with close friends or family, complete with a billiards table, fascinating books and heirlooms that are used too often to gather dust. Every morning, guests at the plantation are treated to a full country breakfast. North Bend Plantation provides a picturesque backdrop for weddings and special events. The Coplands extend their invitation for you to come and acquaint yourself with the rich history of North Bend Plantation, reserve a room and immerse yourself even more in the wonders of this historical home.

12200 Weyanoke Road, Charles City VA
(804) 829-5176
www.northbendplantation.com

Jasmine Plantation Bed and Breakfast

Jasmine Plantation Bed and Breakfast is an elegant but comfortable place to relax and enjoy the rich history of this area. Current innkeepers Eileen and Don Smith have retained many of the beautiful and unique aspects of this home that give it such significant historical value. Guests will enjoy an incredible upscale breakfast while still feeling relaxed and at home. Jasmine Plantation was originally settled on 5,000 acres in 1680 by George Morris, who was a member of the House of Burgesses from 1660 to 1662. Although it is not the original house on the property, the current Jasmine house was built in 1750 and was headquarters for the Revolutionary Army in October 1779. Jasmine was purchased in 1918 by Henry and Mattie Brenneman. Mattie was quite the painter and examples of her artwork are on display in the parlor. She painted a mural on the stairway landing which has been restored to its original splendor. The house has been a bed-and-breakfast since the 1990s and offers six bedrooms, each with private baths and air conditioning, filled with antiques and nostalgic pieces of Americana. There are 47 acres of beautiful woods to explore and nearby attractions to complete your stay. Visit the Jasmine Plantation Bed and Breakfast and relive a piece of history.

4500 N Courthouse Road, Providence Forge VA
(800) 639-5368 or (804) 966-9836
www.jasmineplantation.com

Boxwood Inn

While you are enjoying a Friday night getaway at the Boxwood Inn, consider that this marvelous building was on the verge of being demolished before Barbara and Bob Lucas bought it. Barbara and Bob point out that their initials spell B & B, suggesting that innkeeping has always been their destiny. Certainly it's something they perform with style and creativity. The special Friday package is one of their many great ideas. It includes dinner, a night in one of the four guest rooms and a gourmet breakfast for two for the same price as a night's lodging. Another Boxwood Inn favorite is the Dinnertainments, for groups of 35 or more. These themed events showcase the singing and acting talents of local entertainers, who dress in costume to perform a Murder Mystery Evening, a Dickens Christmas Dinner or Pirates of the Pennisula. The four-course meal coordinates with the entertainment, so guests feast on such Southern favorites as peanut soup, baked chicken and caramel bread pudding while enjoying an Evening in Old Virginia. As for the building itself, it was built in 1896 as a 21-room mansion for Simon Curtis, the so-called Boss of Warwick County. He collected the taxes. The Lucases have preserved much of the home's original charm by using furniture and antiques that they found in the attic. Go to the Boxwood Inn, and pat Barbara and Bob on the back for saving this old beauty.

10 Elmshurst Street, Newport News VA
(757) 888-8854
www.boxwoodinn.com
d-inn.com

Newport House Bed & Breakfast

Take an exciting trip back in time when you stay at the Newport House Bed & Breakfast. Located in historical Williamsburg, the Newport House was built to museum standards in 1988 from an original 1756 design by the famous architect Peter Harrison. Newport House is totally furnished with period English and American antiques and reproductions. You'll stay in spacious, luxurious rooms that feature four poster canopy beds and private bathrooms. Even the blankets and carpeting

are historically authentic. In the mornings you can enjoy a full breakfast served in the formal dining room that includes delicious dishes made from authentic colonial recipes. Fruit and honey from their own garden are also featured. At the same time, if you wish, you can enjoy an interesting and informative historical seminar given by your host John Fitzhugh Millar. He's a former museum director, the author of many historical books and captain of an historic square-rigged sailing ship. Newport House is only a five-minute walk from Colonial Williamsburg and it's near all the historic attractions of the area. It's the only one of 24 bed-and-breakfasts in Williamsburg that embraces the area's historical theme. This allows guests to be immersed in the colonial period completely without sacrificing comfort. John, his wife Cathy and their son Ian invite you to stay at Newport House Bed & Breakfast and experience the full richness of this historical area.

710 S Henry Street, Williamsburg VA
(757) 229-1775 or (877) 565-1775
www.newporthousebb.com

The Moss Guest Cottage

The Moss Guest Cottage in Yorktown has the warmth and charm of a bygone era. Designed as a romantic getaway for couples, this one-bedroom Colonial cottage is furnished with antiques that are both lovely and comfortable. Guests here can enjoy a cup of hot tea in the beautifully manicured garden or a stroll along the Riverwalk. While you are out, be sure to try one of the many fine restaurants along the river or do some shopping in the antique stores and art galleries. The cottage is centrally located with convenient access to historic Williamsburg and Jamestown via the scenic Colonial Parkway. Golf enthusiasts will want to visit some of the finest golf courses that Virginia has to offer. Guests here never tire of beach combing, swimming, biking, fishing and amusement

parks. After a day of sightseeing, you can look forward to returning to your lovely little cottage, fully stocked with amenities for your convenience and enjoy a fine collection of books and movies. All the comforts of home are provided, including linens and towels, a washer and dryer and a well-appointed kitchen. Call and make your reservation for a second honeymoon at the Moss Guest Cottage.

224 Nelson Street, Yorktown VA
(757) 229-5606
www.mossguestcottage.com

Attractions

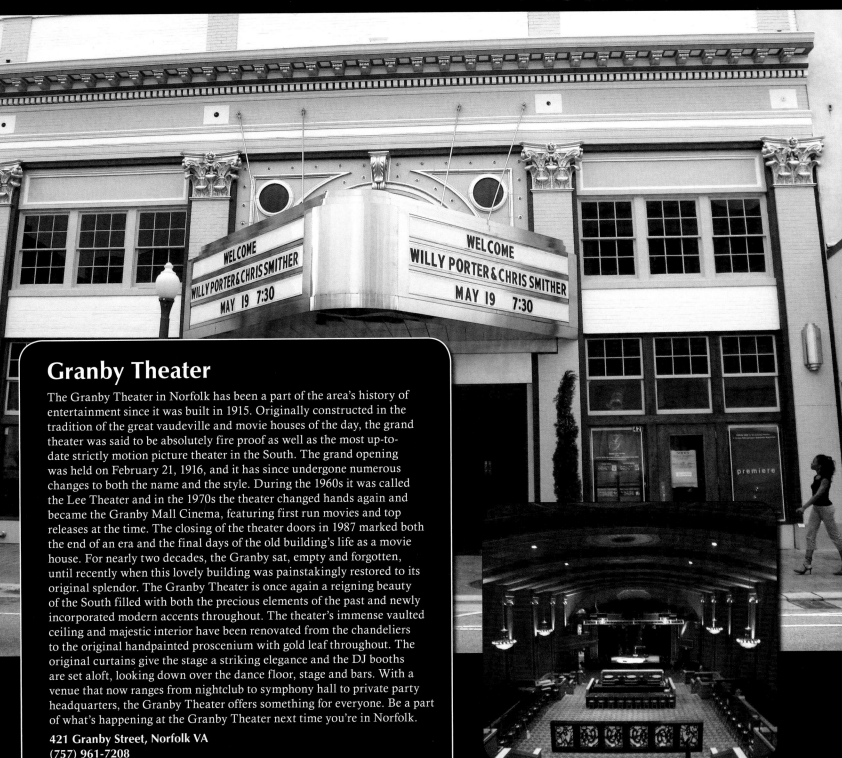

Granby Theater

The Granby Theater in Norfolk has been a part of the area's history of entertainment since it was built in 1915. Originally constructed in the tradition of the great vaudeville and movie houses of the day, the grand theater was said to be absolutely fire proof as well as the most up-to-date strictly motion picture theater in the South. The grand opening was held on February 21, 1916, and it has since undergone numerous changes to both the name and the style. During the 1960s it was called the Lee Theater and in the 1970s the theater changed hands again and became the Granby Mall Cinema, featuring first run movies and top releases at the time. The closing of the theater doors in 1987 marked both the end of an era and the final days of the old building's life as a movie house. For nearly two decades, the Granby sat, empty and forgotten, until recently when this lovely building was painstakingly restored to its original splendor. The Granby Theater is once again a reigning beauty of the South filled with both the precious elements of the past and newly incorporated modern accents throughout. The theater's immense vaulted ceiling and majestic interior have been renovated from the chandeliers to the original handpainted proscenium with gold leaf throughout. The original curtains give the stage a striking elegance and the DJ booths are set aloft, looking down over the dance floor, stage and bars. With a venue that now ranges from nightclub to symphony hall to private party headquarters, the Granby Theater offers something for everyone. Be a part of what's happening at the Granby Theater next time you're in Norfolk.

421 Granby Street, Norfolk VA
(757) 961-7208
www.granbytheater.com

Newport News—Preserving a Dynamic and Diverse Heritage
Discovery Tour

More than 140 years ago, the area around Newport News underwent a mighty transformation as thousands of Civil War soldiers tramped the Great Warwick Road; cannon fire filled the air along with the cries of the wounded and dying. Today, Newport News remembers the people who fought here with the preservation of historic homes, battle sites, fortifications, monuments and artifact collections. A discovery tour of Newport News is an opportunity to immerse yourself in this poignant conflict with visits to such museums as the Virginia War Museum and the Mariner's Museum, which celebrates the 2007 opening of the USS Monitor Center, an exhibition that takes a close look at the battle between the ironclads, the USS Monitor and the CSS Virginia. The Peninsula Campaign Museum resides in the Lee Hall Mansion, because the Confederate Army headquartered here while preparing to challenge the Army of the Potomac's advance on Richmond in 1862. The museum provides an overview of the campaign, from the Battle of the Ironclads to the Battle of Seven Pines. A 70-mile driving tour of the 1862 Peninsula Campaign takes you to dramatic battle sites and fortifications, all easily reached from Newport News. Continue your exploration of Newport News history with visits to Endview Plantation and the Newsome House Museum. Newport News is just minutes from Williamsburg and a short drive to Virginia Beach. The city invites you to take a close-up look at the history that shaped it and rocked the country.

Newport News Visitor Center 13560 Jefferson Avenue, Newport News VA (757) 886-7777 or (888) 493-7386. *www.newport-news.org*

Newport News— Preserving a Dynamic and Diverse Heritage

Lee Hall Mansion

Just three years after Richard D. Lee moved his family into their new home in Newport News, a war came raging in its direction, and the Confederacy came knocking on the door. With its commanding view of the countryside, Lee Hall Mansion served as Major General John Magruder and General Joseph Johnston's headquarters during the 1862 Peninsula Campaign. In preparing for the Union's advance, the Confederate Army rented several buildings on the property, tore down eight miles of Lee's fences and destroyed 85 acres of wheat. Did the Union reach Lee Hall? Find out when you tour the grounds. Lee was an affluent planter whose home is significant not only for its role in the Civil War but for its plantation history and antebellum architecture. The architecture is a marriage of styles, including Italian and Georgian as well as Greek Revival. Due to *Gone with the Wind* and other fictional accounts of the South, Greek Revival is the style typically associated with plantation houses. Lee Hall is the only large antebellum plantation house remaining on the lower Virginia Peninsula. Volunteers lead visitors through seven rooms, which are beautifully decorated in the style of the mid 19th century. Add Lee Hall Mansion to your Newport News discovery tour.

163 Yorktown Road, Newport News VA
(757) 888-3371
www.leehall.org

Newport News—Preserving a Dynamic and Diverse Heritage

The Newsome House Museum

The Newsome House, which became the nation's first black historic site to receive the National Historic Preservation Award, was the home of Joseph Thomas Newsome, whose quick wit and sharp logic served him well throughout his distinguished career as a lawyer. He often opened his elegant Queen Anne home, built in 1899, to community leaders and civil rights activists. Therefore, he would no doubt be delighted that the house continues to be used today as a center for intellectual and artistic activity. The Newsome House honors the legacy of this man, who was one of the first African American attorneys to argue before the Virginia Supreme Court, by engaging the public in an ongoing study and remembrance of African American history and culture. Featured events may include exhibits of contemporary art and tributes to civil rights leaders. In November, the Newsome House holds an annual holiday gift show with fine wares from local craftspeople, followed by a festive open house throughout the month of December. An African American Santa Claus drops by for an event in December known as a Soulful Christmas, which also features a Kwanzaa observance, seasonal music and praise dancers. Celebrate, discover and remember at the Newsome House Museum.

2803 Oak Avenue, Newport News VA
(757) 247-2360
www.newsomehouse.org

Newport News—Preserving a Diverse and Dynamic Heritage
Endview Plantation

If they were to make a movie based on the human drama that has been played out at Endview Plantation, it would definitely be an epic. This T-frame Georgian-style house has stood since 1769, when it was built for William Harwood, whose family provided Warwick County with political leadership for more than 200 years. A militia encampment of 3,000 soldiers drew water from the spring at Endview during the Revolutionary War. The property was used as a training ground in the War of 1812. By the outbreak of the Civil War, Endview had been purchased by William's great-grandson, Dr. Humphrey Harwood Curtis. According to 1860 census records, he owned $8,000 worth of real estate, $21,000 worth of property and 12 slaves. In other words, this young doctor was just the kind of prominent citizen who would help organize a volunteer company, the Warwick Volunteers, of which he was elected captain. Indeed, the Civil War came right to Endview's doorstep when the plantation was used as a hospital by both armies. A tour of Endview provides details concerning its human history plus facts on architecture, and glimpses into the lives of owners and slaves. You may even learn how Endview got its name. To explore a Virginia home with an epic past, visit Endview Plantation.

362 Yorktown Road, Newport News VA
(757) 887-1862 *www.endview.org*

Shirley Plantation

Shirley Plantation gives visitors a rare glimpse of a southern plantation and the historical perspective of the family who has owned and operated it since the early days of British colonization. This privately owned plantation, located on the James River 35 miles west of Williamsburg, is the oldest family owned business in North America. A land grant from the King of England to the Governor of Virginia carved Shirley Plantation out of the Virginia frontier in 1613, just six years after the settlement of Jamestown. By 1638, Edward Hill had started agricultural operations on Shirley soil. Construction on the present mansion began in 1723 when Edward's great-granddaughter Elizabeth married John Carter. Completed in 1738, the mansion is largely in its original state and remains the home of the Carter family. It survived the Indian Uprisings, Bacon's Rebellion, the Revolutionary War, the Civil War and the Great Depression and so remains an architectural treasure. A guided tour of the house reveals a square-rigged flying staircase that rises three stories with no visible means of support as well as original 18th-century carved woodwork, family portraits and furniture. The grounds provide the opportunity to see eight original buildings including four brick structures that form a symmetrical Queen Anne forecourt, the only example of its kind in the country. Immerse yourself in American history at Shirley Plantation.

501 Shirley Plantation Road, Charles City VA
(804) 829-5121 or (800) 232-1613
www.shirleyplantation.com

Photos by Shirley Plantation in Charles City, Virginia

Westover

An outstanding example of 18th century Georgian architecture and one of the most beautiful homes in the United States, William Byrd II built Westover in 1730. Its elegant brickwork, steeply sloping roof and tall paired chimneys are all significant design motifs from that era. Today, Westover is a private residence owned by the Bruce C. Fisher family. Most of the furniture is from the 18th century. There are no pieces remaining from the Byrd family. Two volumes from the once famous library containing over 4,000 volumes, belonging to William Byrd II remain in the house today. Some of the past owners have loved this house so much they never left, such as the ghost of Evelyn Byrd, who has been spotted by different guests on numerous occasions. Located approximately 150 feet from the James River, the house is flanked by tulip poplars over 150 years old. Westover participates in Historic Garden Week in Virginia, one of the few times of the year the house is open to the public. The grounds and outer buildings are open to the public year-round. It is a magnificent place to have a wedding. Several motion pictures and miniseries have been filmed at Westover. Come tour the grounds and enjoy the breathtaking beauty of a house that has been loved for hundreds of years. Westover welcomes groups of 12 or more for house tours by appointment.

7000 Westover Road, Charles City VA
(804) 829-2882
www.jamesriverplantations.com

Historic St. Luke's Church

Historic St. Luke's Church, circa 1632, is the oldest church of English foundation and the oldest surviving Gothic structure in the country. This house of worship welcomed new world colonists who were contemporaries of John Smith, Pocahontas and Chief Powhatan. Revolutionary War soldiers marched across its grounds and Confederate troops camped beneath its great cedars. For nearly four centuries, Historic St. Luke's Church has persevered through war, destruction, misuse and abandonment, witnessing the great events of our nation's history. Originally known as Old Brick Church, Historic St. Luke's Church was one of only five parishes, including Jamestown, where the General Court of the Colony was permitted to convene. The church houses a rare 17th century American altar and minister's chairs, 16th and 17th century Bibles and a 1630 English chamber organ—the only surviving, intact instrument of its kind in the world. Chosen in 2005 as an official restoration project by The Garden Club of Virginia, today the church is used for weddings, baptisms and other special ceremonies, and on the fifth Sunday of the month, and Episcopal service is held. Historic St. Luke's Restoration, Inc. is a non-profit foundation that relies upon the generous support of others to maintain this extraordinary building for future generations to enjoy. It is a Registered National Historic Landmark and a Virginia Historic Landmark. Visit today and learn more about this inspiring site. The church is open for tours every day except Monday.

14477 Benn's Church Boulevard, Smithfield VA
(757) 357-3367
www.historicstlukes.org

Photos: Keith Lanpher

Chippokes Plantation State Park
Chippokes Farm & Forestry Museum

The graceful acreage of Chippokes Plantation State Park has been continually cultivated since 1619 when Captain William Powell received a grant for the land. Directly across the James River from Jamestown and about five miles from the Jamestown/Scotland Wharf ferry, the plantation and bordering creek are named after an Indian chief who befriended early settlers. Today, visitors can stroll through the grounds and along two miles of riverfront, tour the Jones-Stewart Mansion with its Victorian antiques and formal gardens and visit the Farm & Forestry Museum and a sawmill exhibit. A campground with water and electric hookups and bathhouses with hot showers and a laundry facility are open from March through November. An Olympic-size swimming pool is a favorite destination during the summer months. In the historic area, refurbished historic tenant farm houses are available as rental cottages year-round. Complete with kitchens and baths, the cottages are fully furnished, heated and air conditioned. The plantation, donated to the Commonwealth of Virginia in 1969 by Evelyn Stewart in memory of her husband Victor, remains a working farm with grazing cows, hay fields and crops, including corn, peanuts, wheat, soybeans and cotton. The mansion was built in 1854 by Albert Carroll Jones, the first owner to live on the plantation. Jones produced and shipped peach and apple brandy and cider. According to local legend, the mansion survived the Civil War because Jones sold his brandies to both armies. The Museum interprets life in rural Virginia through a collection of farm and forestry equipment, tools and hardwares from the 17th to the early 20th century. You can visit the Chippokes Plantation State Park grounds year-round and take in the mansion and the museum from April to October.

695 Chippokes Park Road, Surry VA
(757) 294-3625 or (800) 933-PARK (7275)
www.dcr.virginia.gov/parks/chippoke.htm

Photos by Carlton S. Abbott

Wessex Hundred

This 300-acre historic property is home to The Williamsburg Winery, the Gabriel Archer Tavern, and Wedmore Place, a Country Hotel. Gabriel Archer, a leader of the first successful Virginia expedition in 1607, proposed this James River site for the initial settlement, but was overruled by Captain John Smith, who placed the settlement at the more easily defended Jamestown site two miles upstream. Archer's proposed settlement site, a 500-acre neck of land marked off by creeks and ravines, became known as Archer's Hope. For two centuries the farm was a grain and cattle operation. In 1983, the Duffeler family purchased the farm and renamed it Wessex Hundred, following the tradition of early settlers in naming a farm that could provide living space and food for one hundred persons. In 1985, they planted the first vines. Today, most of the farm is a forested wildlife and nature preserve. The winery, restaurant and hotel complex is situated in the middle of the farm, and offers venues for visitors, wine enthusiasts, receptions, private dinners, executive meetings and cultural events.

5800 Wessex Hundred, Williamsburg VA
(757) 258-0899

Wedmore Place, A Country Hotel at the Williamsburg Winery

Near the restored Colonial capital at Williamsburg, Wedmore Place can be found surrounded by acres of woods, pasture and vineyards. The hotel is an environmentally oriented project, as evidenced by the careful selection of its site. The entrance is nestled among tall trees, and the hotel encases an interior cobblestone courtyard. Accommodations include three suites as well as 25 guest rooms decorated in the style of European provinces or cities for which they are named. Each is enhanced by the wood-burning fireplace and imported antique furniture. Murals, paintings and tapestries abound. The elegant library invites study and reflection. The pool, spa and exercise room, and nearby walking trail contribute to a healthy lifestyle. Conceptualized for the discerning traveler and executive groups, there are meeting rooms with state-of-the-art technology available. The hallmark of Wedmore Place is its commitment to providing guests with impeccable customer service in an elegant, healthy and enjoyable environment.

5810 Wessex Hundred, Williamsburg VA
(866) WEDMORE (933-6673)
info@wedmoreplace.com
www.wedmoreplace.com

Williamsburg Winery, Ltd.

Founded in 1985 by the Duffeler family, the Williamsburg Winery is the largest in the state, producing more than 60,000 cases annually. Situated on a 300-acre farm located between historic Jamestown and the restored Colonial capital of Williamsburg, the vineyards occupy a unique spot at the birthplace of our nation. When you open the doors of the Williamsburg Winery, you enter a world where time-honored methods and the best practices of modern viticulture have combined to create an exciting new Virginia wine tradition. Besides a visit to the production area and a stroll through the barrel cellars, the guided tour of the facilities includes a video presentation on winegrowing and winemaking, a sample tasting of selected releases, and an etched wine glass as a keepsake of your visit. The Winery cellars offer a comprehensive group of wines that exhibit the individuality and elegance expressed in the fine handcrafted wines of Europe, from the flagship Gabriel Archer Reserve, to the most popular white wine produced in Virginia, the Governor's White. The Winery is open daily for tours and tastings. Reserve wine tastings are available only by appointment in the Private Wine Cellar. You can take a virtual tour of the Winery at their website, browse the on-line wine shop, and enjoy, even at a distance, the Virginia tradition and quality of life.

5800 Wessex Hundred, Williamsburg VA
(757) 229-0999
info@williamsburgwinery.com
www.williamsburgwinery.com

Gabriel Archer Tavern

Nestled amongst the vineyards of the Williamsburg Winery, the Gabriel Archer Tavern offers casual dining in a comfortable setting. Seating is available, weather permitting, on the outside terrace under a canopy of wisteria, in the Tavern itself, or in the enclosed Vineyard Room overlooking the oldest vineyard at the Winery. Lunch is served daily from 11:00 to 4:00 and dinner is offered on Thursday, Friday and Saturday evenings from 5:30 to 9:00, April through October. Menu items include a French Country Platter with paté, cheese and sausage, or smoked duck on a spring salad, both recommended by *The New York Times*, as well as a variety of freshly prepared sandwiches served with baby green salad that is topped with dried cherries, sugared pecans and Raspberry Merlot vinaigrette. Located just minutes from the restored area of Colonial Williamsburg and historic Jamestown, the Gabriel Archer Tavern has become a favorite of both local residents and visitors to the Williamsburg Winery.

5800 Wessex Hundred, Williamsburg VA
(757) 229-0999 ext. 117
info@williamsburgwinery.com
www.williamsburgwinery.com

Virginia War Museum

Some wars have been viewed as necessary evils; others, as heroic fights for freedom. The Virginia War Museum studies and explores the full range of American military conflict in its outstanding collection of uniforms, weapons and memorabilia. Founded just after World War I to help people understand the impact of that war on the world, the museum has continued to expand, so visitors now encounter nine galleries in all. Your tour of the exhibits begins at the America and War gallery, which provides an overview of United States military history from 1775 to the present. Other galleries tell the story of prisoners of war, interpret the role of women in the military and chronicle the military importance of the area's own Hampton Roads region. A highlight of the Fowler Gallery of Arms is a small group of Civil War presentation swords. Among the weapons on display in the Evolution of Weaponry gallery are an 1883 Gatling gun, an American light tank from World War II and a German howitzer from World War I. The Visions of War gallery shows how posters and other artwork attempted to persuade and solidify public opinion regarding war. Overall, the museum's artifacts comprise one of the most comprehensive collections of items relating to American military history in the world. Visit the Virginia War Museum today.

9285 Warwick Boulevard, Newport News VA
(757) 247-8523
www.warmuseum.org

Dominion's Nuclear Information Centers

Whether you are a curious youth wanting to know what energy is and how it works or an educated adult with questions about safety, security or environmental issues surrounding your community's nuclear energy production and use, a visit to one of Dominion's Nuclear Information Centers will satisfy every question you have. Virginia boasts educational centers at the Surry power station in Surry County and the North Anna power station in Louisa County. These centers reach more than 10,000 people a year through their programs. Whether through a scheduled educational tour or an individual visit, Dominion's Nuclear Information Centers demystify nuclear energy by exploring misconceptions and truths about nuclear power and its alternatives. The centers' educational materials and knowledgeable staff provide detailed information about local nuclear power stations. Although tours of Surry and North Anna Power Stations are not allowed for security reasons, you'll feel like you know them inside and out once you've explored the educational resources available at Dominion's Nuclear Information Centers. Programs here cater to school groups of all ages and programs match learning standards required by the state of Virginia. Students participating in educational tours here score an average of ten points higher on their SOL tests. Each center caters to the needs of your group, and guided presentations are free to school, youth and community organizations. Contact a Dominion's Nuclear Information Center before visiting to learn what information and presentations may be available to you.

5570 Hog Island Road, Surry VA
(757) 357-5410
1022 Haley Drive, Mineral VA
(540) 894-2029
www.dom.com

Honey Bee Golf Club

Honey Bee Golf Club was designed by world-renowned architect Rees Jones. This beautiful championship course lays claim to being one of the premiere courses in the Virginia Beach area. The course plays 6,075 yards and is a par 70. There's water on 10 holes and expansive bunkers and elevated tees that make it a vigorous challenge for experienced golfers while still not overwhelming novice players. There's a great practice facility available, complete with separate putting and chipping greens, a grass driving range and a practice bunker. In addition to the excellent course conditions, you'll always find the staff to be friendly and helpful. There's an impressive clubhouse that has a grill and a dining area with a variety of menu items. You'll also find two hard surface tennis courts and an Olympic-sized swimming pool and patio that are perfect for a casual get together or private party. The area's year round mild temperatures and plentiful sunshine make for ideal golfing conditions most of the year. Be sure to stop in and play a relaxing round of golf at the Honey Bee Golf Club while you're in Virginia Beach.

2500 South Independence Boulevard, Virginia Beach, VA
(757) 471-2768 or (877) 563-7888

Heron Ridge Golf Club

You're in for a spectacular round of golf when you play at Heron Ridge Golf Club. Designed by renowned golf course architect Gene Bates and P.G.A. Tour Star Fred Couples, it was the first new public golf course in Virginia Beach in more than 10 years when it opened in the spring of 1999. This outstandingly designed course features 13 of its 18 holes with water hazards, rolling hills and wetlands. The front nine winds links-style through rolling hills with bunkers and water hazards that are strategically placed. When you make the turn to the back nine the topography changes to a setting with mature stands of oaks, elms, beeches and yet more water. The course measures 7,010 yards from the "Boom-Boom" (Fred Couples' nickname) tees. Not to worry if you play a shorter game, because there are four other sets of tees to play from on every hole. This ensures that golfers at any skill level will be put to the test. Heron Ridge's open to the wind links-style quality, unique topography, elevation changes and meandering streams all combine to give course players a great round of golf in a matchless beach course setting. Be sure to stop in and play a challenging round at Heron Ridge Golf Club.

2973 Heron Ridge Drive, Virginia Beach VA
(757) 426-3800
www.heronridge.com

Signature at West Neck

The Signature at West Neck, a masterful Arnold Palmer-designed golf course is destined to become a timeless classic. "Equal parts beauty and challenge, The Signature features 13 lakes and several picturesque natural wetlands. It's all accented by wooded and dramatically landscaped terrain and highlighted by yawing bunkers," is how Virginia Golf Guide described the course in 2002. It's a beautiful and challenging par 72, 7,010 yard championship course with meticulously maintained Tifsport Bermuda tees and fairways. The greens are smooth A-4 bent grass. There are 13 lakes, several picturesque wetlands and dramatically landscaped terrain lending their beauty to the course as well. Jim Ducibella of The Virginian-Pilot said in June 2002, "All the flowers are incredible. They should change the name to 'The Signature Botanical Gardens.' " The granite-wall bulkheads fronting the 11th and 18th greens are spectacular and beach bunkers on many holes offer a unique golfing challenge and visual appeal. There are five sets of tees on each hole so that no matter your skill level you're sure to have fun. "The Arnold Palmer designed golf course is excellent, the service first-rate, the amenities exceed your expectations and the location's very convenient to locals and vacationers," said Jeffrey A. Rendall from TravelGolf.com in July 2002. Be sure to play on this outstanding and beautiful golf masterpiece while in the Tidewater area.

3100 Arnold Palmer Drive, Virginia Beach VA
(757) 721-2900 or (877) 348-6810
www.signatureatwestneck.com

Red Wing Lake Golf Course

A facelift is coming to an old friend: the classic Red Wing Golf Course that once hosted the Virginia PGA Open in 1974 is undergoing major renovations. The course was originally designed by George W. Cobb and now the Kevin Tucker Design Group has assembled a renovation plan that will provide a great golfing experience in a beautifully new environment while at the same time providing up to date amenities. New wetland areas and lakes will not only add beauty to the course, but they'll add additional challenges as well. All the greens will be rebuilt, shaped and seeded with Bent grass. Each fairway is being reworked to improve drainage and enhance character while still remaining within corridors of mature loblolly pines. Multiple tees will give golfers of all abilities maximum opportunity to take advantage of the course. The course is a par 72 and measures 7,187 yards from its championship tees. Scheduled to open in summer of 2006, make sure to put Red Wing Lake Golf Course on your list of places to play while in the Virginia Beach area.

1144 Prosperity Road, Virginia Beach VA
(866) 482-4653
www.virginiagolf.com/redwing.html

Bay Creek Resort

Bay Creek Resort and Golf Club features two 18-hole courses that have stunning views and take advantage of the area's natural terrain. The courses were designed by Arnold Palmer and Jack Nicholas, both extraordinary golfing legends. The Arnold Palmer Signature Golf Course at Bay Creek intermingles a modern state-of-the-art golfing facility with historical landmarks from the Cape Charles' 19th and 20th century railroad era. It features four outstanding holes on the shores of the Chesapeake Bay and several holes are framed by sand dunes and giant beach bunkers. There's an abundance of native hardwoods, loblolly pines and dogwoods that make Bay Creek a nature lover's delight. Its golf cars feature a GPS system that displays a detailed graphic of each hole as well as distance to the pin. The 7,204 yard par 72 course offers smooth A-4 greens and perfectly manicured Tifsport Bermuda fairways. There are five sets of tees on each hole to ensure the course is fun and challenging for players of all skill levels. The Jack Nicklaus course also has tremendous views of the bay and Old Plantation Creek. There are acres of dunes and more than 100 bunkers. This course measures 7,417 yards, has Tifsport Bermuda fairways, smooth A-4 greens and five sets of tees as well. Both courses share a world class practice range with eight bunkered target greens, a short range practice area and large chipping and putting greens. Come play on these outstandingly beautiful courses and experience golfing at its finest!

1 Club House Way, Cape Charles VA
(757) 331-9000
www.baycreekgolfclub.com

Hell's Point Golf Club

Hell's Point Golf Club is a great place to go if you're ready to heat up your game. Rees Jones, the renowned golf course architect, had a devilish inspiration when he designed this course. The 18-hole par 72 course plays to 6,776 yards, has 61 sculptured sand traps, challenging greens and interesting fairway angles. It's nestled between tall Virginia Pines, has narrow fairways and several lakes. The course has won many awards including Golf Digest's One of the Best New Courses rating when it first opened in 1982 and their prestigious One Hundred Best Courses in the USA award. In addition, it was voted Best of the Beach for 13 years running by the Virginian Pilot Readers Poll. The entire staff is dedicated to creating a legendary experience for its golfers, both on and off the course. They can assist you with all your golfing needs from PGA instruction to arranging your next golf outing. Hell's Point lures you in to the first tee with the promise of adventure and holds you through to the last hole with its many masterful challenges and beautiful surroundings. Stop in and play this wonderful course and discover for yourself why many golfers visit, but few want to leave.

2700 Atwoodtown Road, Virginia Beach VA
(757) 721-3400
www.hellspoint.com

Isle of Wight County Museum

At Main and Church Streets in Smithfield is a prominent stone dwelling built in 1913 to house the Bank of Smithfield in the Isle of Wight County. This beautiful historic edifice began serving a new purpose in 1978, when it became home for the area's historic treasures and was dubbed the Isle of Wight County Museum. The museum was officially created in 1976, though housed elsewhere, and is dedicated to all aspects of local history. The museum places emphasis on the daily life of the county's residents with collections that utilize both ancient and modern materials concerning the county's broad history. Look for a reproduction of an old-fashioned general store, and exhibit on early boat building and Civil War artifacts. The museum pays special attention to the area's agricultural industries during the 17th, 18th and 19th centuries and includes exhibits dedicated to water usage and, of course, the county's famous hams. Isle of Wight County Museum further broadens community awareness with off-site exhibits and archaeological investigations, as well as educational programs, local history publications and other special and historically minded activities. Museum administrator Joann Hall, along with curator Dinah Everett and their staff of terrific volunteers and weekend docents are always on hand to share additional information and answer any questions about the exhibits, including the world's oldest Smithfield Ham, which was cured in 1902. A gift shop offers antique reproductions, jewelry, books and collectibles. Immerse yourself in living history with a visit to Isle of Wight County Museum.

103 Main Street, Smithfield VA
(757) 357-7459 *www.co.isle-of-wight.va.us/park_rec/museum.html*

Westover Parish Church

A harmonious echo of a thousand voices whispers through time to lend its song to those who gather in worship at Westover Parish Church, where history and a deep, abiding love of God merge into a joyful and inspiring crescendo. Westover Church, now called Westover Episcopal Church, was originally established near the Jamestown settlement in 1613 and, throughout history, has been a place of worship for presidents, slaves, plantation owners and country farmers. Sadly, the history of Westover Episcopal Church has not always been a happy one. The Civil War brought great battles to the parish, and by the end, not a door, window or floor was left, according to the vestry book, which was miraculously saved along with the Communion silver and bibles by an unknown benefactor. By September 15, 1867 Westover Episcopal Church was once again ready to receive parishioners and remains today a place where anyone, regardless of race, can come to worship. To date the parish church has around 160 active communicants, many of whom are fifth, sixth and seventh generation parishioners. Westover Episcopal Church offers services each Sunday at 8:30

a.m., with additional summer services at 10:00 a.m., presided over by the rector, Reverend Virginia Heistand Jones. For the congregation's youth the church provides a nursery, playground and short sermons, as well as Sunday school classes and an active and joyful youth group. Lend your voice and prayers to the historic Westover Episcopal Church.

6401 John Tyler Memorial
Highway, Charles City VA
(804) 829-2488

Brandon Plantation

Robert W. Daniel, Jr. and his wife understand the historic significance of their home at Brandon Plantation and open it for many public tours and special events. The historic Virginia plantation, founded in 1616, first belonged to John Martin, one of the last survivors of Jamestown. The property changed ownership several times, all the while functioning as a non-resident-owned plantation that produced tobacco for the English market. Over time and by the hands of different owners, the Brandon Plantation residence changed its style. It is possible that Thomas Jefferson, an admirer of the Georgian style, contributed to Georgian elements in the home's design. During the Civil War, Brandon bore the brunt of Union occupation. Several buildings and their contents were destroyed. Afterwards, the plantation fell into ruin, as did many others. Eventually, Brandon Plantation was restored and became a National Historic Landmark. Its gardens abound with roses, yellow jasmine and old growth cedar, making Brandon Plantation one of the most magnificent estates in the area. It's also a working farm, growing corn, wheat and soy beans. Cattle graze the pastures. Large herds of Virginia deer find shelter in the property's woods and marshes. Daniel, a former congressman who served in the US House of Representatives, appreciates the history and legacy of Brandon Plantation and opens the home to tours by appointment. Experience our nation's beginnings at Brandon Plantation.

23500 Brandon Road, Spring Grove VA
(757) 866-8486

North Bend Plantation

The North Bend Plantation, circa 1801, is owned by Ridgely and George Copland. Incredibly, George is a descendent of the original owners of the house. The 850-acre plantation grows a strict rotation of corn, wheat and soybeans, attracting all manner of wildlife. An on-site pond draws ducks and nature trails lure visitors to explore the beautiful grounds punctuated by historic landmarks such as civil war trenches. North Bend Plantation is a National Registry property built for the sister of the ninth president of the United States and still contains antiques original to the house and family. Guests can also enjoy the swimming pool on the grounds and the house itself is truly outstanding with its elegant decor and comfort. Ridgely and George exude gracious southern hospitality while they freely share information about the history of the plantation and the family tree. Staying at North Bend Plantation is similar to staying with close friends or family, complete with a billiards table, fascinating books and heirlooms that are used too often to gather dust. Every morning, guests at the plantation are treated to a full country breakfast. North Bend Plantation provides a picturesque backdrop for weddings and special events. The Coplands extend their invitation for you to come and acquaint yourself with the rich history of North Bend Plantation, reserve a room and immerse yourself even more in the wonders of this historical home.

12200 Weyanoke Road, Charles City VA
(804) 829-5176
www.northbendplantation.com

Pork, Peanut and Pine Festival

The Surry County Bicentennial Committee keeps things lively for local families and visitors to this agricultural area with a sensational mid-July festival, held annually since 1976. The Pork, Peanut and Pine Festival, held in historic Chippokes Plantation State Park, pays tribute to three important crops with fun, non-alcoholic family entertainment and activities. Chippokes' Antebellum mansion and the park's many blooming crepe myrtle trees are at the center of festivities. Over 225 artisans display everything from needlework and paintings to garden art and furniture. Activities include working demonstrations and exhibits on pork, peanut and pine products. The sawmill display and chainsaw carving exhibits appeal to everyone, while children are fond of the mule rides. Two stages treat audiences to bluegrass, country and gospel music. You and 20,000 fellow visitors can pay your respects to pork with food choices like char-grilled pork chops and cracklings, chitterlings and pork rinds or ham biscuits. Peanut brittle and peanut pie are festival favorites. You'll also find usual fair food, like funnel cakes and cotton candy or hot dogs and lemonade. It takes hundreds of volunteers each year to make the festival a roaring success. The County of Surry and the festival committee invite you to celebrate Surry County's agricultural heritage at the Pork, Peanut and Pine Festival.

695 Chippokes Park Road, Surry VA
(757) 294-3625
www.toursurryva.com/pppfestival.html

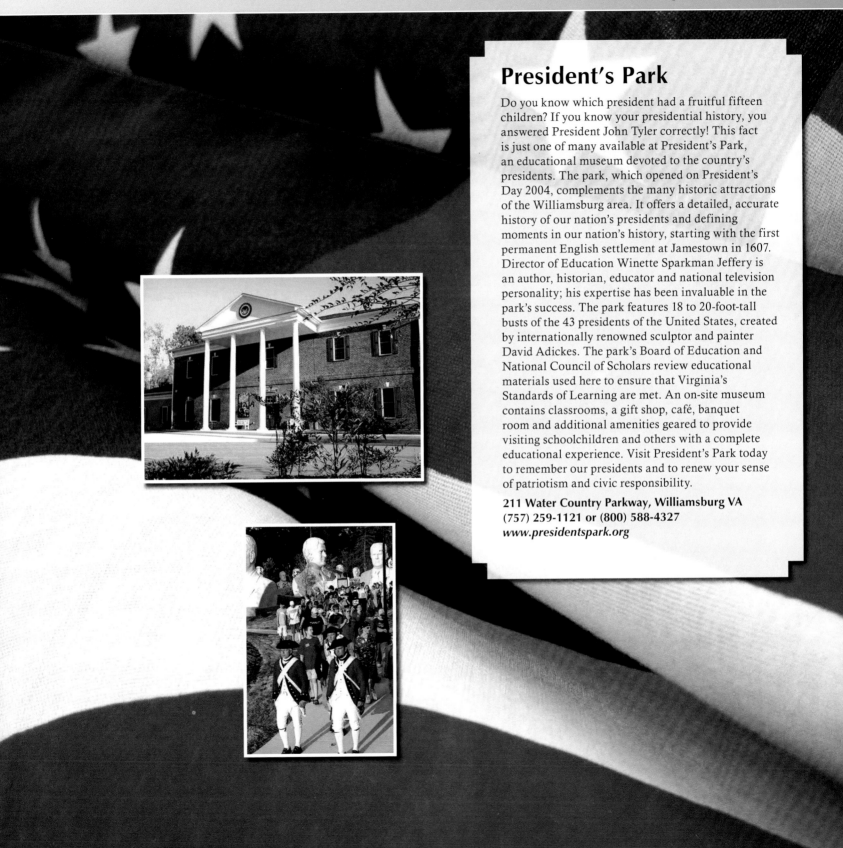

President's Park

Do you know which president had a fruitful fifteen children? If you know your presidential history, you answered President John Tyler correctly! This fact is just one of many available at President's Park, an educational museum devoted to the country's presidents. The park, which opened on President's Day 2004, complements the many historic attractions of the Williamsburg area. It offers a detailed, accurate history of our nation's presidents and defining moments in our nation's history, starting with the first permanent English settlement at Jamestown in 1607. Director of Education Winette Sparkman Jeffery is an author, historian, educator and national television personality; his expertise has been invaluable in the park's success. The park features 18 to 20-foot-tall busts of the 43 presidents of the United States, created by internationally renowned sculptor and painter David Adickes. The park's Board of Education and National Council of Scholars review educational materials used here to ensure that Virginia's Standards of Learning are met. An on-site museum contains classrooms, a gift shop, café, banquet room and additional amenities geared to provide visiting schoolchildren and others with a complete educational experience. Visit President's Park today to remember our presidents and to renew your sense of patriotism and civic responsibility.

211 Water Country Parkway, Williamsburg VA
(757) 259-1121 or (800) 588-4327
www.presidentspark.org

Taste - Tea, Salon & Gifts

Nestled in the Village Shops at Kingsmill, in Williamsburg, lies a charming haven called Taste. Here, the tea and its accompaniments receive the greatest attention to detail. Diana Dean, Cherri Fiorenza and their mother Lillian Croft pooled their talents to create the shop. They love talking with their guests and sharing their knowledge about tea blends and the health advantage of certain teas. Diana's passion is exceptional food and its presentation. You will find herbs and flowers garnishing the four courses of the afternoon tea. Each table is set with a separate china pattern and fresh flowers. The selection of teas offered includes black, green, white and herbals. Lillian is known for her scrumptious lemon pound cake and Cherri for her cheesecake. These are just two of many delectable sweets. While guests can rely on excellent signature dishes, most days bring a surprising addition of a variation on a popular menu item. While the owners are very serious about tea, their tea room is far from stuffy. The bright and airy salon with its colorful French linens and white overlays are accented by soft blue walls. A wrought iron trellis, palms and a rain shower fountain add to the ambiance. The gift shop offers a unique selection of teas, teaware, French linens, baby items, bath and body lines and many other fine gifts. There is also a selection of culinary foods, including fine chocolates. Diana, Cherri and Lillian extend a warm invitation to visit Taste, where tea and its accompaniments are a way of life.

1915 Pocahontas Trail, Williamsburg VA
(757) 221-9550

Aromas Specialty Coffees and Gourmet Bakery

Expect to be delightfully surprised by the atmosphere as well as the coffee, tea and food preparation at Aromas in Williamsburg's Merchants Square. Full breakfasts, lunches and dinners offer much more extensive choice than usually found at a coffeehouse. The live entertainment and a mixed clientele contribute to the fun. Aromas is just enough off the beaten tourist path to retain a personal, hometown appeal, encouraged by the efficient baristas, Executive Chef Jeffrey Kinney and General Manager Dave Burchett, a graduate of the Culinary Institute of America. You might find two gray-haired local women discussing their grandchildren, visitors from abroad discussing Colonial Williamsburg and college students and staff visiting, catching up on their reading or enjoying a local band. Among the sweet specialties of the house are Caramel Aromaccino and chocolate fondue. Aromas also provides marshmallows, graham crackers, chocolate and flame for building America's favorite campfire treat, s'mores. Beyond the bakery's gourmet fare, delicious soups, salads, sandwiches and a full breakfast and dinner menu are available. Beer, wine and spiked smoothies, like Irish cream and coffee, add to the versatility at this hip establishment. Since opening in 2000, Aromas has been making a name for itself among divergent Williamsburg populations. The Flat Hat voted it the best coffee shop in Williamsburg for three years in a row, noting its welcoming atmosphere, food, drink and music. Come alone or with the family, in sweats after jogging or dressed for a show, but by all means come to Aromas.

431 Prince George Street, Merchants Square, Williamsburg VA
(757) 221-6676
www.aromasworld.com

Miss Bessie's Best Cookies & Candies

The quaint and charming town of Smithfield is the embodiment of a Norman Rockwell painting come to life and such a town would not be complete without its own candy store. Miss Bessie's Best Cookies & Candies fits the bill nicely and is the only shop of its kind for miles around. Owner Trey Gwaltney opened this delightful shop in 2005 and offers an astounding array of both contemporary and vintage candies. Miss Bessie's creates many of its confections on-site and customers can view the process through the glass window overlooking the kitchens and then ask Granny Franny, the kindly woman at the front counter, for a sample. Miss Bessie's Best Cookies & Candies carries all of your favorites including homemade lemon cookies and other tasty concoctions alongside old-fashioned treats such as Swedish redfish and horehound drops. They also carry a wide variety of contemporary treats for the younger generation like gummies, lollypops and candy goo. Indulge your sweet tooth with the delicious and decadent selections awaiting you at Miss Bessie's Best Cookies & Candies on historic Main Street.

207-A Main Street, Smithfield VA
(757) 357-0220
www.missbessie.com

Fashion

Keller Fine Jewelers

A status symbol to some people, jewelry has always been a matter of art and beauty for the Keller family. The two rock hounds who started Keller Fine Jewelers, Mary and William Keller, have since passed the business to their son, John. However, their ideal still persists, namely that no one should buy a piece of jewelry based solely on its price, but only if it strikes a deep chord within the beholder. John says that his selection of loose diamonds and natural fine gems, such as rubies, sapphires and topaz, is the largest in Virginia. He and his staff at Keller Fine Jewelers are eager to help each customer find the piece that speaks directly to him or her. They will take the time to explain how color, clarity, carat and cut interact to define a total piece of fine jewelry. Working closely with customers is especially important when choosing a diamond. "It's not enough to have a cursory grading on paper," says John. "One must see aesthetically a diamond's quality in detail to determine a true impression of value." Keller Fine Jewelers began as a hobby that provided personal enrichment for Mary and William. Back in the 1960s, the pair scoured quarries in the Western states, collecting rough stones that they would later polish to reveal their beauty. Find jewelry that stirs your own sense of beauty at Keller Fine Jewelers.

3930D E Princess Anne Road, Norfolk VA
(757) 857-0234 or (800) 255-1144
www.kellerfinejewelers.com

The Precious Gem

When enthusiastic clients think about the Precious Gem in Williamsburg, their thoughts turn to Reggie Akdogan. Reggie is a master goldsmith, designer and seasoned bench jeweler. He's also a true artist, whose pieces celebrate the beauty of fine precious metals and stones. He learned his craft from his uncle in Istanbul and ran a stall in the famous Grand Bazaar. His hard work and natural gift for design have earned him many awards in jewelry design competitions. Reggie travels all over the world in search of the finest materials to use in designing his jewelry. Collectible stones for his pieces come from such exotic locales as Sri Lanka, Thailand, Burma and Madagascar. You can purchase an individual precious gem from the shop or have the stone of your choice incorporated into a custom jewelry creation. Many museum quality stones are on display and available for purchase at the Precious Gem. Reggie loves sharing stories of the history of the stones, their mining and how he went about acquiring them. He understands that the holistic and spiritual aspects of gemstones are part of their intrinsic value and has an infectious passion that helps his customers develop an emotional attachment to their gems and jewelry pieces. Reggie's employees share his enthusiasm and add to the pleasures of shopping here. For fine jewelry and precious stones worthy of fine settings, visit the Precious Gem.

423 W Duke of Gloucester Street, Williamsburg VA
(800) 644-8077
www.thepreciousgems.com

Pink Cabana

The Pink Cabana brings the famous pink and green clothing of the Lilly Pulitzer line to Williamsburg. These stylish essentials can take you from a day of touring the town to an afternoon on the beach or a party with accessories to match. The vibrant prints and classic styling of the Lilly Pulitzer line started in the 1950s, when Lilly was squeezing citrus fruit at her juice stand in Palm Beach. Lilly asked her dressmaker to create a dress that would be comfortable enough to work in and bright enough to cover the stains from the fruit juice. The result was a sleeveless shift that quickly gained the attention of Lilly's customers. Soon, Lilly shifted her focus to the designing and marketing of her dresses, known as Lillys. Jackie Kennedy, a beacon of style, appeared in *Life* magazine wearing a Lilly, which boosted Lilly's fame. Lilly's clothing line expanded, and stores carrying her pink and green preppy creations appeared in resort towns up and down the East Coast, until Lilly's retirement in the mid 1980s. In the early 1990s, Lilly allowed her clothing line to be revived, and in 2005, Pink Cabana, under the ownership of Thea and Derek Robertson, became one of 70 signature stores featuring the Lilly Pulitzer label. Find out what all the pink and green fuss is about with a visit to Pink Cabana, where Thea and her staff will introduce you to simple but oh so intriguing clothing that could turn you into a Lilly Lover.

411 W Duke of Gloucester Street, Williamsburg VA
(757) 229-3961
www.pinkcabanashop.com

Pizazz Jewelry

Costume jewelry is what Jody Greason has been specializing in for the last 20 years at Pizazz Jewelry. Stop by her shop and you are guaranteed to have a sensational time just trying things on whether or not you buy anything. Sparkles and lots of them is the philosophy behind Pizazz Jewelry. Pizazz's raison d'être is definitely its stylish selection of costume jewelry with pieces for casual day or eveningwear and special occasions. Jody and her fabulous staff can guide you through the huge selection of bangles, brooches, charms, cameos, chokers and coronets. The collection of stunning rings and earrings is too overwhelming to list. Pizazz also features evening bags, handbags and belts to complete any accessory ensemble. Jody is particularly adept with suggestions for bewildered mothers looking for trendy accessories for a daughter's first formal. One grateful mother was so successful with the bracelet and earrings she found for her daughter's sophomore prom that she came back and bought the jewelry for her daughter's senior prom as well! Pizazz Jewelry definitely does more than one thing exceptionally well. A visit to Pizazz Jewelry will have you accessorized for any event.

738 Hilltop North Shopping Center, Virginia Beach, VA
(757) 422-1201
4000 Virginia Beach Boulevard, Virginia Beach VA
(757) 431-0700

Galleries & Fine Art

Shirley Pewter Shop Inc

A classic American craft is alive and well in contemporary Williamsburg. For over 50 years, Shirley Pewter Shop has been creating cherished masterpieces with time-honored methods of pewter craft passed down through the generations. In 1953, Shirley Robertson opened his craft shop in his garage and began creating original designs as well as reproduction pieces, such as the ever-popular Jefferson Cup, a Thomas Jefferson design. By 1955, he moved his workshop to the current building on Jamestown Road. American colonists refined pewter quality with a stronger, safer and more brilliant metal combination known as Britannia pewter, an alloy consisting of tin, copper and antimony. American Pewter is a lead-free product. The popularity of pewter continues today, thanks to its beauty, ease of care and limitless design possibilities. It fits into many homes and features three basic finishes—polished, satin and a distressed antique look. Shirley and his wife, Doris, pursued excellence in all of their designs. Today, their son Bruce and his family continue the tradition with store locations in Merchants Square adjacent to Colonial Williamsburg and on Jamestown Road, just south of Route 199. The workshop on Jamestown Road offers visitors the opportunity to watch masterpieces being created. Explore the informative website and then view fine pewterware at Shirley Pewter Shop.

417 Duke of Gloucester Street, Williamsburg VA
(757) 229-5356
1205 Jamestown Road, Williamsburg VA
(757) 229-1378 or (800) 550-5356
www.shirleypewter.com

Lazare Gallery - Representing the Best of Moscow's School of Russian Realism

In historic Charles City County, on the banks of the James River, art dealers John and Kathy Wurdeman have spent years assembling a collection of works of enduring relevance by the greatest Soviet Era and Russian Era master artists. Advocates of tradition and academic training and affiliated with the Moscow School of Russian Realism, these master artists collectively have more than 1,000 paintings in major museums worldwide. The style of painting represented by the Moscow School of Russian Realism was strongly influenced by the philosophy of the late 19th century French Academy of Art, along with the exploration of color pursued in the Russian Impressionist Academic painting. First-time visitors are pleasantly startled by the uniqueness of Lazare Gallery. Located in a forested, waterfront setting between Richmond and Williamsburg, Virginia, the 8,200-square-foot gallery welcomes art collectors and connoisseurs from all over the USA. For collectors, multiple guest rooms are available on the property to allow for overnight stays. Instead of representing paintings of secondary importance by great artists, Lazare Gallery's emphasis has been to seek out the very best Russian Realism and Impressionism from the Soviet Era to present. With an inventory of more than 1,300 fine Russian paintings, Lazare Gallery invites dealers, collectors, and lovers of fine art to view and select treasures from this outstanding collection. Open by appointment only.

4641 Kimages Wharf Road, Charles City VA
(804) 829-5001
www.lazaregallery.com

Health & Beauty

Gary Allen Hair and Skin Care Centre

When it's time to leave the day's stresses behind, head for Gary Allen Hair and Skin Care Centre. Here, you'll enter a world filled with elegant décor, soothing music and a staff waiting to pamper and style you from head to toe. Services at Gary Allen include hairstyling, cuts and color, manicures, pedicures, facials and massages. Gary Allen Riffe, the spa's namesake and owner, takes pride in the center by offering first-rate professionalism, cleanliness and efficiency. Gary Allen constantly looks toward the future, staying up to date with the ever-evolving needs of his clients as well as with the newest treatments and products that are available. Gary Allen's team resembles the harmony and grace found in a well-practiced ballet company. It is because of this synchronicity and competence that clients are never kept waiting and always receive gracious, personalized and expert attention. Plus, the staff regularly attends classes to build new skills and stay abreast of the latest styles and products. Treat yourself to the very best by making an appointment today at Gary Allen Hair and Skin Care Centre in the Marketplace at Hilltop.

741 First Colonial Road, Suite 102, Virginia Beach VA
(757) 425-1641 *www.garyallen.net*

Body Balance Studio

Williamsburg's Body Balance Studio assists individuals in the development of physical, mental and spiritual well-being through a combination of Pilates and yoga classes that focus on the connections between the mind, the body and the breath. Co-Directors Becky Crigger and Missy Kerner encourage their students to use both disciplines, since the benefits of a strong core that come from Pilates increase the control and stability needed for yoga poses. Classes are tailored to meet various needs and experience levels. Body Balance is the only place in Williamsburg that offers Hot Yoga, a style of yoga that originated in Calcutta, India, where outdoor temperatures can reach 120 degrees Fahrenheit. Body Balance Studio employs a specialized heating and air conditioning system that quickly brings a room to 100 degrees with the right level of humidity. Hot yoga is based on the theory that heat allows a deeper stretch by warming muscles and soothing tendons and joints. Sweating also helps clear the body of potentially harmful toxins. The specialized flooring at Body Balance is designed for a safe and healthy yoga experience. It's made of a special matting material that is comfortable and slip-resistant underfoot and allows quick moisture evaporation to prevent the growth of mold, mildew or bacteria. Besides hot yoga, look for gentle and Vinyasa yoga, yoga for toddlers, prenatal yoga and restorative yoga for individuals with physical injuries or health issues. Pilates with or without props plus meditation round out the options. Put balance into your life with a visit to Body Balance Studio.

370 McLaws Circle, Williamsburg VA
(757) 221-0774
www.bodybalancewilliamsburg.com

Home & Garden

Williamsburg Floral

Elgin C. Morris, owner of Williamsburg Floral, comes from a long line of green thumbs. With a family tree blooming with gardeners and groundskeepers, Elgin adopted a knack for foliage. He leads a design team who makes every special occasion pop with bloom. Known for floral designs of distinction, Williamsburg Floral has provided freshly cut inspiration for such dignitaries as Margaret Thatcher, Prince Charles and Sandra Day O'Connor. The team of creative designers helps you surprise a loved one with a single orchid or a gourmet fruit basket. They also turn their creativity on full blast to make a mark on large events, including golf tournaments, corporate parties and bridal showers. They pride themselves on turning your ideas into reality. For once-in-a-lifetime events like weddings and anniversary parties, the team adorns wedding chuppahs, chapel archways and seatbacks with roses, foliage, herbs and exotics in a show of opulent beauty. Order your favorite nosegay of white roses and blue violets or a series of tall centerpieces with oriental lilies soaring gracefully from them. Picture a column or topiary adorned with hundreds of hydrangeas or a simple headdress for a country flower girl. As a full-service florist, Williamsburg floral rents such items as fountains, wrought iron stands and blooming plants. To ensure delivery of the freshest product possible, the shop cuts from its own garden and buys from local growers. For blooms fit for a prince, visit Williamsburg Floral.

701 Merrimac Trail, Williamsburg VA
(757) 229-9844 or (800) 228-2837
www.williamsburgfloral.com

Le Marché – Importers of Fine French Furnishings

At Le Marché–Importers of Fine French Furnishings, the luxury goods for the home begin where department-store inventories leave off. Le Marché features country French antiques, home accoutrements and gifts. The French iron beds are among the most striking and desirable items in the store. Le Marché furnishes the beds with down comforters, high-thread-count Egyptian cotton sheeting and washable Italian silks. Other options include monogrammed blanket covers and matelassé white cotton coverlets. For the table, the shop offers dazzling sterling silver flatware, stemware and china from Fabergé and other top European vendors. Le Marché also stocks tabletop goods for everyday use, from the oven to the table. The shop's attractive baby section includes French iron cribs and cradles, crib ensembles and baby silver. Neuhaus chocolates are a customer favorite. Le Marché provides a complete bridal, nursery and gift registry. Crane stationery for bridal and birth announcements and other social occasions is enormously popular. Le Marché is a Norfolk institution, and yet it also draws customers from up and down the seaboard. The shop opened for business in 1975, and the local owners have more than 30 years of experience in serving customers. Children of the store's original brides have opened their own wedding registries, as Le Marché services a third generation of Norfolk families. Come to Le Marché–Importers of Fine French Furnishings, and let it bring the extraordinary into your everyday life.

1607 Colley Avenue, Norfolk VA
(757) 625-1211
www.lemarcheva.com

G. Bates of Williamsburg Ltd

For tasteful, cutting edge home décor and a store that reflects the discerning eye of its owner, take the time to find G. Bates of Williamsburg, where Gail Bates has gathered together a cornucopia of specialty items. This extraordinary shop is a bit hidden, on the second floor behind the Trellis Restaurant in Merchant's Square. In an effort to represent an international mix of design styles, Gail has picked fine Oriental rugs and an assortment of home furnishings, including Chinese cabinets, painted chests and English pine cupboards. Gift items abound, from lighted china birthday houses to hand painted glassware and accent lamps. G. Bates extends its embellishments to gardens with an international mix of fountains, feeders, statues and arbors. You'll even find personal adornments here, including glamorous and affordable jewelry and accessories similar to those seen on the fashion runways in London, Paris and New York. Her store offers an extensive collection of Vera Bradley bags and licensed accessories, including stationery, rugs, furniture and lamps. Strolling through 4,000 square feet of individually themed rooms while listening to carefully chosen background music is an adventure that shopping connoisseurs will relish. The staff at G. Bates is capable and friendly and always happy to share their knowledge and enthusiasm with you. An online store puts G. Bates at your fingertips, even from afar. For a shopping experience that promises impeccable selections for the home and garden, visit G. Bates of Williamsburg.

413 Duke of Gloucester Street, Williamsburg VA
(757) 229-5400
www.gbates.com

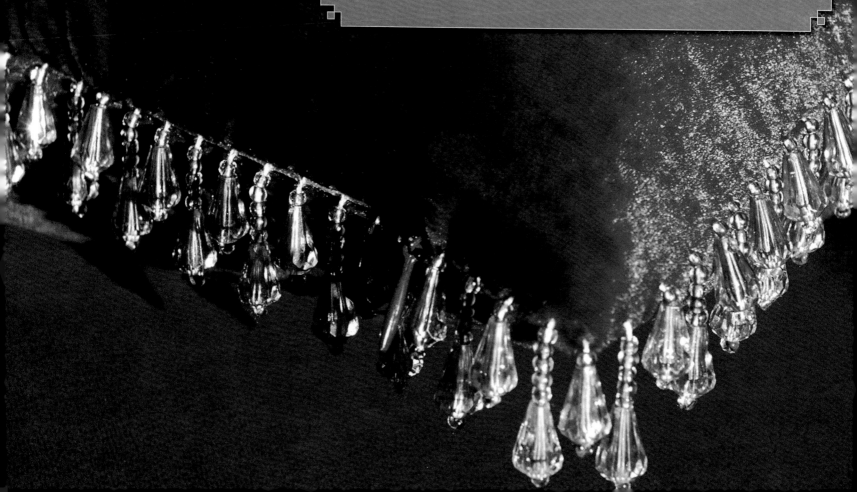

The Guild Hall of Williamsburg

The Guild Hall of Williamsburg is an interior design firm with a collaborative approach. The Bristow family that began the business and continues to run it wants to help you create the memories that make a home. Your imagination is the only limit. Rather than having the feel of a design firm, their store is a place to see ideas. The store is in a house built by an executive of Colonial Williamsburg in the 1940s. Signature pieces are on display that you can buy regardless of whether you make use of the firm's services. These include a palette of fabulous fabrics, both traditional items and unusual textiles. You can also see fine furnishings and original artwork that may spark your imagination. The goods on display change regularly. The Bristows try to meet your wants and needs while creating timeless beauty. Their hope is that people can tell that they did the work because it looks so good, rather than because it has their look. The look should be all yours. Visit the Guild Hall of Williamsburg, where you can browse, conjure up exiting ideas and if you desire, obtain the professional assistance of a talented team.

1300 Jamestown Road, Williamsburg VA
(757) 565-0221 *www.yorkcounty.gov/riverwalk/yto.htm*

Garden Art, Etc.

Add a touch of whimsy and style to your yard with the incredible statuary and garden art available at Garden Art, Etc. Located in a charming and lovingly restored cottage on Laskin Road, this elegant shop has everything you need to brighten up your home and garden along with a fabulous selection of delightful gift ideas. This original shop was opened in 2000 by Donna Beale who just couldn't shake the image of the little house after showing it to a friend who had an interest in opening a clothier. When the friend passed up opportunity, Donna pounced on it and moved her two-year-old statuary art business from her garage into its new home. Donna had previously enjoyed a 13-year career as a probation officer, but wanted to spend more time with her family. Unfortunately, she was diagnosed with breast cancer almost simultaneously and turned to her artwork as an outlet for coping with arduous chemotherapy treatments. She began by creating works of art for friends but soon the demand grew, so she obtained a business license and the rest is history. Each room of the cleverly decorated house has a personalized theme, including the Vacationer's Retreat and the Tex Mex room, where the walls are lined with eclectic and exciting décor items that Donna has hand selected to enhance each room's theme. Add a touch of whimsy and joy to your home and garden with a visit to Garden Art, Etc., just three blocks from the oceanfront.

518 Laskin Road, Virginia Beach VA
(757) 422-6223

Belle Cose

Decorating your home to truly reflect your own sense of style and personality isn't as easy as it sounds. Belle Cose is available to help you with all your decorating needs. Owner and Designer Bobby O'Bryan has created an exciting and inspiring shop filled with interesting, original home accessories and furnishings that will attract your attention as well as your imagination. Belle Cose offers an astounding array of flora and botanicals that can be custom arranged on-site to your specifications. This creative home design resource also offers an exciting collection of pieces for Chelsea House, a well-known importer of Italian and English reproductions along with Jay Strongwater picture frames, accessories and a huge selection of lamps, occasional tables and interesting pieces. Belle Cose further has an extensive collection of candles from top names such as Slatkin Candles. O'Bryan chooses only the best quality fabrics for the shop, including Scalmandre, Old World Weavers and Schumacker. The company is also very well-known for their elegant and sophisticated window treatments. Trust your home to the experts and create a whole new space that reflects the real you with the inspring designs and furnishing available at Belle Cose in Virginia Beach.

1620 Hilltop W, Virginia Beach VA
(757) 437-4303

Topiaries

Let your search for something new and wonderful end at Topiaries in Virginia Beach. Owner Gail Arnold has been creating fabulous centerpieces and offering customers original and exciting home décor and gift ideas for more than 12 years. Gail and her cheery staff are dedicated to providing exceptional customer service every step of the way. They each truly love what they do. Their dedication shines through to make your shopping experience an exciting and enjoyable adventure in treasure hunting. Topiaries' warm and comfortable surroundings easily draw visitors into the magic provided by this elegant shop. You can delight in the fountains, fun music and soft fragrances from Lampe Berger that fill the air. Displays are redone weekly to reflect the often changing inventory of well-known lines, including Votivo, Bethany Lowe and Mark Roberts Fairies. Topiaries is perhaps best known for the incredible topiaries and centerpieces that Gail creates herself. Among the most popular are the whimsical animal topiaries and the truly fantastic Santa designs. With an extensive selection of both permanent and real flowers available, Topiaries can create the ideal centerpiece for any occasion to beautifully compliment your décor. Even the least creative among us can add style and flair to any room of the house with the wonderful design ideas, gifts and exquisite flora available at Topiaries.

301 25th Street, Virginia Beach VA
(757) 437-1183 *www.topiaries.biz*

Lifestyle Destinations

Edinburgh Premier Living

Have you ever dreamed of living among the sights and sounds of waterfalls, bridges and dusk 'til dawn scenery that begs a daily neighborhood stroll? Located in Edinburgh, within the Hickory School District and offering easy access to the Chesapeake Expressway, Edinburgh Premier Living offers some of the most exclusive home sites in the area. Developer and Owner W. Preston Fussell with Precon Development Corporation, Inc. now offers custom upscale homes sites built by a select group of builders to your exact specifications on half to three-quarter acre sites. Lakefront sites are still available. These home sites are only 17 minutes from downtown Norfolk and the Chesapeake General Hospital is an easy nine minutes away. Edinburgh is no ordinary development, though. There are triple fountains bursting delightfully from one lake and an absolutely breathtaking 20-foot, three story high waterfall is featured in the second lake. Homes can provide up to 7,000 square feet of living space and can supply amenities rarely available in other developments in the Hampton Roads area. Gourmet kitchens, home theaters, wine cellars and three-car garages are just a sample of the custom creations available in each home. With its exceptional quality and the endless upgrades and services, these home sites possess the most desired addresses in the area. If you are ready to own a dream home in an entirely upscale community, then Edinburgh Premier Living is yours for the taking. For further information on this community, contact Rose and Womble Realty.

5857 Harbour View Boulevard, Suite 200, Suffolk VA
(757) 421-2107

The Governor's Land at Two Rivers

In one of the most singularly beautiful regions of Virginia, just miles from Colonial Williamsburg, lies the Governor's Land at Two Rivers. This private residential community can accommodate 700 homes among 1,400 acres of gently rolling hills and a 200-acre wildlife and beach sanctuary. As if that isn't enough, the Governor's Land includes a master golf course designed by respected golf course architect Tom Fazio. The country club offers two Junior Olympic sized pools, lighted tennis courts and elegant, heart-healthy dining. A well-maintained marina provides boat access, while miles of walking trails bring you about as close as you can get to heaven on earth. The community, conveniently located just off the John Tyler Highway, honors its heritage with a rich palette of cultural and historical events. Living here allows exposure to the enchantments of the James and Chicahominy Rivers and access to the many charms of the Williamsburg area. Call ahead and set up an appointment to view one of the country's finest planned communities at the Governor's Land at Two Rivers.

2700 Two Rivers Road, Williamsburg VA
(757) 258-4653 or (800) 633-5965
www.govland.com

Gatling Pointe

Located where the James and Pagan Rivers meet, Gatling Pointe is a waterfront community in Isle of Wight County, adjacent to the Historic town of Smithfield. Timeless and classic architectural designs are found throughout the quiet cul-de-sac streets and along one of the many waterfront home sites. You can rediscover a small town atmosphere as you wind through this maturely landscaped community. Three times selected Community of the Year by the Peninsula Housing & Builders Association, Gatling Pointe features the best in waterfront living. Residents enjoy many social and recreational opportunities at their neighborhood yacht club, which offers spectacular views across the James River. The Gatling Pointe Yacht Club has become the social hub of the community and really adds to the overall sense of neighborhood. It's a place where friends and neighbors gather and enjoy many family activities and the natural beauty of the river. There's a 68 slip deep water marina, riverfront swimming pool, volleyball and tennis courts, playground and even a restaurant. The Yacht Club offers fabulous dining along with wine tasting events and a plethora of activities that are designed to keep the whole family involved year round. You can take your kid or grandkid for a stroll down the neighborhood bike trail to go fishing, or attend one of the many summer camp events. You can sail, ski, swim, play tennis, or just sit back and enjoy the view. Be careful, one trip through Gatling Pointe and you just might want to drop anchor for good.

903 Gatling Pointe Parkway, Smithfield VA
(757) 357-2200
www.eastwestreality.com/hamptonrodscommunity/gatlingpointe
www.gatlingpointe.com

Ford's Colony at Williamsburg

With a multitude of amenities and recreational opportunities, residents of Ford's Colony at Williamsburg feel like vacationers year-round. The American Resort Development Association recognizes Ford's Colony, founded in 1985 by developer Richard J. Ford, as the number one master planned community in the United States. Mr. Ford's two sons, Richard J. Ford, Jr. and Brian Ford, now manage the community and all three enjoy living in the custom Colonial, Greek revival, Federal and Georgian style homes. The active community boasts two Olympic size swimming pools, 14 tennis courts and more than 50 groups, organized by members of the activities committee, to bring together community members with such interests as bird watching, theater and bowling. A 54-hole championship golf course, designed by Dan Maples, challenges pros while also accommodating beginners. The Ford Colony Country Club's Dining Room offers upscale American cuisine with an emphasis on fresh and locally grown ingredients and features handcrafted wine brewed for Ford's Colony. For a more casual dining experience, the Grille Room offers bistro style specials, like coconut and cashew crusted fried shrimp and stuffed grilled portobello mushrooms. This diverse nature preserve area is perfect for quiet walks and runs through the center of the 3,000-acre property. The United States Department of Agriculture recognized Ford's Colony's efforts to protect it with a Certificate of Excellence for conserving America's natural and cultural resources. Visit Ford's Colony at Williamsburg and discover the many benefits of living in this engaging community.

1 Ford's Colony Drive, Williamsburg VA
(757) 258-4000
www.fordscolony.com

The Riverfront/East West Partners

With an outstanding golf course and an award-winning swim club facility, the Riverfront is the Suffolk area's most awarded new home community with numerous awards from the Tidewater Builders Association and recognition for Best Club in the country by the Resort & Commercial Recreation Association. The Riverfront golf course community overlooks the Namsemond and James Rivers in the Hampton Roads area. It consists of more than 1,000 upscale homes and luxury condominiums. At least two-thirds of its properties offer premium views of the lake, creek, river or golf course. The homes here feature timeless architectural designs and uncompromising construction by eight of the area's premier custom homebuilders. Recreation is at your doorstep at the Riverfront with a full-time activities director and many special features, including two lakes, a lakeside park with an amphitheater, two riverfront parks with gazebos and piers, plus playgrounds, tennis and volleyball courts. The Riverfront Swim Club activities director coordinates numerous events and a monthly social calendar. The Riverfront is one of four planned communities developed by East West Partners in the Hampton Roads area. East West focuses on developing planned communities, marketing and selling homes and managing club amenities. Come by to tour the Riverfront's unrivaled, natural setting and the many amenities of this quality community.

6101 Walkers Ferry Lane, Suffolk VA
(757) 638-9100
www.the-riverfront.com

Markets

College Run Farms

Surry's long growing season gives visitors to College Run Farms three seasons of pick-your own pleasure. In spring, you can pick your own strawberries. In summer, corn taken right from the stalk promises sweet delights and in fall, families return for pumpkins and gourds. Steve Berryman, the son of a longtime Surry farmer, started College Run in 1999, shortly after completing an independent study class in strawberry production that concluded his Virginia Tech degree. Today, his farm is a favorite destination for Surry families seeking a country outing, offering picnic and picking opportunities. For those who prefer to let someone else do the picking, Steve and his wife, Jordan, also sell baskets of fresh strawberries and other seasonal favorites from an on-site farm market. In summer, the market carries butter beans, watermelon, peppers, tomatoes, and other fruits and vegetables of the season, all grown at College Run Farms. The Berrymans also transport their freshly picked produce to the Williamsburg Farmers Market in Merchant Square every Saturday morning from May through October and during holidays. College Run Farms, named after a creek at the back of the farm, is a favorite destination for school field trips. Children can learn about food production and develop an appreciation for the incomparable flavor and sweetness that accompanies food that has just been harvested. Seasonal variations in weather and crops changes the market hours, so the Berrymans suggest you call for hours and check the website for what crops are currently available before heading their way.

Alliance Road, Surry VA
(757) 294-3498
www.collegerunfarms.com

Jamestown Pie Company

Jamestown Pie Company specializes in pies of all kinds, including pecan pies, gourmet pizzas and deep-dish potpies. Owners Reggie Akdogan, Stephen Smith and Christopher Raven offer freshly baked pies made with products grown in Virginia. They bake 20 kinds of specialty pizzas and 10 varieties of potpies. Many of the deep-dish pies and pizzas contain novel ingredients. For example, seafood pizzas can include locally caught bay scallops, shrimp or crabmeat. You can create your own pizza with a healthy selection of veggies, tasty sausages or ham. Jamestown Pie Company offers chicken or beef potpies, as well as specialty veggie and pork loin potpies. The dessert pies are the stars, whether made from such fruits as berries, dark cherries or apples, or from nuts, including peanuts or hazelnuts. First time visitors should try Jamestown's version of the South's great delicacy, pecan pie. The Jamestown version is made using an 80-year-old recipe from a Williamsburg family. It's not too sweet and will stay fresh on the counter for up to 60 days, so there is no need to freeze it. When you visit, ask about seasonal pies, gift certificates and catering. Jamestown offers carry out and local delivery, as well as nationwide shipping, via the website. Jamestown Pie Company, located between Colonial Williamsburg and the Jamestown Settlement, invites you to Buy a Pie.

1804 Jamestown Road, Williamsburg VA
(757) 229-7775
www.buyapie.com

The Peanut Shop of Williamsburg

Located on the Prince George Street corridor, The Peanut Shop of Williamsburg is the second oldest business in Merchant Square. The Peanut Shop makes and distributes 60 percent of the products they sell and although most people roast peanuts in vegetable oil, The Peanut shop uses peanut oil. This makes the peanuts very tasty and healthy. These hand cooked peanuts out sell anything else in the store, but the other products they sell, such as tavern foods and gifts, help to make the store even more interesting. Retail Manager Terri Morgan says that they are a licensee of Colonial Williamsburg so they make some Colonial Williamsburg products, too. The Peanut Shop helps their patrons to have a great experience at the shop by providing a sampling program where almost all of their nut products and a few other items are out for sampling daily. They are also a part of Smithfield Foods and sell Smithfield hams at the shop. The Peanut Shop sells Virginia Peanuts, which are the best in the world, because of their extraordinary flavor, large size and good response to the cooking process. Aside from their peanuts served in different seasoned or spicy varieties, you can purchase nut confections and specialty gifts such as linens and kitchen accessories. Come sample some of the nuts or other things at The Peanut Shop of Williamsburg.

414 Prince George Street, Williamsburg VA
(757) 229-3908
http://thepeanutshop.com

Edwards Virginia Ham

It has taken a dedicated family and a tried-and-true curing method to bring about a product so flavorful and consistent that households from one end of the country to the other make a Virginia country ham from Edwards of Surry a traditional part of their most important celebrations. The Edwards family started its business in 1926 when young Captain Samuel Wallace Edwards of the Jamestown-Surry ferryboat served a ham sandwich to a passenger using ham cured on the family farm. It wasn't long before Captain Edwards was curing and selling his ham on a full-time basis and supplying nearby country stores and gracious manor homes. His son and, today, his grandson Samuel Edwards III with wife Donna and sister Amy continue PopPop's commitment to quality close to the spot where American Indians first taught colonists their curing secrets. Most of the country orders Edwards ham, smoked meats and specialty foods from the family's Virginia Traditions catalog or through prestigious catalog stores, but anyone can visit the company's Surry or Williamsburg shops to buy the famed products directly from the source. You can even take a tour of the Surry plant in the summer. Edwards hams consistently win top honors at the Virginia State Fair and are the personal favorites of *New York Times* food writer Johnny Apple. *Gourmet* magazine voted them the best mail order hams in 2005. When consumers, restaurants and wholesalers want fine Virginia ham, they buy Edwards Virginia ham. Taste a tradition from a proud Virginia family.

11381 Rolfe Highway, Surry VA
1814 Richmond Road, Williamsburg VA
(757) 294-3121 or (800) 222-4267
www.virginiatraditions.com (Retail)
www.edwardsvaham.com (Wholesale)

The Wine and Cheese Shop at Kingsmill

The Wine and Cheese Shop at Kingsmill is a comfortable place to enjoy lunch, to shop for gifts or to bring home the ingredients for a party. Locals go on to become regulars here and soon know each other by name. Owners Carol and Aaron Hill serve up a fabulous selection of sandwiches, made with their very own fresh baked bread and special sauce. A pleasant patio with a park-like setting makes a great location for enjoying your deli fare. You'll find a large selection of imported, domestic and Virginia wines. Once a month, the shop holds a wine dinner and a wine tasting to familiarize participants with fine wines. Pick up a party tray for your next celebration or a gift basket to satisfy someone on your gift list. For a basket that meets all your expectations, choose from the shop's extensive selection of gourmet food items, including wines, cheeses, sauces, nuts and crackers. The staff will package your selections and arrange to ship them anywhere in the continental United States. The Wine and Cheese Shop carries such specialty gifts as wine accessories, decorative lap trays and placemats. Carol and Aaron retired from the medical industry and settled in Williamsburg, where they bought the shop and, with the help of longtime manager Cindy Cesil, created a happy gathering place. Treat yourself to the Wine and Cheese Shop at Kingsmill, where good times begin.

1915 Pocahontas Trail, Williamsburg VA
(757) 229-6754 *www.potterywineandcheese.com*

The Genuine Smithfield Ham Shoppe

In their mission to showcase and introduce people to Smithfield Hams, The Genuine Smithfield Ham Shoppe sells many varieties of hams. Located on Main Street in the heart of the Smithfield historic shopping district, the shop carries dry-cured Smithfield hams, country hams and spiral sliced hams. They also sell smoked specialty bacons that are handcut, as well as regional foods and gourmet gifts. Store Manager Virginia Wade says that they like to introduce people to other specialty food items of the state as well. They let patrons sample different types of peanuts and other featured foods. The shop is very quaint and has a genuine Smithfield feeling, giving it the essence of southern elegance and hospitality. Visit the Genuine Smithfield Ham Shoppe to purchase delicious food and gifts and you will leave with a smile on your face and quality food that the whole family will enjoy.

224 Main Street, Smithfield VA
(757) 357-1798
www.smithfieldhams.com

Bon Vivant Market

If you're looking for the perfect wine for your next party or just interested in trying something new, then head for the little red brick building known as Bon Vivant Market. Husband and wife co-owners Mike Adams and Kate Bouvier offer patrons a spectacular selection of wines priced to meet any budget. Additionally, Mike takes all of the guesswork out of choosing the ideal vintage by carefully sorting through the available wines and selecting the one that best suits your occasion. Along with fabulous vintages, Bon Vivant Market also houses an extensive collection of world-class microbrews. These specialty beers come from microbreweries that are passionate about what they do and Mike and Kate choose the best of these to sell in their spirited boutique. Bon Vivant Market hosts both beer and wine tasting events each month that feature guest speakers who are informative, imaginative and make each event unique and delightfully entertaining. Bon Vivant further offers a great selection of loose spices at far lower than grocery store prices along with fresh coffee beans and a wonderful gift basket service. Mike has you select which items will be included and uses only full size, award winning products displayed in clever, original containers like decorated flower pots and eight-quart buckets. Become a devotee of the finer things in life with a visit to Bon Vivant Market, or come to their new location called Bon Vivant at Governor's Pointe.

1504 S Church Street, Smithfield VA (Market) (757) 365-0932
1901 Governors Pointe Drive, Suffolk VA (Governor's Pointe) (757) 238-7038
www.bonvivantmarket.com

Plantations

Shirley Plantation

Shirley Plantation gives visitors a rare glimpse of a southern plantation and the historical perspective of the family who has owned and operated it since the early days of British colonization. This privately owned plantation, located on the James River 35 miles west of Williamsburg, is the oldest family owned business in North America. A land grant from the King of England to the Governor of Virginia carved Shirley Plantation out of the Virginia frontier in 1613, just six years after the settlement of Jamestown. By 1638, Edward Hill had started agricultural operations on Shirley soil. Construction on the present mansion began in 1723 when Edward's great-granddaughter Elizabeth married John Carter. Completed in 1738, the mansion is largely in its original state and remains the home of the Carter family. It survived the Indian Uprisings, Bacon's Rebellion, the Revolutionary War, the Civil War and the Great Depression and so remains an architectural treasure. A guided tour of the house reveals a square-rigged flying staircase that rises three stories with no visible means of support as well as original 18th-century carved woodwork, family portraits and furniture. The grounds provide the opportunity to see eight original buildings including four brick structures that form a symmetrical Queen Anne forecourt, the only example of its kind in the country. Immerse yourself in American history at Shirley Plantation.

501 Shirley Plantation Road, Charles City VA
(804) 829-5121 or (800) 232-1613
www.shirleyplantation.com

Photos by Shirley Plantation in Charles City, Virginia

College Run Farms

Surry's long growing season gives visitors to College Run Farms three seasons of pick-your own pleasure. In spring, you can pick your own strawberries. In summer, corn taken right from the stalk promises sweet delights and in fall, families return for pumpkins and gourds. Steve Berryman, the son of a longtime Surry farmer, started College Run in 1999, shortly after completing an independent study class in strawberry production that concluded his Virginia Tech degree. Today, his farm is a favorite destination for Surry families seeking a country outing, offering picnic and picking opportunities. For those who prefer to let someone else do the picking, Steve and his wife, Jordan, also sell baskets of fresh strawberries and other seasonal favorites from an on-site farm market. In summer, the market carries butter beans, watermelon, peppers, tomatoes, and other fruits and vegetables of the season, all grown at College Run Farms. The Berrymans also transport their freshly picked produce to the Williamsburg Farmers Market in Merchant Square every Saturday morning from May through October and during holidays. College Run Farms, named after a creek at the back of the farm, is a favorite destination for school field trips. Children can learn about food production and develop an appreciation for the incomparable flavor and sweetness that accompanies food that has just been harvested. Seasonal variations in weather and crops changes the market hours, so the Berrymans suggest you call for hours and check the website for what crops are currently available before heading their way.

Alliance Road, Surry VA
(757) 294-3498
www.collegerunfarms.com

Westover

An outstanding example of 18th century Georgian architecture and one of the most beautiful homes in the United States, William Byrd II built Westover in 1730. Its elegant brickwork, steeply sloping roof and tall paired chimneys are all significant design motifs from that era. Today, Westover is a private residence owned by the Bruce C. Fisher family. Most of the furniture is from the 18th century. There are no pieces remaining from the Byrd family. Two volumes from the once famous library containing over 4,000 volumes, belonging to William Byrd II remain in the house today. Some of the past owners have loved this house so much they never left, such as the ghost of Evelyn Byrd, who has been spotted by different guests on numerous occasions. Located approximately 150 feet from the James River, the house is flanked by tulip poplars over 150 years old. Westover participates in Historic Garden Week in Virginia, one of the few times of the year the house is open to the public. The grounds and outer buildings are open to the public year-round. It is a magnificent place to have a wedding. Several motion pictures and miniseries have been filmed at Westover. Come tour the grounds and enjoy the breathtaking beauty of a house that has been loved for hundreds of years. Westover welcomes groups of 12 or more for house tours by appointment.

7000 Westover Road, Charles City VA
(804) 829-2882
www.jamesriverplantations.com

Chippokes Plantation State Park
Chippokes Farm & Forestry Museum

 The graceful acreage of Chippokes Plantation State Park has been continually cultivated since 1619 when Captain William Powell received a grant for the land. Directly across the James River from Jamestown and about five miles from the Jamestown/Scotland Wharf ferry, the plantation and bordering creek are named after an Indian chief who befriended early settlers. Today, visitors can stroll through the grounds and along two miles of riverfront, tour the Jones-Stewart Mansion with its Victorian antiques and formal gardens and visit the Farm & Forestry Museum and a sawmill exhibit. A campground with water and electric hookups and bathhouses with hot showers and a laundry facility are open from March through November. An Olympic-size swimming pool is a favorite destination during the summer months. In the historic area, refurbished historic tenant farm houses are available as rental cottages year-round. Complete with kitchens and baths, the cottages are fully furnished, heated and air conditioned. The plantation, donated to the Commonwealth of Virginia in 1969 by Evelyn Stewart in memory of her husband Victor, remains a working farm with grazing cows, hay fields and crops, including corn, peanuts, wheat, soybeans and cotton. The mansion was built in 1854 by Albert Carroll Jones, the first owner to live on the plantation. Jones produced and shipped peach and apple brandy and cider. According to local legend, the mansion survived the Civil War because Jones sold his brandies to both armies. The Museum interprets life in rural Virginia through a collection of farm and forestry equipment, tools and hardwares from the 17th to the early 20th century. You can visit the Chippokes Plantation State Park grounds year-round and take in the mansion and the museum from April to October.

695 Chippokes Park Road, Surry VA
(757) 294-3625 or (800) 933-PARK (7275)
www.dcr.virginia.gov/parks/chippoke.htm

Photos by Carlton S. Abbott

Lazare Gallery - Representing the Best of Moscow's School of Russian Realism

In historic Charles City County, on the banks of the James River, art dealers John and Kathy Wurdeman have spent years assembling a collection of works of enduring relevance by the greatest Soviet Era and Russian Era master artists. Advocates of tradition and academic training and affiliated with the Moscow School of Russian Realism, these master artists collectively have more than 1,000 paintings in major museums worldwide. The style of painting represented by the Moscow School of Russian Realism was strongly influenced by the philosophy of the late 19th century French Academy of Art, along with the exploration of color pursued in the Russian Impressionist Academic painting. First-time visitors are pleasantly startled by the uniqueness of Lazare Gallery. Located in a forested, waterfront setting between Richmond and Williamsburg, Virginia, the 8,200-square-foot gallery welcomes art collectors and connoisseurs from all over the USA. For collectors, multiple guest rooms are available on the property to allow for overnight stays. Instead of representing paintings of secondary importance by great artists, Lazare Gallery's emphasis has been to seek out the very best Russian Realism and Impressionism from the Soviet Era to present. With an inventory of more than 1,300 fine Russian paintings, Lazare Gallery invites dealers, collectors, and lovers of fine art to view and select treasures from this outstanding collection. Open by appointment only.

4641 Kimages Wharf Road, Charles City VA
(804) 829-5001
www.lazaregallery.com

Edgewood Plantation

Edgewood Plantation is an inviting bed-and-breakfast and a fascinating place to learn about local history and folklore, complete with a resident ghost. The plantation gets its name from its location—on the edge of the woods of Berkeley Plantation, ancestral home of Benjamin Harrison V, a signer of the Declaration of Independence, and his grandson, William Henry Harrison, ninth president of the United States. A comfortable blend of primitive 18th century, Victorian, and Chippendale furnishings fill the home. Several guest units have fireplaces, and all have private baths. In Lizzie's Room, visitors can see the name Lizzie Roland etched into a windowpane. She was the daughter of the man who built the house and made the etching while waiting for her true love to return from the war. He never did, and legend has it that she died of a broken heart and her spirit still roams the halls. In keeping with the Victorian surroundings, Edgewood offers Victorian tea parties and lunches, where guests can try on period hats while enjoying the traditional food selections. They host a Queen's Tea on Thursdays and Fridays, a Jamestown Luncheon on Wednesdays, and an Early Settler's Breakfast on Saturdays and Sundays. In November and December, among the 18 Christmas trees in the house, they do a Candlelight Tour and Dinner, and a Somewhere in Time Christmas Tea. All of these events require at least a two day advance notice. Owners Dot and Julian Boulware seek to make each visit as enjoyable as possible. To experience the history and hospitality of Virginia firsthand, visit Edgewood Plantation.

4800 John Tyler Memorial Highway, Charles City VA
(804) 829-2962
www.edgewoodplantation.com

North Bend Plantation

The North Bend Plantation, circa 1801, is owned by Ridgely and George Copland. Incredibly, George is a descendent of the original owners of the house. The 850-acre plantation grows a strict rotation of corn, wheat and soybeans, attracting all manner of wildlife. An on-site pond draws ducks and nature trails lure visitors to explore the beautiful grounds punctuated by historic landmarks such as civil war trenches. North Bend Plantation is a National Registry property built for the sister of the ninth president of the United States and still contains antiques original to the house and family. Guests can also enjoy the swimming pool on the grounds and the house itself is truly outstanding with its elegant decor and comfort. Ridgely and George exude gracious southern hospitality while they freely share information about the history of the plantation and the family tree. Staying at North Bend Plantation is similar to staying with close friends or family, complete with a billiards table, fascinating books and heirlooms that are used too often to gather dust. Every morning, guests at the plantation are treated to a full country breakfast. North Bend Plantation provides a picturesque backdrop for weddings and special events. The Coplands extend their invitation for you to come and acquaint yourself with the rich history of North Bend Plantation, reserve a room and immerse yourself even more in the wonders of this historical home.

12200 Weyanoke Road, Charles City VA
(804) 829-5176
vwww.northbendplantation.com

Westover Parish Church

A harmonious echo of a thousand voices whispers through time to lend its song to those who gather in worship at Westover Parish Church, where history and a deep, abiding love of God merge into a joyful and inspiring crescendo. Westover Church, now called Westover Episcopal Church, was originally established near the Jamestown settlement in 1613 and, throughout history, has been a place of worship for presidents, slaves, plantation owners and country farmers. Sadly, the history of Westover Episcopal Church has not always been a happy one. The Civil War brought great battles to the parish, and by the end, not a door, window or floor was left, according to the vestry book, which was miraculously saved along with the Communion silver and bibles by an unknown benefactor. By September 15, 1867 Westover Episcopal Church was once again ready to receive parishioners and remains today a place where anyone, regardless of race, can come to worship. To date the parish church has around 160 active communicants, many of whom are fifth, sixth and seventh generation parishioners. Westover Episcopal Church offers services each Sunday at 8:30 a.m., with additional summer services at 10:00 a.m., presided over by the rector, Reverend Virginia Heistand Jones. For the congregation's youth the church provides a nursery, playground and short sermons, as well as Sunday school classes and an active and joyful youth group. Lend your voice and prayers to the historic Westover Episcopal Church.

6401 John Tyler Memorial Highway, Charles City VA
(804) 829-2488

Brandon Plantation

Robert W. Daniel, Jr. and his wife understand the historic significance of their home at Brandon Plantation and open it for many public tours and special events. The historic Virginia plantation, founded in 1616, first belonged to John Martin, one of the last survivors of Jamestown. The property changed ownership several times, all the while functioning as a non-resident-owned plantation that produced tobacco for the English market. Over time and by the hands of different owners, the Brandon Plantation residence changed its style. It is possible that Thomas Jefferson, an admirer of the Georgian style, contributed to Georgian elements in the home's design. During the Civil War, Brandon bore the brunt of Union occupation. Several buildings and their contents were destroyed. Afterwards, the plantation fell into ruin, as did many others. Eventually, Brandon Plantation was restored and became a National Historic Landmark. Its gardens abound with roses, yellow jasmine and old growth cedar, making Brandon Plantation one of the most magnificent estates in the area. It's also a working farm, growing corn, wheat and soy beans. Cattle graze the pastures. Large herds of Virginia deer find shelter in the property's woods and marshes. Daniel, a former congressman who served in the US House of Representatives, appreciates the history and legacy of Brandon Plantation and opens the home to tours by appointment. Experience our nation's beginnings at Brandon Plantation.

23500 Brandon Road, Spring Grove VA
(757) 866-8486

Recreation

The Corner Pocket

Majority owner and managing partner Lynn Allison has rebuilt the Corner Pocket into the ultimate upscale pool hall. Serving food and fun for all ages, the Pocket is a classy yet casual place to take a date, watch the Monday night pool tournament or enjoy live music by nationally known artists. The Corner Pocket combines Italianate architecture with the relaxed Southern style of the French Quarter. The open floor plan has separate, defined areas for pool, drinking and smoke-free dining. The 12 Connelly pool tables and one snooker table attract up to 70 shooters who play in two weekly in-house leagues. For live music, visit on Thursday, Saturday or Sunday. The California Guitar Trio and Buckwheat Zydeco have both played at the Pocket, and author James Elroy has given live readings here. The Pocket always celebrates Mardi Gras and St. Patrick's Day in style. It's a dedicated member of the Williamsburg community, and each year holds a bluegrass concert to raise money for the local food bank. Leave your tank tops at home when you visit the Pocket, where the dress code is casual but neat attire. Children ages 10 and older are allowed to play pool here, making the Corner Pocket a good spot for a family affair. For food, games and entertainment, make a night of it at the Corner Pocket.

4805 Courthouse Street, Williamsburg VA
(757) 220-0808
www.thecornerpocket.us

Wasabi Charters LLC

Imagine that you are going on a fishing trip. Further imagine that you can customize your day right down to telling your captain what you want to catch. Sign on with Captain Joe Mora of Wasabi Charters and Yacht Sales, and your imagined adventure can be a reality. Whether you want to sight-cast for cobia, bounce the bottom for flounder, or troll the blue water for tuna and marlin, Wasabi Charters has the trip for you. Wasabi is a 36-foot Custom Pro Sports boat with an average cruising speed of 35 knots. She's perfect for getting you to the fishing grounds quickly and comfortably. Wasabi Charters also uses a 2004 24-foot Pro Sports Cat for in-shore fishing and light tackle fights. Captain Mora has fished in Puerto Rico, New York, North Carolina, California, Chesapeake Bay and the offshore waters of Virginia Beach for most of his life. His expertise makes him a valued speaker at sports fishing clubs across the country. Why leave your fishing to chance? Book a tour with Captain Joe at Wasabi Charters, and assure your success.

5601 RiverBluff Drive, Suffolk VA
(757) 635-6146 (cell) *www.wasabi-charters.com*

Restaurants & Cafés

The Black Angus Restaurant

Since 1953 The Black Angus Restaurant has been serving Virginia Beach denizens the finest steak and seafood dishes around. This casually elegant restaurant first opened under the ownership of Christy Harriton and Chris Patsalides, who had a dream of building an eatery that focused on fabulous steaks and above par service. That dream quickly became reality and by 1960 they were ready to expand. Over the years many things have changed, including ownership, and The Black Angus now belongs to Christopher and Michael Savvides, nephews to Chris Patsalides. What hasn't changed is the fantastic food and incredible service. The Black Angus offers patrons a delicious and complementary hors d'oeuvres tray featuring crackers, liver paté and sprats with feta cheese along with pickled mushrooms and marinated asparagus tips. As you whet your appetite you can browse the extensive menu of Angus beef, seafood or pasta dishes and choose your favorite from among the list of delectable choices such as rack of lamb or the Black Angus beef kabob. Other delectable choices include the Grecian baked chicken or the calf's liver sautéed with bacon and onions. The Black Angus is equally well known for its fabulous catering services and can happily accommodate large or small parties for special events like bridal suppers and corporate gatherings. Treat yourself and your guests to a meal that deserves a standing ovation at the popular and delicious Black Angus Restaurant located on the beautiful Virginia Beach oceanfront.

706 Atlantic Avenue, Virginia Beach VA
(757) 428-7700
www.blackangusrestaurant.com

Il Giardino Ristorante

Since 1980, Il Giardino Ristorante has been a popular favorite for Virginia Beach residents and visitors alike. Located on Atlantic Avenue, Il Giardino offers an inviting and beautifully appointed atmosphere that is highlighted by the excellent staff. The varied menu features a wonderful selection of succulent steaks, superb seafood and tender veal dishes such as the *Vitello alla Francese*, which is comprised of veal Scalopine with lemon, butter and white wine. Further menu favorites include fabulous pasta dishes and pizzas from the wood-burning oven. Nestled into a corner of the eatery is the striking oven itself, which Co-owner and President Anthony Gargulio found on a trip to Florence, Italy, in 1983. Since it was installed, the wood-burning oven has been used to bake their signature *focaccia* bread that is then served to each table. Both Anthony and Vice-president Maureen Murphy are proud to use only the freshest and highest-quality ingredients in every dish, including Il Giardino's famous sauces, which are made each day from scratch. In addition to the fabulous cuisine, Il Giardino Ristorante further offers a terrific selection of wines, each chosen to complement the excellent array of appetizers and entrées. Il Giardino also has valet parking and a lively piano bar, making this fine dining eatery a welcoming and delightful place to spend an evening. Make your next outing extra special with fine dining at Il Giardino Ristorante.

910 Atlantic Avenue, Virginia Beach VA
(757) 422-6464
www.ilgiardino.com

Captain George's Seafood Restaurant

If your idea of heaven on earth includes endless Alaskan snow crab legs, steamed spiced shrimp, and freshly prepared fish, then head to Captain George's Seafood Restaurant, the original World Famous Seafood Buffet. In 1979 George Pitsilides and his wife, Sherry, opened the first of these Virginia favorites in Hampton. In the years that followed, they added locations in Virginia Beach, Williamsburg and even Myrtle Beach, South Carolina to their fleet. You will encounter a mouthwatering all-you-can-eat seafood buffet that is sure to please any palette. The buffet features over 70 items including steamed shrimp, oysters rockefeller, prime rib, steamed clams and mussels, a variety of fresh fish, seafood casseroles and homemade salads. Despite the decadent array of sumptuous delights that line the buffet table, you will want to be sure to save room for a selection from the Captain's dessert bar. Choose from an array of fresh Greek pastries, creamy puddings and rich cakes, not to mention pies and berry cobblers. With a visit to Captain George's Seafood Restaurant, you will experience a 26-year-old tradition that will leave you reflecting in fond memory.

1956 Laskin Road, Virginia Beach VA
(757) 428-3494
www.captaingeorges.com

Aldo's Ristorante

From the excellent Old World service, intimate lighting and tasteful settings to the fabulous cuisine and wine selection, Aldo's Ristorante is the locals' favorite for fine Italian dining in Virginia Beach. Co-Owners Deborah Kassir and Jim Farsi have given Aldo's a rich history of serving first-rate cuisine since its inception in 1988. Aldo's beckons its guests to savor a one-of-a-kind gastronomical experience with fresh and homemade signature dishes such as pescatore, shrimp gorgonzola, fantastic hand-cut filets and myriad pasta concoctions. Ask the chef to create perfectly seasoned pizzas and delicious focaccia bread baked in their wood-burning brick oven. Make room to sample delectable desserts such as crème brulee, tiramisu, napoleons and chocolate grand sequoia. Aldo's is also proud to offer its guests an extensive wine selection that has won the coveted Wine Spectator Award of Excellence since 1995. Aldo's has also been the recipient of numerous accolades such as Port Folio Weekly Crystal Stem award, Best of the Beach and Viewer's Choice awards for Best Fine Dining and Best Italian Restaurant. Aldo's successful venture never hindered its owners from giving back to the community. Throughout the year, it fulfills its active civic duty by participating in numerous charitable events that support schools, children's research and local organizations. Experience fine dining in a whole new way. You know you are someplace special when you walk through Aldo's doors. Come to Aldo's Ristorante, located in La Promenade Shoppes.

1860 Laskin Road, Suite 104, Virginia Beach, VA 23451
(757) 491-1111

O'Sullivan's Wharf

O'Sullivan's Wharf in Norfolk has been a favorite of locals and visitors for more than 20 years. This fabulous restaurant features a terrific menu filled with spectacular seafood, steaks and tasty entrées to satisfy any appetite. Due to its location on the banks of the famous Lafayette River in the historic Ghent district, patrons of this popular eatery can arrive by land or by sea and either park in the spacious lot or tie up at the docks before heading inside to enjoy the comfortable atmosphere, friendly staff and great food. The menu features a variety of dishes that will make your mouth water including Oysters Rockefeller, fried shrimp, juicy steak specials and prime rib. It also offers deli sandwiches and catering for your special events and family get-togethers. In addition to the indoor dining room, patrons can dine alfresco on the open-air deck while gazing at the beautiful scenery and watching the boats glide by. This Norfolk landmark has a large wraparound bar in the center lounge which is an ideal place to sip your favorite drink while chatting with friends or colleagues. During any given visit, you will see everyone from folks just in off the river in shorts and sandals to elegantly dressed couples on their way to the theater. Owner Joseph Bambery prides himself on providing nothing but the best for his customers, so come see for yourself why O'Sullivan's Wharf has been a Norfolk favorite since 1981.

4300 Colley Avenue, Norfolk VA
(757) 423-3746

The Whitehall Restaurant and King's Lounge

The Whitehall presents fine European dining in a relaxing elegant atmosphere. After living for 20 years in London and the Near East, Karin and Roy Moor knew just the elegance they wanted to create when they opened the Whitehall in 1997. They combined many of the features of their favorite European restaurants with an extensive wine list and dedicated staff. Whitehall has received Golden Stem awards and five star ratings for both food and atmosphere. Beautiful antique furniture and mahogany Chippendale chairs compliment the white linen service. With close to 30 years experience in the operation of five star restaurants, Manager Ernest Green is committed to providing patrons with delicious meals and outstanding service. In addition to intimate dining, with four separate dining rooms the restaurant makes it possible to accommodate parties from 10 to 150 people. The Whitehall is also a popular venue for rehearsal and wedding dinners, corporate functions and banquets. The Whitehall also boasts the new King's Lounge & Terrace. The entire room and bar are hand crafted in solid Cherry used from trees removed from the grounds of the Capitol in Washington, D.C. Drink specialties include fresh fruit martinis and exotic champagne cocktails. The building itself is about 100 years old and it has housed a wealthy private family, an Art Gallery and a Weapons Museum. It was also the site of a pottery factory operated by a master potter from England. The potter, Palin Thorley, and his wife also had their residence in the building until his death at age 94. Located one mile east of Colonial Williamsburg, visit the Whitehall Restaurant and King's Lounge for an evening you will savor.

**1325 Jamestown Road,
Williamsburg VA**
(757) 229-4677
dine@thewhitehall.com
www.thewhitehall.com

Lynnhaven Fish House

Lynnhaven Fish House, overlooking the Chesapeake Bay, has been serving incredibly fresh and delectable seafood to Virginia Beach residents for more than 25 years. Today, under the management of Owner Christopher Kyrus and Executive Chef John Chapman, this casual, elegant family restaurant retains its reputation for excellence by focusing on providing a large selection of fresh fish at a great value and combining that with fabulous service and quality. Kyrus considers Lynnhaven's staff to be its biggest asset and many staff members have been with the restaurant for well over a decade. In conjunction with an extensive menu of fresh fish and seafood dishes, Lynnhaven also offers a savory selection of succulent beef dishes and fantastic salads along with delicious side dishes that are worth the trip all by themselves. Lynnhaven Fish House is designed in such a way that every patron has a view of Chesapeake Bay and the Bridge Tunnel from their seat and the welcoming dining room is filled with light, making it seem as though you were dining right by the water. This popular eatery has been named the Best of the Beach for the past 12 years and is committed to honoring its loyal customers through several customer appreciation services that they have in place. Lynnhaven further contributes by choosing one day per year to donate an entire day's gross receipts to a Hampton Roads area charity organization. If you want to enjoy fresh fish at its best, then come to Lynnhaven Fish House.

2350 Starfish Road, Virginia Beach VA (757) 481-0003 *www.lynnhavenfishhouse.net*

Wisteria

Wisteria at Thoroughgood Commons in Virginia Beach offers an innovative menu complemented by caring, attentive service in a relaxing atmosphere. This dynamic restaurant is a dream come true for Owner and Operator George Butler who has been providing hospitality to the folks of the Hampton Roads area for more than 20 years. Butler was formerly the manager for The Harbor Club as well as part owner of The Garden House, both in Norfolk. In 2002, he teamed up with Chefs Jon Kenyon and Jon Scott and Manager Becky Blair to create a truly memorable dining experience in the form of Wisteria. The graceful and elegant dining room, complete with crisp linens, wood and wrought iron accents, has a Southern Gothic feeling that is welcoming and relaxing. Above the main room is a fantastic loft, which is ideal for intimate gatherings and private functions. During warmer weather, you may dine alfresco on the stunning terrace. The menu at Wisteria offers entrées that are as stylish and varied as the atmosphere, including signature items such as the four cities shrimp and brie cigars, which are deep-fried phyllo-wrapped brie served with a raspberry dip. Wisteria also pays homage to the time-honored tradition of a formal afternoon tea with all of your favorites like scones served with clotted cream and crustless finger sandwiches. Wisteria is the perfect place to entertain a small group of friends or stage an intimate bridal shower. Enjoy a dining experience that's unparalleled at Wisteria.

1658 Pleasure House Road (Thoroughgood Commons), Virginia Beach VA
(757) 216-2900
www.wisteriarestaurant.com

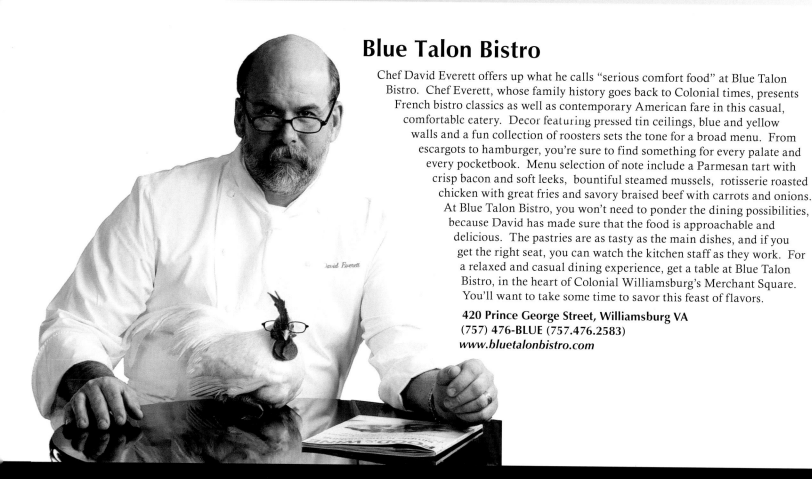

Blue Talon Bistro

Chef David Everett offers up what he calls "serious comfort food" at Blue Talon Bistro. Chef Everett, whose family history goes back to Colonial times, presents French bistro classics as well as contemporary American fare in this casual, comfortable eatery. Decor featuring pressed tin ceilings, blue and yellow walls and a fun collection of roosters sets the tone for a broad menu. From escargots to hamburger, you're sure to find something for every palate and every pocketbook. Menu selection of note include a Parmesan tart with crisp bacon and soft leeks, bountiful steamed mussels, rotisserie roasted chicken with great fries and savory braised beef with carrots and onions. At Blue Talon Bistro, you won't need to ponder the dining possibilities, because David has made sure that the food is approachable and delicious. The pastries are as tasty as the main dishes, and if you get the right seat, you can watch the kitchen staff as they work. For a relaxed and casual dining experience, get a table at Blue Talon Bistro, in the heart of Colonial Williamsburg's Merchant Square. You'll want to take some time to savor this feast of flavors.

420 Prince George Street, Williamsburg VA
(757) 476-BLUE (757.476.2583)
www.bluetalonbistro.com

Rockafeller's

Rockafeller's of Virginia Beach offers casual dining with a magnificent view overlooking the majestic Rudee Inlet. This popular eatery features the freshest, highest quality seafood, steaks and pasta dishes available along with a fabulous selection of signature homemade desserts. Rockafeller's opened in 1990 under the late veteran restaurateur Frank Baumann, who envisioned a casual, comfortable restaurant that focused on delicious, high-quality cuisine. His wife, BJ Henley-Baumann took over in 1999 and succeeded in making their vision a reality and has gone on to receive numerous awards including the Women in Business award given by *Inside Business* in 2003. During Virginia Beach's National Tourism Week Awards Luncheon, Rockafeller's received a record of three awards for service and hospitality. The nonchalant yet colorful décor gives Rockafeller's the appearance and ambiance of a beachfront summer home and is as warm and inviting and the food is delicious. Daily specials feature regional classics that have made Rockafeller's a destination for locals and tourists alike and the indoor and outdoor seating options allow guests to enjoy the best of Virginia's beautiful seasons. Whether you prefer to relax in the wooden rockers on the porch while sipping a cocktail or bask in the cozy atmosphere of the main dining room, you are sure to enjoy the incredible entrées and exemplary service that await you. Enjoy a perfect dining experience highlighted by impeccable service and extraordinarily divine cuisine at Rockafeller's.

308 Mediterranean Avenue,
Virginia Beach VA
(757) 422-5654
www.rockafellers.com

Seasons of Williamsburg

Just as each season of the year brings its own set of sights, sounds and smells, Seasons of Williamsburg captures the beauty of each season with quality gift items and fresh floral designs. Since 1991, Seasons of Williamsburg has been accessorizing homes and gardens with classic touches of lamps, mirrors, prints, containers, seasonal décor and custom silk floral arrangements. A recent addition to the mix has been a wonderful collection of vintage and antique silver, china, glass and estate linens. Owners Kent Harrell and Kendall Kerby and their seasoned staff pride themselves on the personal attention they give their customers, which has earned them a loyal following from local residents and visitors. A visit to Seasons of Williamsburg is a delight that begins with the easy parking and continues with the large selection of flowers, gifts and accessories. A November open house rings in the holiday season by transforming the shop into a Christmas wonderland. Seasons of Williamsburg moved to its present location in 2000. The building has all the modern amenities, but is constructed in a classic styling that makes it look as though it were a longtime Williamsburg fixture. A stop into Seasons of Williamsburg embraces each customer with year-round beauty.

1308 Jamestown Road, Williamsburg VA
(757) 565-4600
http://theseasonsofwilliamsburg.com

Le Yaca French Restaurant

Le Yaca French Restaurant in Williamsburg has changed owners and crossed the sea, but remains as charming and French as ever. When Danielle Bourderau and her husband, Gerard, decided to open a restaurant in a tiny village in the French Alps, friends said people would not drive eight kilometers over icy winter roads for dinner. After three months of indecision, they finally said, "Yaca le faire," which basically means *let's do it.* They called their restaurant Le Yaca as a gag. Guests from the nearby ski resort at Courchevel came because of the whimsical name, but came back for the excellent food. Danielle and Gerard opened a second Yaca in St. Tropez for the summer season and a third location in Williamsburg in December 1980. In 1989, Danielle sold the Williamsburg Le Yaca to Jane Dunston, a family friend. In 2001, Daniel Abid, one of the original chefs at Williamsburg, bought the restaurant with his wife, Joy Anderson Abid. Trained by some of the best chefs in the world, Abid prepares authentic French food that looks beautiful on the plate and tastes even better. Savory entrées include whole duck breast with black truffle sauce and succulent leg of lamb with rosemary garlic sauce. Le Yaca's signature dessert, Marquis au Chocolat, pairs dense chocolate truffle with French vanilla bean sauce. Everything about Le Yaca is first-rate, from the exceptional wine list to the attentive service and intimate atmosphere. To experience French cuisine at its finest, make a reservation at Le Yaca.

1915 Pocahontas Trail, Williamsburg VA (757) 220-3616

Stephanos Pizza and Subs

Put several favorite categories of comfort food together at one location, and the result is Stephanos Pizza and Subs, a quick, easy and inexpensive meal option in Colonial Williamsburg. Stephanos is somewhat more upscale than a traditional pizzeria, but it is still comfortable and casual. Several big screen televisions throughout the restaurant create the feel of a sports bar. Stephanos sells large wedges of its New York style pizza by the slice. House pizzas include Thai chicken and the Mediterranean, with feta and other cheeses, pesto and fresh spinach. Stephanos also serves subs, including a club sub, a popular Italian sub and an oven-baked cheese and steak sub. You can change any sub into a wrap and fill out your order with chicken wings, salad and coleslaw. Beer and wine are available. You can dine in or carry out; either way, Stephanos guarantees fast service. Stephanos Pizza and Subs is located next to Seasons Restaurant, a first-class restaurant under the same ownership and management as Stephanos. The two restaurants differ in style and atmosphere, but both offer great food. Stop by Stephanos Pizza and Subs for fast food with extraordinary flavor and choices in Colonial Williamsburg.

110 S Henry Street, Williamsburg VA
(757) 476-8999
www.stephanospizza.com

Old Chickahominy House

Old Chickahominy House features authentic Southern fare, and locals and visitors alike come for the house specialties as well as the 18th century charm and hospitality of owners Melinda Barbour and Maxine Williams. If you visit in the morning, you must have Virginia country ham from Virginia's own Wallace Edwards. The Plantation Breakfast is a favorite way to try the ham, but if you prefer something simpler, you can order the ham with two eggs and biscuits. The Virginia flat biscuits are designed to complement the ham, although you can also enjoy them with jam. At lunch, try Miss Melinda's Special, which adds a cup of famous Chickahominy House Brunswick stew and a fruit salad to the ham and biscuits. Chicken and dumplings are popular, and buttermilk pie is Melinda and Maxine's signature dessert. Resident house cat Mr. Biscuit has been greeting customers for more than 15 years and is probably the most famous and best loved animal in Williamsburg. You can most likely find him napping in the gift shop. The Old Chickahominy gift shop is actually larger than the restaurant and contains antiques, handwoven placemats and other unique gifts. The ham and specialty foods are available to buy and ship. For hospitality and food in the Southern tradition, visit the Old Chickahominy House.

1211 Jamestown Road, Williamsburg VA
(757) 229-4689

Carrot Tree Kitchens

An enthusiastic love of cooking and a lack of shortcuts are at the heart of Carrot Tree Kitchens. Owners Debi and Glenn Helseth treat their customers to cakes and breads, sandwiches and soups that are made from scratch with garden-grown herbs and vegetables. The restaurant specializes in baked goods and continues to make a superior carrot cake. In 1984, Debi was challenged by a restaurant owner to produce a carrot cake to beat what he was serving. She called her grandmother at midnight for the family recipe, then baked until 3 am. The cake was delicious, and her cooking adventures continued. Debi wore out several home ovens and turned a garage into a commercial kitchen before opening the Jamestown Road Carrot Tree Kitchens in 1995. Debi's baking and all of Chef Gabe Walker's food preparation are done at the Williamburg location. Customers can enjoy the delicious results there or at Carrot Tree's second location, in the circa 1720 Cole Digges House in Yorktown. Carrot Tree Kitchens treats its guests to freshly made Brunswick stew, ham biscuits, tomato basil soup, carrot tea sandwiches and its regionally renowned crab cakes. Breads, cakes, pastries and all sorts of baked dessert items remain popular

reasons to visit Carrot Tree. The restaurant also offers custom wedding cakes and catering services. Enjoy a meal or a snack in the café or out on the terrace. Anyway you slice it, you'll love eating at Carrot Tree Kitchens.

1782 Jamestown Road, Williamsburg VA
(757) 229-0957
411 E Main Street, Yorktown VA
(757) 246-9559

The Whaling Company

After a long day of touring Colonial Williamsburg or Busch Gardens, stop in at the Whaling Company to refresh your spirits and energy levels with fresh seafood in an old New England style boathouse. Expect a casual atmosphere with impeccable service and delicious fare that suits many tastes. Owner Steve York has spent the past 25 years operating the Whaling Company, and Chef Tony has been invaluable for making fresh, delectable cuisine a reliable standard here. Begin your dining experience with the hot and spicy shrimp or crab cakes made from jumbo lump crabmeat and fried to perfection. Seasonal vegetables and fresh baked bread complete such dinner entrées as Virginia sea scallops baked in garlic butter or the cornmeal-breaded North Carolina farm raised catfish. Such delicacies as South African lobster tail, steamed in the shell and served with drawn butter, Alaskan king crab and traditional steaks served with whiskey peppercorn sauce will satisfy even the hardiest of appetites. Save room for the tempting homemade desserts, brought to

your table for individual selection. The Whaling Company welcomes larger groups for banquet style luncheons and dinners and offers several packages for tour groups. Sail into the Whaling Company for a whale of a good seafood or fresh water fish experience.

494 McLaws Circle, Williamsburg VA
(757) 229-0275
www.thewhalingcompany.com

Second Street An American Bistro

A good rule of thumb when dining out is to eat where the locals do. For more than 20 years Second Street Restaurant and Tavern in Williamsburg has been the place where the locals gather and visitors turn into regulars. Owners Mickey and John Chohany are very passionate about what they do, and their dedication shows. They see themselves not simply as order takers, but helpful food consultants who want your meal to be unforgettable. Many of their staff members have been working at Second Street for years, and know the secrets of offering a superior dining experience. Second Street specializes in hearty All-American cuisine that includes seafood, poultry, beef and pasta. Virginia Gazette readers have voted Second Street home of Williamsburg's best burger ever since the voting began. The restaurant features plenty of room for large groups and bus tours, and the menu offerings are designed to get you back to your vacation quickly without breaking your budget. Beers and microbrews are popular tavern offerings. Second Street also can cater an event on your street. Enjoy Second Street's old-fashioned comfort food in two convenient locations, just blocks from the historic district and in Newport News. Visit Second Street, where the locals turn for generous portions of their favorite fare.

140 2nd Street, Williamsburg VA
(757) 220-2286
115 Arthur Way, Newport News VA
(757) 872-7887
www.secondst.com

A Chef's Kitchen

Come and experience performance art that you can eat! A Chef's Kitchen in Williamsburg is a one-of-a-kind interactive cooking class and dining establishment rolled into one. The dining room itself is set up very much like a television studio cooking show. Top chefs prepare hors d'oeuvres and five delectable courses, including a sumptuous dessert, and then they serve it to you, the audience. Champagne and wine selections are carefully chosen for their quality, value and ability to complement the cuisine. The menus at A Chef's Kitchen change frequently and feature fresh seasonal ingredients. The chefs gladly answer questions and keep a friendly and relaxed tone, which makes the evening entertaining and informative. After dinner, be sure to visit the retail store to take home some wines that A Chef's Kitchen recommends as "great finds." This is the restaurant's name for inexpensive wines that have received national recognition. A Chef's Kitchen also offers a best-selling cookbook by owner and Executive Chef John Gonzales plus cooking gadgets of every description. John is a graduate of the Culinary Institute of America with 30 years of professional experience, including executive chef positions at Washington D.C.'s Watergate and Ritz Carlton Hotels. He has been featured on HGTV, the Discovery Channel, the Fox network and NBC's morning show. He's also been a guest speaker on nationally syndicated radio. Hampton Roads Magazine voted A Chef's Kitchen one of the top 50 restaurants in the region. Be sure to include A Chef's Kitchen in your Williamsburg experience.

501 Price George Street, Suite 102, Williamsburg VA
(757) 564-8500
www.achefskitchen.biz

Indian Fields Tavern

Indian Fields Tavern meets the requirements of travelers looking for some place distinctive to eat lunch while visiting the plantations or while driving to Williamsburg. At dinner, it becomes many people's special occasion restaurant, a destination out in the country that guarantees a fine meal. *Bon Appétit* and *Gourmet* magazines have praised the quality of the regional dining experience that owner Erich von Gehren and his team offer. The location is halfway between Williamsburg and Richmond on Route 5. The setting is a restored 1890s farmhouse with a porch overlooking the rural landscape. The fare is innovative Virginia cuisine that relies upon local seafood and seasonal produce. Although the menu changes to reflect what is fresh at the moment, mainstays include the signature jumbo crab cakes served with ham and hollandaise, called Crabcakes Harrison, as well the Angus filet mignon medallions, called Steak Lyons Den. Indian Fields Tavern takes its name from a fascinating piece of Virginia history. After Christopher Newport landed on the *Susan Constant*, he led his charges along the Indian trails, where they came to this spot. On it, they viewed the first corn that they had ever seen, which was being grown by Native American farmers. No doubt it filled them with curiosity and made them more than just a little hungry. Don't be surprised if you react the same way to the menu at Indian Fields Tavern.

9220 John Tyler Memorial Highway, Charles City VA
(804) 829-5004
www.indianfields.com

Shopping & Antiques

Freckled Fox, LTD

Are you looking for a unique store that caters to the cutting edge shopper? The Freckled Fox has it all, with home and garden accessories with a distinctive European flavor, great gifts and wonderful permanent florals by the stem or arrangement. Only five blocks from the ocean front at the end of route 264, the Freckled Fox is on the corner of 21st and Cyprus Streets. This shop has a helpful and knowledgeable staff, managed by Katherine Grones, who can guide you through choices compatible with your home décor. Floral Designers Becky Lockery and Molly Rueger do floral designs with floral buyer Lynda Briggs for the home and for commercial businesses. The president of the Freckled Fox, Kaye Taylor, and the vice president, secretary and treasurer, Jan Fine, focus on leading in trends and having versatile product styles. In short, the owners and staff of the Freckled Fox are in business to serve you, so visit the shop and see how they can improve your home or office.

700 21st Street, Virginia Beach VA
(757) 422-3045

Camelot Bears of Williamsburg

Enter the Camelot castle of Tom "Lancelot" and Pam "Guinevere" Jones for an unusual visit with thousands of bears. Camelot Bears of Williamsburg devotes separate chambers to four of the eight bear species. There is also an area for koala Bears, even though they are not really bears, and a large section in the back of the store promotes the ninth species: the Teddy Bear. You'll find apparel, books, collectibles, plush toys and home decor items for each bear. Steiff, Hatley, Gund, Russ, and Ditz are some of the most popular brand names. Camelot Bears is dedicated to the preservation of bears worldwide, and visitors can view display boards and watch an educational DVD presentation on a large plasma television to learn about bears and their plight in today's world. Expect a friendly greeting from the Grizzly-size ExcaliBear, and choose from a huge selection of bears and outfits in the Make-A-Bear section. Bear parties are popular for birthdays and the store offers special rates to groups making bears for charities. Camelot's party room allows groups to bring in refreshments. Expect a group photograph and a bear hug from a costumed bear named King Arthur, often seen tossing out souvenir bears at William and Mary ball games. The Camelot Bears website is filled with bear facts and brings a new dimension to shopping for bear-related products. Let the world's bears and the beautiful products that honor them capture your heart at Camelot Bears of Williamsburg.

3044-106 Richmond Road (Patriot Plaza), Williamsburg VA
(757) 565-9060
www.camelotbears.com

Stars and Stripes Forever

It is fitting that Williamsburg should be home to one of America's foremost patriotic stores. Stars and Stripes Forever exists to promote a sense of patriotism and appreciation for the United States through merchandise with patriotic, political and military themes. Owner Robin McNamara encourages others to value American history and patriotism through the products she selects. Robin started this store in 1995 with the aim of including finer items she could not find in other patriotic stores across the country. Many of the products are custom-made and are of heirloom quality, perfect as gifts for family or business clients. The classy product line includes home décor, artwork, jewelry, clothing and stationary. When you visit this store, the main thing you will notice is the excellent customer service and the environment. The staff is always happy to order anything you don't find in stock, and the ambiance is purely patriotic. A model of the American Freedom Train charges through the store, and Uncle Sam interacts with customers as they shop at the Yorktown store location. The most popular items at Stars and Stripes Forever are the fine art prints and artwork. Visit Stars and Stripes Forever at either location, and you will likely remain a customer for life and find yourself inspired by the patriotic products available for display in your home or office.

3044 Richmond Road, Suite 101, Williamsburg VA
(757) 565-7827
Water Street, Riverwalk Landing, Yorktown VA
(757) 898-0288
www.starsandstripesforever.us

Mrs. Bones Boutique

Paris Hilton isn't the only person who likes to spoil her dog, located here in Virginia Beach is the original Mrs. Bones Boutique retail location, frequented by numerous celebrities who like to spoil their pets. Mary Alexander, owner of Mrs. Bones Boutique, could give Hilton a run for her money. Her high-end pet boutique offers a plethora of fashionable accessories and clothing to pamper your favorite pup. For instance, there are seven different lines of collars, from the Scottish tartan-inspired International Collection to the tasteful designs of the Masterpiece Collection. Each is fully lined and has sturdy, solid brass hardware. For extra pizzazz, add a charm featuring Swarovski crystals in the shape of a heart, butterfly, star or dozens of other custom designs. You can choose your favorite color velvet leash, a Mrs. Bones couture T-shirt and a set of matching LilybootsT to finish off the ensemble. Your dog will be the talk of the town. Mrs. Bones Boutique is more than just clothing and collars, however, you will find car seats, strollers, plush beds and stylish carriers as well. There is also a quality health and beauty section to keep you furry friend looking and feeling its healthiest. You'll also be hard-pressed to find more intricate, royalty-worthy dog bowls than the choices here. To help show off your love of man's best friend, they also offer retro and giclee prints, dog-shaped handbags and glass ornaments. If you're a sophisticated dog lover with discriminating taste, take your dog on a walk through Mrs. Bones Boutique.

1616 Hilltop W Shopping Center, Virginia Beach VA
(877) 767-1308 or (757) 412-0500
www.mrsbones.com

Mansion House Art and Antiques

The charm of a bygone era combined with the elegance of Victorian times is the ticket to a perfect getaway at the Mansion on Main bed and breakfast, located in Smithfield's beautiful historic district. Guests can choose from three exceptionally furnished rooms plus an optional adjoining room to the Master Suite. A stay at Mansion on Main is a journey back to the style and grace of the past and manager Dawn Riddle invites you to make yourself

at home amongst stunning antique furnishings and classic décor. In addition to its distinctive overnight accommodations complete with a home cooked breakfast buffet, Mansion on Main can also play host to intimate gatherings such as weddings, group meetings or even a children's birthday tea party complete with a costumed hostess. Mansion on Main holds the distinct honor of being the first "painted lady" in Smithfield, meaning it was the first Victorian home in the area to proudly showcase a multi-colored paint job. Mansion on Main is located in the heart of Smithfield and within original colonial limits. Right next door is Mansion House Art and Antiques, a beautifully restored Victorian treasure that is home to a wide variety of original oil paintings ranging from the 1800's to the mid 1950's, estate jewelry including Victorian mourning pieces, and porcelain and glass collectibles such as Royal Dalton, Lladro and Waterford. Owner Betty Clark also offers a pattern matching service for sterling flatware, plus painting restoration. Betty credits her daughter Marie with much of the restoration work on Mansion House and with her determination to preserve the integrity of the renovation by using the original Victorian color scheme. Sadly, Marie passed away in April of 1998 at the age of twenty-six. Mansion House's quality collection of antiques and art rivals what could be found in major metropolitan areas. In fact, dealers often purchase items here and then sell them at inflated prices in the larger cities. The highways or the waterways lead to straight to Mansion on Main and Mansion House. Neither should be missed.

36 Main Street, Smithfield Virginia (757)357-0006 *www.mansion-on-main.net*
120 North Church Street, Smithfield Virginia (757)357-3968 *www.mansiongallery.net*

Seasons of Williamsburg

Just as each season of the year brings its own set of sights, sounds and smells, Seasons of Williamsburg captures the beauty of each season with quality gift items and fresh floral designs. Since 1991, Seasons of Williamsburg has been accessorizing homes and gardens with classic touches of lamps, mirrors, prints, containers, seasonal décor and custom silk floral arrangements. A recent addition to the mix has been a wonderful collection of vintage and antique silver, china, glass and estate linens. Owners Kent Harrell and Kendall Kerby and their seasoned staff pride themselves on the personal attention they give their customers, which has earned them a loyal following from local residents and visitors. A visit to Seasons of Williamsburg is a delight that begins with the easy parking and continues with the large selection of flowers, gifts and accessories. A November open house rings in the holiday season by transforming the shop into a Christmas wonderland. Seasons of Williamsburg moved to its present location in 2000. The building has all the modern amenities, but is constructed in a classic styling that makes it look as though it were a longtime Williamsburg fixture. A stop into Seasons of Williamsburg embraces each customer with year-round beauty.

1308 Jamestown Road, Williamsburg VA
(757) 565-4600
http://theseasonsofwilliamsburg.com

The Mole Hole

For a little bit of everything you could imagine in gifts and collectibles, Williamsburg residents turn to the Mole Hole. Regina Petit and her behind-the-scenes guy, David, go out of their way to stock surprising specialty gifts. They recognize repeat customers, provide local delivery and a free gift wrap service. They deal with over 400 vendors to stock the Mole Hole, one of the many reasons Williamsburg residents have voted the Mole Hole the best locally owned gift store in Williamsburg. Regina and David also have two other locations, one at The Williamsburg Hospitality House and the other in Newport News. Merchandise at the Mole Hole includes Swarovski crystal, Italian music boxes and collectibles by Wee Forest Folk, limited edition figurines adored by mouse lovers everywhere. You'll also find candles, handmade jewelry and wonderful ladies apparel. If you're looking for collectible dolls or precision clocks and kaleidoscopes, the Mole Hole is the place to come. Regina can also help you choose a custom designed wreath, wedding gift or picture frame, because her goal is to meet and exceed her customers' expectations. By offering charm, service and unique quality gifts, the Mole Hole is one of Williamsburg's true treasures and a sure bet for finding a gift that will be treasured.

4680 Monticello Avenue, Suite 18C, Williamsburg VA
(757) 220-8609

The Silver Vault

The Silver Vault, which opened in Colonial Williamsburg's Merchants Square in 1976, was a mere tot compared to the large store that exists there today. Having branched out beyond the original focus of silver hollowware, tableware and jewelry, the 21st century version of The Silver Vault has a dazzling array with a larger collection of jewelry and additional choices for formal entertaining and casual dining. From a simple sterling bracelet or chain, to an eye-catching necklace, this shop has items in every price range. You will find jewelry with semi-precious and precious stones. Beautiful sterling baby gifts are also a specialty. Top your selection off with either hand or machine engraving for the personal touch and with free gift wrapping you will have an exceptional gift. For your most memorable occasions, be it a wedding, family reunion, a commemorative birthday, or a retirement gift, choose from a large selection of trays that you and your guests can sign. The Silver Vault will loan you one of their engraving pens for the event; it truly makes a memorable presentation. Have you ever wondered what to do with a silver family heirloom that needs tender loving care? Take it to The Silver Vault's twice yearly Silver Clinic for repair. Services such as this and their bridal registry are what make this shop so distinctive. When a business grows through the years, it sometimes loses the personal touch, this has not happened with this Williamsburg favorite. Find full service shopping for beautiful gifts when you visit The Silver Vault.

416 Duke of Gloucester Street, Williamsburg VA
(757) 220-3777
dwk03@cox.net

Photos by Bob Oller

Nectar

Enrich yourself and your home with the treasures, gifts and home décor pieces that can be found at Nectar, located on Hilltop West in the heart of Virginia Beach's premier shopping district. Owner and entrepreneur Susan Renee Lloyd opened the business in 2003 after leaving a career in social work. A resident of Virginia Beach for more than 20 years, she felt that the store would be an ideal addition to her neighborhood's favorite shopping destination and regards her shop as nourishment for you and your home. Nectar offers patrons a wide selection of incredible products that are hand selected to pamper both you and your environment. Here you can find a full selection of candles by Votivo, Trapp and Archipelago along with fabulous purses and accessories. Nectar also carries Palecek Furniture as well as bath and body supplies. Located less than three miles from Chesapeake Bay, Nectar pays homage to the sea with a wide variety of nautical and travel oriented gifts such as maritime and aviation themed signs and plaques, vintage travel posters and the musical strains of Louis Armstrong's *C'est Si Bon* rising up joyfully from the radio. Lloyd further offers a fine selection of infant accessories and toddler gifts that are ideal for baby showers and birthdays. Whatever the reason, nourish yourself and your loved ones with inspiring and exciting gifts and accessories from Nectar.

1614 Hilltop W Executive Center, Virginia Beach VA
(757) 422-5400

Laura & Lucy's

Exquisite junk is the term that Laura uses to describe the merchandise at Laura & Lucy's. Here you will find an eclectic variety of old merchandise, including antiques. Laura and Bob Redlin opened Laura & Lucy's in 1998, fulfilling Laura's lifelong dream of having a retail store and providing something for everyone at a fair price. The name Lucy came from the family dog who is a mixed breed, but mostly Beagle, even though she looks like a miniature lab. Bob was a career Marine and when the Redlins retired to Smithfield, they purchased a residential duplex on Main Street to serve as their storefront. The 3,000-square-foot house was built in 1902. The Redlins renovated the property and painted it green to match the color of the lawn in the town's seal. The store has a library room which is filled with old books for sale. Guests are invited to take their time browsing through the numerous volumes. The store also has a garden room and a kitchen room. The rest of the house is filled with china, linens, sterling pieces, chandeliers, glassware, old jewelry, vintage clothing, furniture and other home accent items. Smithfield offers many shops, but Laura & Lucy's is the only one for exquisite items at affordable prices.

333 Main Street, Smithfield VA
(757) 357-2068

Mermaid Books

In Merchant's Square of Colonial Williamsburg, Aurise Eaton has gathered new and used books, antiques and her collection of mermaids to create Mermaid Books. Many people love the smell and feel of old books, and Aurise admits she's one of those who does. A former teacher, she started the shop for selfish reasons, yet it has become a way for her to share her passion for books, ephemera and mermaids. A bookstore has existed in this location since the 1970s, and Aurise carries on the tradition of helping people find the particular book they are seeking. Nonetheless, browsing, with nothing particular in mind, might be the most fun way to shop at Mermaid Books. You may leave with a book or two you really wanted, even though you were unaware of the desire when you walked into the shop. Non-bookworms will be enticed by the many shelves of collectibles. Most people who come into Mermaid Books happen upon it by chance when visiting Merchant's Square. It is off the beaten path, around the corner and down the stairs, but it is the best place to find first editions, comic books, children's books and postcards. Venture into Mermaid Books for new and old books, collectibles and, of course, mermaids.

421-A Prince George Street, Willliamsburg VA
(757) 229-3603
www.mermaidbookswilliamsburg.com

Williamsburg General Store

The Williamsburg General Store offers 6,500 square feet of quality gifts, collectibles and souvenirs. It features Williamsburg's only full service Häagen-Dazs ice cream shop, where you can indulge while shopping. You're free to take it easy in an Adirondack chair on the wraparound covered porch. Relaxation is the byword at the Williamsburg General Store. Inside, you'll find T-shirts, hats and toys. The shop specializes in homemade gourmet candy. An electric penny presser can provide you with an ultra-cheap keepsake. If your tastes run a bit more upscale, the store has costume jewelry and sterling silver items. It stocks home décor products from vendors such as Russ and Ganz. There's a Lang products center that displays boxes, calendars and note cards. In season, the shop offers Christmas cards and merchandise, and candles are on display any time of the year. Most evenings, this Williamsburg attraction features live fife and drum performances. Sam Jr. and Cabell Wallace manage the Williamsburg General Store, the culmination of the Wallace family's retail experience dating back to 1920. They want you to tell everyone about your great experience at their store. Come to the Williamsburg General Store and take home a little piece of America.

1656 Richmond Road, Williamsburg VA
(757) 564-5800
(757) 564-5990 (Häagen-Dazs)
www.williamsburggeneralstore.com

The Christmas Shop

The Christmas Shop in Merchants Square, Williamsburg's oldest Christmas store, specializes in unusual and collectible Christmas merchandise. Come see handcrafted ornaments, as well as your favorite collectibles. The Christmas Shop offers new and traditional merchandise, including European items and dated Williamsburg ornaments. You'll Find Byer's Choice goods and collectible lines such as the Cat's Meow, Anri and Sheila's. Scores of Santas and snowmen are ready to charm you. You'll have no trouble finding an angel for the angel lover on your list, although with so many celestial creatures to choose from, you might have some trouble making a decision. At the Christmas Shop, the inventory changes constantly. You'll see attention to detail everywhere and enjoy quality customer service. Each year, families bring out the ornaments to decorate their tree. Often, each ornament has its own story. The ornaments you purchase at the Christmas Shop will remind you of your visit to Williamsburg and may inspire you to return. Sam Jr. and Cabell Wallace, proprietors of the Christmas Shop, invite you to stop by the next time you're in Williamsburg and pick out a new family heirloom.

405 Duke of Gloucester Street, Williamsburg VA
(757) 229-2514
www.christmasshopwilliamsburg.com

Antiques Emporium of Smithfield

Since 1995 Trey Gwaltney, Owner of Antiques Emporium of Smithfield, has been providing area citizens with fabulous antiques in a venue filled with fun, whimsy and wonder. Antiques Emporium of Smithfield is housed inside of a historic brick building that was the home of the Delk's Department Store for 103 years. After purchasing the building in 2001, Trey restored it to the late-Victorian period, retaining the Lamson Air-Line Cash System that had been installed more than 100 years before. Antiques Emporium now encompasses more than 5,000 square feet and offers a plethora of antiques contributed by more than 50 dealers. Whether you are new to the world of antiques or are a dyed-in-the-wool collector, you will find this open and inviting antiques shop to be the ideal place to find all of the treasures you never knew you needed. At any given time you are likely to find silver and china pieces, vintage jewelry, dolls and linens or period tools and timepieces. They also carry books, paintings and collectable coins as well as just about anything else you could desire. Another delightful addition to this wonderful shop is the quarterly newsletter, Antiques Emporium of Smithfield Gazetteer, featuring updates from Trey, great articles about the town along with listing of upcoming events and terrific commentary from area residents. Make new memories for yourself or a loved one with the treasures of yesterday that await you at Antiques Emporium of Smithfield.

223 Main Street, Smithfield VA
(757) 357-3304
www.shopsmithfield.com

Southern Virginia

Accommodations

Cooper's Landing Inn & Traveler's Tavern

Located in the heart of historic downtown Clarksville, Cooper's Landing Inn & Traveler's Tavern is an historical gem that promises a refreshing vacation from life as usual. Nichol and Les Cooper opened the inn in 2004, after completing extensive renovations on the 1830s house. Expect Southern hospitality and gourmet seasonal fare here, along with four, well appointed and romantic guestrooms, each with a patio, a fireplace and either a claw foot or Jacuzzi soaking tub in the master bathroom. Enjoy breakfast from your room or in the sunroom downstairs, then take a stroll around the grounds, the town of Clarksville or to Kerr Lake, eight blocks away, for an afternoon of boating or hiking. Before you leave, pick up a gourmet picnic basket, prepared by Chef Les. Dinner will be waiting when you return with casual fine dining in one of three formal dining rooms or outdoors, under the trellis. On Friday nights in summer, you can dine under the stars and listen to live music on an outdoor patio. Enjoy fresh seafood, hand-cut black Angus beef or wild game, carefully prepared with locally grown vegetables and complemented by wines from the inn's cellar. End your day with a soak in the Cooper's Springs hot tub, located in a restored smokehouse. Cooper's Landing is an excellent location for a wedding or special event, and Nichol can help with planning details. Nichol and Les invite you to Cooper's Landing Inn & Traveler's Tavern, where Southern charm allows you to relax in comfort and style.

801 Virginia Avenue, Clarksville VA
(434) 374-2866
www.cooperslandinginn.com

Three Angels Inn

Three Angels Inn at Sherwood may be named for the owner's three daughters, but it's not the first time the historic building had such a heavenly presence. In the wake of the Civil War, Pattie Buford, a white plantation owner, saw the vast, urgent, unfulfilled basic needs of the newly freed African Americans. Those needs covered the spectrum of basic social services, including food, housing, education and medical care. In 1867, driven by her Christian compassion for these people, Pattie set aside 20 acres of her land in Brunswick County Virginia and began a work to provide those needs. It began as a church/school for the children of freed slaves. Almost immediately, an orphanage was added, as many children did not know where their parents were or had been left behind by family that went looking for work in the cities. Following soon after were facilities for the elderly and the mentally ill. Still, in Pattie's mind, there was more to do. She traveled north and raised funds from wealthy friends and the Episcopal Church to build a hospital for these needy people. In 1883, her vision was fulfilled in the construction, staffing and operation of the hospital. It was known as the Church Home for the Aged, Infirm and Disabled Colored People. It continued to serve the community in this manner for 35 years. Today, it is on the National Register of Historic Places, Virginia Landmarks Register and one of the many stops on Virginia's Civil Rights in Education Heritage Trail. Thanks to two ex-missionaries, Pat and Tom Krewson, it is still a place to find solace and respite. After serving as missionaries in Swaziland, they found this beautiful, Victorian-style hospital-turned-farmhouse on the former Sherwood Plantation and transformed it into a classy, comfortable bed and breakfast. The setting is in the midst of 65 acres of rolling hills of woods and pasture peppered with large oak trees, where peace and quiet are virtually guaranteed. Each room is named for the Krewsons' three daughters and seven grandchildren. The house features wonderful period furniture and artifacts and each guest room has its own private bath and fireplace with gas logs. Breakfast is served in one of two dining rooms and dinner is also available. Come while away the day and rejuvenate at Three Angels Inn at Sherwood.

236 Pleasant Grove Road, Lawrenceville VA
(434) 848-0830
www.threeangelsinn.com

Brunswick Mineral Springs, c. 1785

Get off the interstate, throw away your AAA Tour Book and focus on relaxation. At Brunswick Mineral Springs, time treads very lightly. Brunswick Mineral Springs, Brunswick County's oldest bed and breakfast, was built in 1785. Owners David and Nanette Spears spent two solid years carefully restoring all three floors of the main house and triumphantly opened in 1997. Their extensive renovations created a beautiful bed-and-breakfast that exudes old-fashioned tranquility while providing modern comforts. You can be as pampered or as active as you wish. Whatever your needs are, David and Nanette want to make sure you enjoy yourself. You can choose from three upstairs suites or the colonial hospitality cottage, all with private baths and sumptuously decorated with antiques. Just added is a 20 by 40 foot heated, indoor swimming pool. Well-behaved dogs are welcome, too, as David and Nanette have three of their own that help show guests around the property. Nanette's Southern home cooking alone brings people back year after year. You can take a walk under old oak and magnolia trees, sip sweet tea on the porch rocker or lie in a hammock and enjoy the scenery. If you're feeling more energetic, three lakes are a short drive away and offer clear, fresh water for swimming, fishing or just a place to dangle your feet in the water and daydream. David and Nanette enjoy their guests, and touching people's lives is what they love the most. So come and enjoy real Southern hospitality at Brunswick Mineral Springs.

14910 Western Mill Road, Lawrenceville VA
(434) 848-4010 or (888) 723-7567
www.brunswickmineralsprings.com

Attractions

The Virginia Peanut Festival

Once considered a food for the poor, the peanut has changed the face of Virginia and, in turn, the eating habits of the entire country. For 44 years, Emporia has been celebrating the Virginia peanut and its contributions to the Virginia economy and lifestyle with the annual Virginia Peanut Festival, four days of festivities set for early fall. Expect plenty of food, crafts and music, not to mention games and pony rides for children, a parade, fireworks and numerous exhibits. There is also a carnival, antique farm equipment and the largest car show in Southside Virginia. The first commercial peanuts in Virginia were harvested in the mid-1800s and soldiers from both the Union and Confederate armies relied on the durable, nutritious crop during the Civil War. Harvesting peanuts from the soil was a slow and dirty job until the advent of labor saving farm devices at the turn of the century. This combined with the arrival of the boll weevil and the devastation of the Southern cotton crop in the early 1900s gave Virginia good reasons to grow peanuts and to change the public image of the lowly peanut, a move that has created a multimillion dollar industry in Virginia with over 3,000 peanut farms producing upwards of 250 million pounds of peanuts every year. Celebrate roasted and salted peanuts, peanut candy, peanut oil, peanut butter and the many ways that peanuts are deeply woven into the fabric of Virginia life. As the weather cools and the crops come in, Emporia invites you to come to The Virginia Peanut Festival.

South Main Street (Veterans Memorial Park), Emporia VA
(434) 348-4219
kcallahan@courts.state.va.us

VIRginia International Raceway

Experience the energy and excitement of world-class motersports while enjoying luxurious resort amenities at VIRginia International Raceway. VIR originally opened in 1957, with many of America's most renowned drivers competing on the 3.27-mile road racing circuit nestled among 1,200 acres of rolling hills and meadows alongside the Dan River. After it closed in 1974, the track sat vacant for more than 20 years until real estate developer Harvey Siegel purchased the land in 1998. The vision of Siegel and partner Connie Nyholm went far beyond simply reopening the track, he developed a luxury destination resort centered around motorsports. VIR reopened in 2000, this time with first-class amenities for the racing enthusiast. The view overlooking the racetrack from the comfortable rooms of The Lodge or the Paddock Suites ensures you never miss a minute of the excitement. The VIR Motorsports Country Club, headquartered in a renovated 1840s plantation house, offers dining at the Oak Tree Tavern, which serves such mouthwatering entrees as Carolina crab cakes and grilled Angus burgers, or drinks and light snacks at Connie's Pub. Revisit the tracks storied history and enjoy historic racing cars at the VIR Gallery. Browse the Pro Shop for unique souvenirs and racing accessories. The Plantation Valley Kart Track allows you to sharpen your racing skills on a paved 5.8-mile track. Visit VIRginia International Raceway for full-throttle fun and excitement for the whole family.

1245 Pine Tree Road, Alton VA
(434) 822-7700
www.virclub.com

Taste of Brunswick Festival

Brunswick County is deservedly proud of its quality of life and celebrates the many attributes of the area with several annual festivals, foremost among them the Taste of Brunswick Festival and accompanying Brunswick Stew Cookoff. Families look forward to this early fall event, which has grown from its beginnings at the Brunswick Mineral Springs Bed & Breakfast and now takes place at the Christianna campus of Southside Virginia Community College on the second Saturday of October. The county celebration showcases the area's agricultural life and values along with the many recreational opportunities found on the county's waterways. Exhibits include such favorites as antique cars and farm machinery, civil war reenactments, horse exhibitions and pony rides. Bass fishing takes place in a temporary pond, and festivalgoers delight in local performances of Indian dances and gospel singing, plus booths devoted to arts and crafts and foods. Each year offers its share of surprises, but one beloved event is constant – the Brunswick Stew Cookoff, where approximately 20 contestants vie for the title of Brunswick County Stewmaster. This tasty chicken stew that originated in Brunswick County is a top fundraiser for local organizations and is usually sold out in advance of the contest. According to local historians, in 1828, a black chef named Jimmy Matthews first concocted the stew using squirrels for Dr. Creed Haskins of the Virginia state legislature and his hunting party. Today, it is a proud, and delicious, symbol of what awaits the visitor to Brunswick County.

228 N Main Street, Lawrenceville VA (434) 848-6773 or (866) STEWPOT *www.tourbrunswick.org*

The Prizery

The residents of Halifax County are fortunate to possess an important gathering place for exploring art and history. The Prizery, located in South Boston's historic warehouse district, is a multifaceted complex that contains a community welcome center, a state-of-the-art auditorium, an art gallery and classrooms. A converted 1890s tobacco warehouse, formerly used for prizing, or pressing tobacco into layers for packing and shipping, the Prizery is a massive brick building with a four-story Italianate tower on one end. It has been undergoing several years of extensive renovations, but pays homage to its warehouse beginnings with open ceilings, brick walls and exposed timbers. The Halifax County Little Theatre, with 50 years of continuing performances, performs three or four shows a year here. The intimate 326-seat theatre also offers performances by professional musicians. The Parsons-Bruce Art Association brings exhibits here and uses the facility for art classes for children and adults. The Prizery's welcome center provides an in-depth look at the county's tobacco and river transportation heritage. The center displays maps with suggested cycling routes for those who would like to explore the area on two wheels, and its community calendar features upcoming local events. Visit the Prizery, a place that brings the community together through art, history and education.

700 Bruce Street, South Boston VA   **(434) 572-8339**   *www.prizery.com*

Photos by Anne W. Bryant/Southampton Ag & Forestry Museum

South Hill Depot

South Hill is a delightful historic town that has managed to maintain its Main Street USA charm while still allowing for growth and modernization. One of the ways that the South Hill community has maintained this balance is by supporting historical points of interest and area museums such as the South Hill Depot. This stately building was erected in the center of town in the 1920s, serving as the railway depot for the Atlantic & Danville Railway line, which had added significant growth to the area. Today it is known as the South Hill Chamber of Commerce Building and houses not only the Chamber but also the South Hill Tourist Information Center and museums including the popular South Hill Model Railroad Museum and the Virginia S. Evans Doll Museum. The railroad museum is housed in what used to be the freight station for the depot and features a wonderful collection of train history, collectables and memorabilia. The focal point of this museum is the Atlantic & Danville Model Railroad, which is a scale model of the trains and towns circa the 1950s, representing the Lawrenceville to Clarksville route. Inside the Virginia S. Evans Doll Museum you will be treated to an array of over 500 dolls that range from the 1800s to the 1980s. Take a reminiscent journey back in time and learn more about South Hill with a visit to the South Hill Depot, home of the South Hill Model Railroad and Virginia S. Evans Doll museums.

201 S Mecklenburg Avenue, South Hill VA
(434) 447-4547
www.southhillchamber.com

Danville Attractions

Majestically sited on the banks of the Dan River, Danville is the heart of Southern Virginia. The city was the last capital of the Confederacy. Jefferson Davis and his government relocated to the Sutherlin Mansion in Danville after the fall of Richmond. One week later Lee surrendered, and Davis fled again. The mansion is now home to the Danville Museum of Fine Arts and History, which contains period furnishings as well as changing local and national exhibits. Danville is home to many famous mansions. Millionaires' Row, on the National Register of Historic Places, is one of the preeminent collections of Victorian and Edwardian architecture in the South. Original owners included tobacco barons and the men who founded the world-renowned textile firm Dan River, Inc. A marker identifies the site of another historical event, the 1903 crash of Old 97, which inspired the famous ballad of the same name. An hour late and speeding, the train left the rails on a curved trestle in North Danville. It careened into the stream 45 feet below, killing 11 and injuring six. The Riverwalk on the Dan may define Danville today. Using a converted 1856 railroad bridge, the paved trail offers magnificent views of the river and connects to many centrally located facilities. One of these is the Danville Science Center in the old train station, which delights all ages with its hands-on exhibits and special programs. During the April to October butterfly season, the Butterfly Station and Garden is a beautiful sight. Another Danville attraction is the American Armoured Foundation Tank Museum, the most extensive collection of tank and cavalry artifacts in the world, with items dating from 1509 to the present. With so much to see, Danville is a place you will want to visit.

645 River Park Drive, Danville VA (Danville Welcome Center) (434) 793-4636
www.visitdanville.com
975 Main Street, Danville VA (Sutherlin Mansion) (434) 793-5644
www.danvillemuseum.org
677 Craghead Street, Danville VA (Science Center) (434) 791-5160
www.dsc.smv.org
3401 U.S. Highway 29B, Danville VA (Tank Museum) (434) 836-5323
www.aaftankmuseum.com

Wrights General Merchandise

In the darling town of Valentines, just south of Lawrenceville, sits Wrights General Merchandise and Valentines Post Office. This delightful vintage building encompasses that feeling of the good old days and offers visitors a refreshing step back in time. Wrights General Merchandise is primarily used as a gathering spot and meeting place for the community and houses a wonderful collection of memorabilia, including an antique cash register and vintage bottle collection. The Valentines Post Office was originally established in 1887 in a country store owned by the town's first postmaster, William Henry Valentine. In 1924, the post office was moved one mile east to its current location, which belonged to the town's fourth postmaster, Robert J. Clary. Postmaster number five, William R. Wright, took over in 1951, and in 1972, he and his wife Frances D. purchased the celebrated building. People have always enjoyed mailing their cards from Valentines Post Office, but things really changed in 1978 when a Cheyenne, Wyoming corporation sent 5,000 love stamp panels, requesting that each have a Valentines cancellation. These panels were then sold to collectors and distributed across the nation. Wright decided to have a special Valentines cachet made, and a tradition began. In 1995, the store and post office were selected as the site for the First Day Cancellation of the 1995 Love Stamp and processed over 75,000 requests. Add a touch of whimsy and charm to your next Valentine greeting by sending it through Valentines Post Office, located inside Wrights General Merchandise.

23 Manning Drive, Valentines VA   (434) 577-2257
Valentines Post Office: (434) 577-2456

MacCallum More Museum & Gardens

Located in a gracious neighborhood in Chase City, MacCallum More Museum & Gardens offers a look at artifacts from antiquity and mature gardens. The nonprofit museum opened in 1996 and houses a permanent exhibit of ancient Indian tools and weapons, collected locally by Arthur Robertson. Surrounding the museum are five acres of gardens, an arboretum and a certified wildlife habitat. Lucy Morton Hudgins, wife of Virginia Supreme Court Justice Edward Wren Hudgins, started the gardens in 1929, and the couple's son, William Henry Hudgins, continued the project until his death in 1986. A self-guided tour along paths that wind through flowerbeds devoted to native plants or singular colors reveals the statue of a 17th century samurai warrior, a 1st century Roman bust, a Spanish cloister and imported fountains. Photographers delight in the grounds, which can be rented for weddings and the house for meetings and club activities. A stop on the Virginia birding and wildlife trail, MacCallum More Museum & Gardens hosts monthly lectures, an annual herb festival, Archeology Day and Native American Day for the areas fifth grade students. The herb garden sprouts more than 200 varieties of plants used for medicine, tea, dyes and culinary purposes. The old carriage house is now the home of the Gift Shop featuring handcrafted gifts, books, note cards, and herb, spice and tea blends. Visit MacCallum More Museum & Gardens, where a staff of gardeners, a horticulturist, and guides wait to greet you.

603 Hudgins Street, Chase City VA
(434) 372-0502
www.mmmg.org

Galleries & Fine Art

Lakeside Gallery

Among the many delights on 4th Street in historic Clarksville is the Queen Anne Liipfert House, now home to Don and Rebecca Hall and the Lakeside Gallery. The Liipfert House, built by a German cabinetmaker in the mid 19th century, reveals a decidedly German charm. The Halls continue the tradition of quality craftsmanship started here, operating from their home studios and filling their gallery with their own artistry as well as antique furnishings and collectibles from around the world. The gallery, which opened in 1981, contains Rebecca's original watercolor paintings and Don's intricately carved acrylic, precious opal, paperweights and table sculptures, as well as Christmas ornaments featuring wildlife and religious themes and opal hand carved jewelry set in 14-karat gold. Don enjoys sharing his artistry with others and offers demonstrations in his studio. He uses optical grade acrylic and opal, along with a technique called reverse intaglio, to gingerly craft lifelike scenes of fish and flowers that look so real people sometimes try to smell them. Make a request and Don will be glad to create a custom scene just for you. Don and Rebecca invite you to visit their website or stop by Lakeside Gallery, where the charm of their home and their art are sure to delight your eye.

109 4th Street, Clarksville VA   (434) 374-9190
www.lakecountryacrylic.com
www.hallsart.com

Lifestyle Destinations

The Springfield Place

On the edge of Buggs Island Lake, you'll find a calm retreat for enjoying the simple life. Once part of the home territory of the Occoneechee Native Americans, the Springfield Place is now owned by Don Moore, who is developing the property into a tranquil retirement community of easily maintained English cottages with fieldstone exteriors, a clubhouse for get-togethers and beautifully landscaped grounds. The community dock and beach provide easy access to beautiful Buggs Island Lake. Kinderton Country Club is adjacent to the property and home to a pool, tennis courts and an 18-hole golf course designed by Donald Ross. The Springfield Rosseechee Museum is also located here. It was founded by Don Moore's late grandfather, the Honorable John W. Tisdale, who built the museum on the banks of what was then the Roanoke River (now Buggs Island Lake) and filled its rooms with stone artifacts, from 12,000-year-old Folsom points to 17th century Indian relics. He also wrote several small books on the history of the local area, which are available at the museum. If you are looking for a new place to call home and a charming lakeside retreat for taking advantage of the simple pleasures in life, visit the Springfield Place and talk to Don Moore about making a move to Buggs Island Lake. If you are looking for a weekend getaway, ask about staying in the lakefront lodge, where you will discover spacious accommodations with covered porches that catch gentle breezes. Experience tranquility at the Springfield Place.

289 Tisdale Lane, Clarksville VA   (434) 374-8216
www.springfieldpropertiesinc.com

Markets

Virginia Favorites

Dorothy Bass and Judy Whittington are nuts . . . about Virginia. As owners of Virginia Favorites, a specialty shop that includes a successful e-commerce site, they promote some of Virginia's best exports. First and foremost are the home-cooked peanuts native to the state. These home-cooked gourmet nuts are given an extra special touch by this mother-daughter team and their staff. Because of this extra special touch, the peanuts have earned the Virginia's Finest seal of approval. Choose from salted or unsalted, shelled, boiled, blanched or cajun-spiced in quantities from 22-ounce tins to five-pound bags. The nut choices don't stop here. They also have pecans prepared in a variety of ways, along with roasted and salted cashews. The Virginia's Finest seal of approval can be found on most Virginia products in the store, including the ever-popular Virginia country hams and slab bacon. Salt-cured, these delicious staples need no refrigeration and will make for a memorable meal if you follow the included directions for cooking. For a sandwich like no other, pick up some jams and jellies made from the delicious fruits of the Graves Mountain area. From the large variety, your palette will be more than satisfied with the incredible flavors of these sweet spreads. There are also many different baking mixes, bean soup mixes, cocoa mixes, sauces, honey (including honey comb), and much more to choose from, as well as cookbooks that will help you create authentic Virginia recipes from scratch in your own kitchen. Located at the I-95 and Route 58 crossroads, the shop also features souvenirs and many gift items. You can custom make your own gift baskets or purchase a ready-made one. Visit Virginia Favorites next time you're traveling down I-95 (exit 11-B) or visit their website and spoil your mouth with a taste of the South.

1001 W Atlantic Street, Emporia VA
(888)790-9096 or (866) 838-6257
www.virginiafavorites.com
www.vapeanuts.com

Photos courtesy of Fred Maldonado Photography

Restaurants & Cafés

Cinnamon Cafe

Mary Truman has always loved cooking breakfast. She established a tradition of making a secret family recipe called "cinnamon sauce" for friends and family to top their Christmas morning pancakes, waffles, and French toast. The sauce proved so popular it seemed she was always cooking up more. A time came when the family was planning a move from Virginia Beach to Lawrenceville and Mary and her husband, Jim, were looking for a business to operate. Their original vision eventually evolved into a restaurant, The Cinnamon Café. The café has helped to revitalize the town and provides community events infused with the family's sense of fun. They team up with a local car club for car shows on the street in front of the café. They hold 1950s and 60s era dance contests, encourage karaoke, and feature local musical talents. An open mic night is held for the local college students from nearby Saint Paul's College. A spot for the cozy blending of old and new; the café provides free internet for laptops with a view of the Civil War Museum across the street. In this energetic meeting place, food is made to order, exactly the way you want it. The Trumans and their children enjoy Lawrenceville and invite you to stop in and say hello. Try the cinnamon sauce while you are there. You will be back.

229 North Main Street, Lawrenceville VA
(434) 848-2226

Photo courtesy of Fred Maldonado Photography

Sheldon's Motel and Restaurant

Baked Virginia ham is a delicacy known throughout the United States, and Sheldon's Restaurant is one of the few Virginia dining establishments that ages its own hams. At Sheldon's, the hams are aged from six to nine months in their own smokehouse, built by Buck Sheldon in the 1960s. Buck was one of three Sheldon brothers who built Sheldon's Motel and Restaurant back in 1940. Many things have changed in the 65-plus years that Sheldon's has been in business. The restaurant has tripled in size, and on a busy day serves more people than the entire population of the local town of Keysville. Catering services are also available either in the restaurant or at the location of your choosing. The motel, which started with eight units in 1940, now offers 40 units and is listed as a AAA approved motel. The second generation of Sheldons, Grover Sheldon, Jr. and his wife Jenness now own and operate the business. Yet many things have not changed. The meals are still delicious, including the heavenly homemade biscuits, rolls and pies baked fresh daily and the down-home southern hospitality can't be beat. Located on Route 360 halfway between Richmond and Danville, be sure to stop by Sheldon's Motel and Restaurant for a mouthwatering meal and a quiet comfortable room for the night.

1450 Four Locust Highway, Keysville VA
(434) 736-8434 or (877) 417-7075
www.sheldonshospitality.com

Kennon House Restaurant

Local residents of Gasburg call the Kennon House Restaurant by another name, the Mud House. This house was built in 1792 out of 16 inch thick clay walls thrown over a mold. In 1877, the house was deeded to Richard Byrd Kennon by his mother-in-law and the Kennons lived in the house for many generations. Eventually, Dennis Monds and Cory Carlisle bought the establishment in 2003. Dennis and Cory have rejuvenated it into an upscale, quality restaurant for the community, while keeping the prices reasonable in this coveted Lake Gaston setting. Lake Gaston, one of three lakes formed by the Gaston Dam, is a popular site for many outdoor activites such as fishing, boating and water sports. The Kennon house is one of the oldest dwellings in this picturesque area. The Kennon House Restaurant reflects the history that runs deep throughout the house as well as in the classic southern recipes served within. Grilled steaks and chops, as well as shrimp and grits fill the air with an unmistakable aroma reminescent of the style of cooking you can only find in the South. Enjoy delicious meals and the occasional jazz performance in the authentic historic home that is the Kennon House Restaurant while you relax at this vacation oasis.

7001 Gasburg Road, Gasburg VA   (434) 577-2680

Kahill's Restaurant

Kahill's Restaurant is one of those surprising gems that you stumble onto in the middle of a long road trip. It's an absolutely fabulous dining experience and it's not where you'd expect it. South Hill is a great little town with great people and Owner Tom Flowers believes this is what makes his restaurant what it is. Tom started Kahill's Restaurant in 1991, naming it after his mother, Kahill Flowers. With beautiful brick walls, hardwood floors and ceilings and a raised marble-top bar, Kahill's Restaurant has a warm and welcoming feeling. The menu is surprisingly broad with herb-crusted fresh fish, steaks and breakfast offerings like crab omelets. The chef at Kahill's has an artistic flair with spices, wine and butter. Try his bacon-wrapped ahi tuna with chipotle chile butter, it'll knock your socks off. The freshness and creativity of the food will make you feel like you've won the culinary lottery. To top it all off, Kahill's staff members are down-home cheery, caring and eager to please. They're quick to offer helpful suggestions and obviously happy when you have a good time. Kahill's is a great little place to meet a friend, have a beer and get something absolutely delicious to eat. More surprises are Kahill's live jazz and blues music events. If you're planning to be on the road in Virginia, look up Kahill's Restaurant. You won't want to miss it.

1791 N Mecklenburg Avenue, La Crosse VA *(434) 447-6941*

Shopping & Antiques

Country Store Antiques

Housed in the historic E.P. Jolly store building in Edgerton is the quaint and curious Country Store Antiques. Antique enthusiasts and shop owners Brenda and Steve Browder say that their inventory is always expanding because they buy more than they sell while feeding their antiques addiction. The Browders travel all over the east coast to find the wonderful and interesting pieces that fill the shop from floor to ceiling. When they're not traveling, they live right next door to the antiques shop in a house that always stood across the field from where Steve grew up. Country Store Antiques has an oft-changing inventory full of eclectic and surprising treasures such as vintage stoneware and a wonderful array of glassware. The Browders also have a great selection of antiques from primitives to sterling silver. Something for every taste can be found at their shop. A second building was opened in October of 2005, so if you're a true lover of the antiquing hobby, come over and spend some time visiting with Steve and Brenda while exploring all of the treasures that await you at Country Store Antiques.

366 Belfield Road, Lawrenceville VA
(434) 848-2900

J's Antiques

J's Antiques, located in the popular destination community of South Hill, is the ideal place to while away a few hours as you search for that perfect treasure. Owners Lucy A.G. and Garnet Queen opened the delightful shop in 1985 and quickly gained a following of faithful antique hunters who delight in the shop's often-changing inventory. You will find a terrific array of antiques that represent the 18th and 19th century, as well as pieces from the early 20th century through the end of the Great Depression. Collectibles include a bevy of glassware and art glass pieces including Wedgwood from England, decanters and Blue Willow pieces, along with cut glass and exquisite porcelain. Additionally, you will find a great selection of lamps, clocks and quality furnishings. Lucy and Garnet are passionate about antiques and bring more than 50 years of antique-buying experience to their enterprise. The shop is housed in a historic building that was home to Yancy's department store circa 1903, which adds a nostalgic feeling to the warm and inviting shop. Share your passion for antiquities with fellow aficionados with a visit to J's Antiques.

106 N Mecklenburg Avenue, South Hill VA
(434) 447-7089

Sallie and Sonny's Florist

Sally and Sonny's Florist has been proudly serving Lawrenceville for over 40 years. Its present location, close to St. Paul's College, was formerly a dress shop owned by Lillian Smith with apartments upstairs. Sally and Sonny's Florist is currently owned by Jerry and Dale Glasscock, who believe in superior customer service and delivering what they promise. Sally and Sonny's is a good-sized operation with

a lot of local appeal and the shop also ships its eye-catching flower arrangements throughout the country. This is also a business with a heart. Once a month, they make arrangements for each member of a local nursing home and they often donate flowers to local charity events. Sally and Sonny's Florist is a member of the Virginia Professional Floral Association. They stock a variety of gift items including hand-painted glass, gourds and Old Virginia candles. Willow Tree figurines grace their shelves along with RAZ brand decorative imports. The shop creates trendy and traditional fresh floral arrangements for every occasion and can customize arrangements to vividly accent your special event. Racecars, anchors and animals are some of themes the floral experts have used in the past. This friendly, fun atmosphere is a hotbed for new ideas and heartwarming gifts. The Glasscocks invite you to browse Sally and Sonny's Florist for inspiration.

319 N Main Street, Lawrenceville VA
(434) 848-2085 or (800) 840-2085
www.sallyandsonnysflorist.com

Strum & Co. Antiques & Uniques

Three friends, Jean Strum Crowe, Betty Rae Norwood and Phyllis Griffith, turned their common interest in antiques and one-of-a-kind items into an uncommon business. Today, Strum & Co. Antiques & Uniques is a showcase for their discerning eyes and talents, as well as a must see in

Clarksville. Since 1999, they have offered a constantly changing array of indoor and outdoor furnishings, antiques, collectibles and works by artisans. Occasional demonstrations by artists and book signings by authors add to the ambiance. The shop is located in the buildings where Jean's late father, J.V. Strum, established Strum's Supermarket and Strum's Feed & Seed Store, 70 years ago. Betty Rae's eye for finding the unusual, Phyllis' talent for turning everyday objects into art and Jean's down-home friendliness keep customers (both local and out-of-towners) coming back for more. Traditional, eclectic or arty, Strum & Co. Antiques & Uniques has something for every taste.

612-614 Virginia Avenue, Clarksville VA
(434) 374-5090

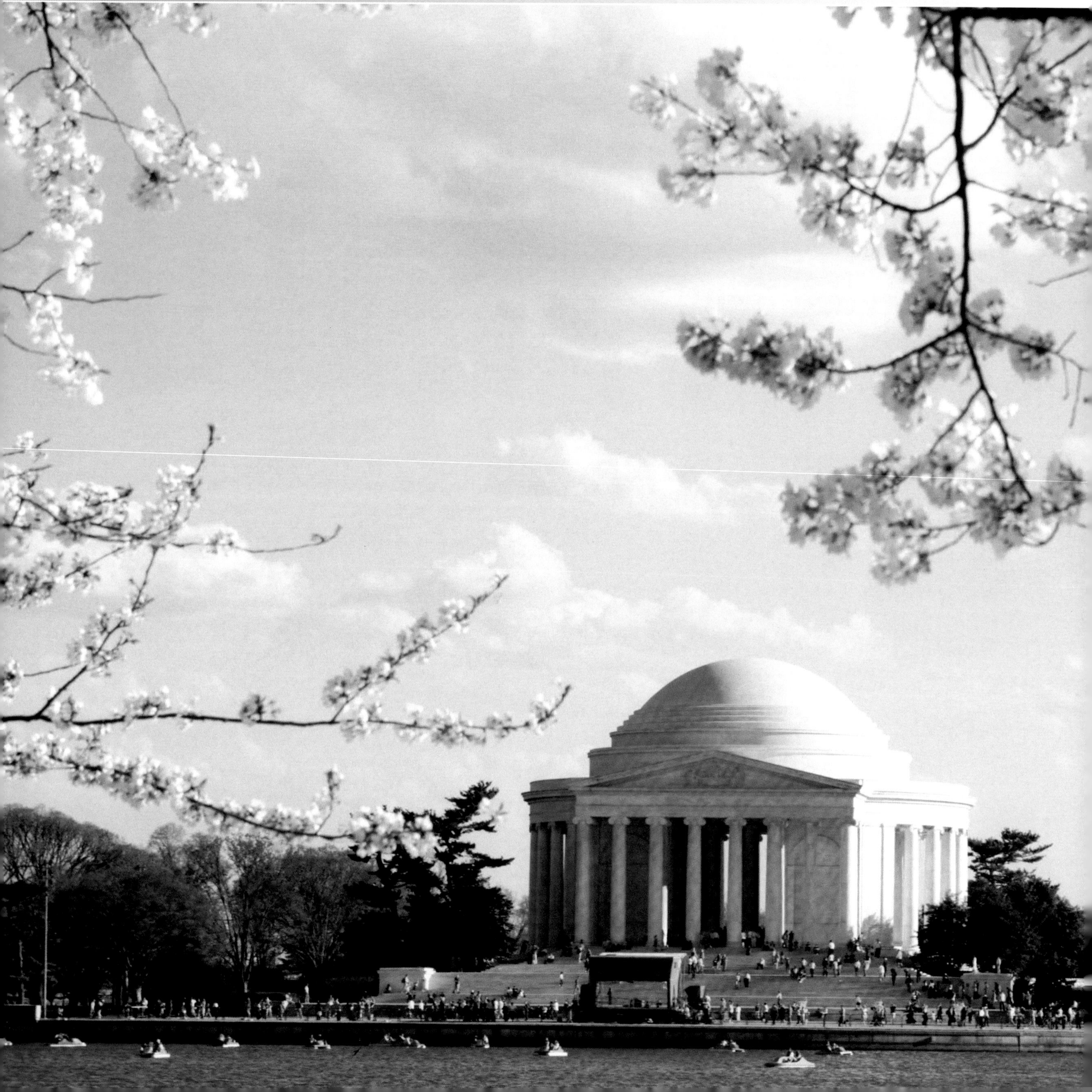

Southwest Virginia

Accommodations

Victoria & Albert Inn

Richard Cano and Hazel Ramos-Cano must be doing something right. Their Victoria and Albert Inn has placed in Arrington's Inn Traveler's Book of Lists for four consecutive years and earned AAA's four diamonds for six consecutive years. Since 1987, Hazel has made it her personal mission to see that all her guests at Victoria & Albert Inn feel at home and have a fabulous time and her standards are extremely high. Hazel is an executive chef and owns the famous Withers Hardware Restaurant, so absolutely fantastic food is guaranteed. Well-known actors and playwrights often stay at the Victoria & Albert when they're working at the world-class Barter Theatre close by. The beautifully renovated 1892 home sits on a quiet, tree-lined residential street in Abingdon's Historic district, well within easy walking distance of all the great attractions Abingdon has to offer. Five elegant suites are comfortably furnished with gorgeous traditional furniture and luxurious amenities that include spacious private baths, whirlpool tubs, gas fireplaces, king and queen size beds, sitting areas, cable television, VCR and CD players and high-speed Internet access. Every guest is pampered with homemade breakfasts. Concierge services will arrange for any activity, including theatre tickets, dinner reservations, spa services or outdoor activities. No doubt about it, the comfort and gracious hospitality of Victoria & Albert Inn will keep you coming back again and again.

224 Oak Hill Street, Abingdon, VA
(276) 623-1281 or (800) 475-5494
www.abingdon-virginia.com

A Tailor's Lodging Bed and Breakfast

You can find A Tailor's Lodging Bed and Breakfast in the middle of Abingdon's 20-block historic district, just a short walk from great craft and antique shopping, art galleries, museums, fine dining and the world famous Barter Theatre. Owners and Innkeepers Rick and Susan Humphreys spent almost two years restoring the fine old house that was first built in 1840 by the Sandoe family who were tailors by trade. The Humphreys took great care to keep architectural details intact so the house still tells the story of Abingdon in the mid 1800s. Each of the three beautiful guest rooms has unique features to suit personal tastes. All rooms come equipped with a queen sized bed, fireplace, private bath, cable television and computer port. Almost everything in the house is pre-Civil war, from the beautiful antique furniture to the silverware. Susan and Rick have kept the warmth and charm of the kitchen and enhanced it with an open expanse of porch outside. The magnificent Virginia Creeper Trail is one short block away and gives those with an affinity for the outdoors a chance to go hiking, biking, jogging or horseback riding. Rick and Susan will make arrangements and take care of details for anything you need, whether it's bicycle rentals, hot air balloon rides or horse drawn carriage outings. The Humphreys want you to feel comfortable, relax and have fun. Stay at A Tailor's Lodging Bed and Breakfast and you'll feel as if you've come home.

119 Park Street, Abingdon VA
(276) 628-7119
www.atailorslodging.com

Maxwell Manor Bed & Breakfast

In 1996, Nancy Steel was looking for the perfect place to live and open her own vision of a bed-and-breakfast. She wanted abundant cultural offerings, historical charm, character and beautiful countryside. She found what she was looking for in the rolling hills and antebellum grace of Abingdon. She fell in love with the Georgian Colonial manor house that was first built in 1819 by the Maxwell family. Maxwell Manor Bed & Breakfast is a rarity in Abingdon because it sits on three beautiful acres of lawn and duck ponds. It's just far enough away to feel like it's out in the country yet conveniently close to all the wonderful things to see and do in Abingdon. The two-story Georgian home has a gorgeous double front porch complete with charming swings, while inside you find fireplaces in the living and dining rooms. Guests receive afternoon tea and full homemade breakfasts, plus amenities that include an indoor heated swimming pool. Each of the four beautifully decorated suites is furnished in antiques from the same period and has a private bath. Romantic and peaceful, Maxwell Manor is a true getaway spot where guests can come and go as they please, enjoy all that Abingdon has to offer in the way of fine arts, shopping and outdoor activities or simply rest and relax. This delightful bed-and-breakfast offers the comfortable atmosphere of home as well as features that make it feel similar to a quiet resort. Let Maxwell Manor Bed & Breakfast work its many charms on you.

19215 Old Jonesboro Road, Abingdon VA
(276) 628-3912 or (888) 851-1100
www.maxwellmanor.com

Shepherd's Joy

Abingdon is a picturesque mountain town full of colorful history, fine and performing arts and wonderful attractions for the entire family. If you really want to enjoy your stay, experience the quaint hospitality of days gone by at Shepherd's Joy. Shepherd's Joy is a bed and breakfast home on a three and a half acre farm-estate complete with sheep and sheep dogs Buzz and Meg. Owner Joyce Ferratt actually grew up right in this beautiful old home which has been in her family for the last century. Together with her husband Jack, she turned the 1892 home into a bed and breakfast in 1994. The house was lovingly restored to retain its historical authenticity and beauty. Guests will find old-fashioned Virginia charm in family antiques and memorabilia plus four lovely bedrooms with queen beds and private baths as well as thoroughly modern amenities. The leisurely grace and unhurried pace of the South invite you to rest and relax. Join Jack and Joyce on their wraparound porch or stroll the beautiful grounds and gardens after you enjoy the gourmet breakfast served every morning. Shepherd's Joy is right in the middle of the historic district and only a mile from most of the places you'll want to see in Abingdon. Joyce and Jack treat every guest like one of their own family. As Joyce says, "We want them to come in as strangers and leave as family." Come stay at Shepherd's Joy and enjoy the warmth and charm of this bed and breakfast.

254 White's Mill Road, Abingdon, VA
(276) 628-3273
www.shepherdsjoy.com

Attractions

Carter Family Memorial Music Center

Classic country songs such as "Wildwood Flower" and "Wabash Cannonball," sung by The Carter Family, hold a special place in many people's hearts. Now you can learn more about this incredible and talented First Family of Country Music with a visit to the Carter Family Memorial Music Center. Founded in 1979 by Janette Carter, daughter of A.P and Sara Carter and niece to Maybelle Carter, the center was established in tribute to the famous trio who first recorded for the Victor Talking Machine Company in August of 1927. From then until 1942 the trio recorded more than 300 songs. In addition to the Carter Family, Jimmie Rodgers also auditioned at the historic Bristol recording sessions of 1927, which laid the foundation for what we now call country music. Every Saturday night the Carter Family Fold, a rustic music hall which seats nearly 900, offers a terrific show. The shows were originally held in A.P.'s old store, now the home of the Carter Museum. Only acoustic instruments are allowed at the Fold and the dance floor quickly fills up as audience members get down to hoedown tunes and other popular favorites. Patrons come from all over the world for a taste of this fabulous gathering where family time is encouraged and alcohol is strictly forbidden. At the Carter Family Museum you can view photographs, instruments and awards that the family received along with other personal family heirlooms, recordings and show clothes. Explore the humble beginnings of American country music with a visit to the Carter Family Memorial Music Center.

A.P. Carter Highway, Hiltons VA (276) 386-6054 (Tickets) or (276) 645-0035 (Museum) www.carterfamilyfold.org

Barter Theatre

With its unique beginnings during the Great Depression, Barter Theatre, one of this nation's oldest professional theatres, is located in beautiful historic Abingdon, nestled in the foothills of Appalachia and overlooking the Blue Ridge. Barter Theatre is a theatre of firsts; one of this nation's first professional regional theatres, the first professional theatre to be designated a state theatre, and, among many other firsts, the first theatre ever to perform Shakespeare's "Hamlet" at the original Elsinore Castle in Denmark. Barter Theatre opened its doors on June 10, 1933, founded by a young visionary named Robert Porterfield who proclaimed, "With vegetables you cannot sell, you can buy a good laugh." The concept of trading "ham for Hamlet" caught on quickly. By the end of Barter's first season, the Barter Company cleared $4.35 in cash, two barrels of jelly and enjoyed a collective weight gain of over 300 pounds. Playwrights including Noel Coward, Tennessee Williams and Thornton Wilder accepted Virginia hams as payment for royalties. An exception was George Bernard Shaw, a vegetarian, who bartered the rights to his plays for spinach. Robert Porterfield, director of this historic theatre for almost 40 years, gave birth to a legend and his ghost is said to pleasantly witness every performance at Barter. Barter's legendary past also includes the many alumni who began their careers at Barter. Their pictures don the halls of Barter including notables Gregory Peck, Patricia Neal, Ernest Borgnine, Hume Cronyn, Ned Beatty, Gary Collins, Larry Linville, Kevin Spacey, Barry Corbin, Frances Fisher, Jim Varney and James Burrows, the creator of "Cheers." Today, Barter's professional company offers a mix of musicals, classics, comedies, dramas and new southern and Appalachian plays are performed on two stages: Barter Theatre and Barter Stage II. The Barter Players, Barter's young professional actors, also produce family programming in both theatres geared especially for young audiences. Barter Theatre, built in 1833 - the nation's second oldest continually operating theatre building, features traditional theatre in a luxurious setting. Barter Stage II, located in beautiful Stonewall Square and operating in a converted brick church first built in 1827, offers a wonderfully intimate setting for more adventurous theatre. History is still in the making as Barter Theatre continues to be one of the nation's most vibrant and exciting professional theatre experiences.

127 West Main Street, Abingdon, Virginia
(276) 628-3991 *www.bartertheatre.com*

William King Regional Arts Center

Known for its changing exhibitions, William King Regional Arts Center displays everything from African masks and Mexican retablos to quilts from the region and fine art paintings from around the world. It has a line of authentic reproduction heritage and contemporary crafts from the southwest region of the state and nearby northeast Tennessee for sale in a great museum store called The Looking Glass. The Arts Center is located on beautiful grounds that include outdoor sculptures. The property is the historic site of a 19th century school called the Abingdon Male Academy, which operated until Circa 1911. The current building, which houses the museum, was built on the same site in 1913 as William King High School, a public school named for an early Irish settler and businessman who left the Abingdom Male Academy a large gift in his 1808 will. That's why the public school was named for him and continues today as the museum's name. William King Regional Arts Center is known for its Cultural Heritage Project, which has surveyed the decorative arts legacy of the region, its art educational programs, and its top-notch exhibitions displayed in multiple galleries. The museum is accredited by the American Association of Museums.

415 Academy Drive, Abingdon VA
(276) 628-5005 *http://wkrac.org*

Bakeries, Coffee & Tea

Java J's

Java J's introduced the latte and the mocha to Bristol and in the process they created a new gathering place for the community. The excellent coffees, salads and paninis satisfy customer appetites as well as enticing them back for more. Java J's also carries some of the best Italian gelato to be found stateside, using only local ingredients to produce the cold, creamy delight. Gelato is an ice-cream with more flavor and less fat. The warm atmosphere inspires group discussions and provides a comfortable meeting place for locals and visitors alike. There are three locations, including the Express for busy coffee-drinking drivers. The Abingdon Java J's Stone Mill location is steeped in an Italian theme with outdoor terrace seating overlooking a gazebo, a tranquil pond and romantic footbridge crossing the fish stream. The downtown Bristol location highlights the area's historic ambiance. In addition to the various coffee beverages, coffee beans are sold by the pound or half pound along with an inventory of coffee mugs. Island Rose teas are imported directly from the Bahamas. Special dietary concerns are accommodated with a variety of choices such as no fat, no sugar, no caffeine or no carbohydrates. Java J's supports the artistic community as well, selling books by local writers and displaying local art work. A preferred customer card gives the cardholder year-long discounts, and can be recharged. Students pay a lower price for the card. Happenings include live music performances and Java J's is WiFi enabled. Visit Java J's to get connected while drinking in an exquisite cup of coffee.

Java J's Abingdon Stone Mill: (276) 623-1119
Java J's Bristol Downtown: (276) 466-8882
Java J's Express: (276) 821-0051 *www.javajs.net*

Galleries & Fine Art

Arts Depot

When a group of artists join together and create, magic ensues. The Arts Depot is a fine example of artistry and teamwork. In 1990, after 5,000 hours of volunteer work by Depot Artists Association members and friends as well as community contributions, the 19th century Norfolk and Western Railroad depot was transformed into the Arts Depot. The organization has seven resident artists and more than 250 volunteers working to make local and regional art available to visitors and to offer hands-on art classes to the community. The Arts Depot displays a large quantity of the highest quality work with accommodations for three-dimensional art. The Spotlight Gallery, an invitational gallery for outstanding regional artists, changes exhibits every six weeks. The Members Gallery showcases the work of member artists. Resident artists work in their on-site studios within Arts Depot. These artists spend an impressive amount of their time talking with interested visitors, providing a rare, intimate connection between the art and the viewer. Classes and workshops are offered throughout the year. Every March, Arts Depot celebrates National Youth Art month by featuring art from a Washington County school. Outreach and scholarship classes are funded from their budget to enrich the community and foster the arts. This historic building and noteworthy group of innovative artists beckon you to take in the masterpiece of creation that is the Arts Depot itself.

314 Depot Square, Abingdon VA
(276) 628-9091
www.abingdonartsdepot.org

Photos by Mike Pierry Jr.

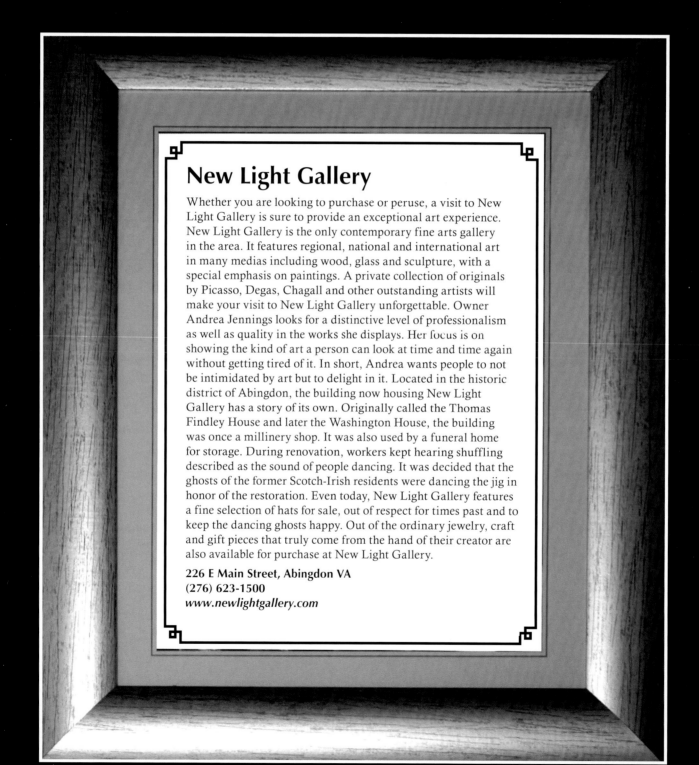

New Light Gallery

Whether you are looking to purchase or peruse, a visit to New Light Gallery is sure to provide an exceptional art experience. New Light Gallery is the only contemporary fine arts gallery in the area. It features regional, national and international art in many medias including wood, glass and sculpture, with a special emphasis on paintings. A private collection of originals by Picasso, Degas, Chagall and other outstanding artists will make your visit to New Light Gallery unforgettable. Owner Andrea Jennings looks for a distinctive level of professionalism as well as quality in the works she displays. Her focus is on showing the kind of art a person can look at time and time again without getting tired of it. In short, Andrea wants people to not be intimidated by art but to delight in it. Located in the historic district of Abingdon, the building now housing New Light Gallery has a story of its own. Originally called the Thomas Findley House and later the Washington House, the building was once a millinery shop. It was also used by a funeral home for storage. During renovation, workers kept hearing shuffling described as the sound of people dancing. It was decided that the ghosts of the former Scotch-Irish residents were dancing the jig in honor of the restoration. Even today, New Light Gallery features a fine selection of hats for sale, out of respect for times past and to keep the dancing ghosts happy. Out of the ordinary jewelry, craft and gift pieces that truly come from the hand of their creator are also available for purchase at New Light Gallery.

226 E Main Street, Abingdon VA
(276) 623-1500
www.newlightgallery.com

Markets

Inari Wines

The state line between Tennessee and Virginia follows the center stripe of Bristol's State Street. On the Virginia side of the street sits Inari Wines, a specialty store featuring fine wines, foods and gifts. Owners Paul and Aulikki Brandt opened the store in 2003 with wines from Virginia, California, Oregon, Europe, Australia and South Africa. You'll find an excellent assortment of over 60 cheeses as well as caviar, olive oils, vinegars, Italian chocolates and specialty beer. The couple also bring samples of their individual heritages to the store with products from Paul's native Texas and Aulikki's native Finland. The foods, wines and gift baskets are pleasantly arranged on a backdrop of hardwood floors and brick walls in an 1890s building. Apparently the Brandts weren't the first people to sell wine from this building. An old sign found under the plaster reads: "Heller Brothers Mail Order House – Wines, Liquors, Beers, Pure Corn Liquor. Choice Brandies for Family Use." A wine and gourmet shop proved the perfect match for the Brandts, who are learning to make wine and have planted grapes on their property. They left Houston several years ago in search of a smaller town where they could open a business. Bristol won their hearts and captured their imaginations. A visit to Inari Wines with its fine selection and personalized service is certain to capture your heart as well.

507 State Street, Bristol VA
(276) 821-WINE (9463)
www.inariwines.com

Wines of Distinction

Looking for a little European charm? Located in historic Abingdon is a lovely shop that offers just that. Wines of Distinction has many surprises that make it so much more than just a place to purchase everyday wines and fine wines. Incorporated in 1995, Wines of Distinction is located in the old Washington House Hotel, circa 1850. The building has hosted a variety of businesses over the years, including an old time grocery, the quaintness of which is still maintained by the current business, including old time charm with personal service and a knowledgable staff to match. Planning to host a proper tea? You will find those specialty products there as well as many coffees, cheeses, imported chocolates and specialty beers. They also have epicurean products such as olive oils, vinegars, pastas, pestos and a number of other distinctive items to aid you with any entertaining endeavor. Exquisite glassware and tabletop accessories are also available for purchase to make any occasion special. This inviting atmosphere is also home to a small coffeeshop that serves a true European coffee from beautiful Italian pottery. Fresh homemade pastries complete the scenario. Take time out from the everyday hustle and bustle to enjoy life and the good things it has to offer by visiting Wines of Distinction.

230 East Main Street, Abingdon, VA
(276) 623-0001

Recreation

Virginia Creeper Trail Bike Shop

There aren't many mountain biking adventures as enjoyable as the Virginia Creeper Trail. The Virginia Creeper Trail Bike Shop is where to go to make the most of your experience. Owners Gary and Jennifer Camper and Jerry and Tina Camper would be glad to help you select an appropriate, high quality bike to get you up and down the trail. The shop rents and sells the finest Haro, Fuji and Marin models for all shapes and sizes and even has comfort bikes. If you have your own wheels, but need a little tightening up here and there, they'll be more than happy to help you with the necessary adjustments. They carry a full line of accessories, components and even commemorative t-shirts for remembering your visit. The Virginia Creeper Trail stretches 35 miles from Abingdon through Damascus to the North Carolina state line near Whitetop. This is a biking adventure that the entire family will enjoy. Try to keep focused on this former railway corridor of the Virginia-Carolina line, but don't miss out on the beautiful scenery that surrounds you! You'll also have plenty of company, since the trail averages 2,000 to 3,000 bicyclists a day on weekends in the peak month of October. The bike shop provides several shuttles to and from Damascus and Whitetop Station for those who aren't prepared to make the nearly 70-mile round trip. Before you start the incredible journey, visit the Virginia Creeper Trail Bike Shop for the tips and tools to make your ride even more memorable.

201 Pecan Street, Abingdon VA
(888) BIKEN4U (245-3648)

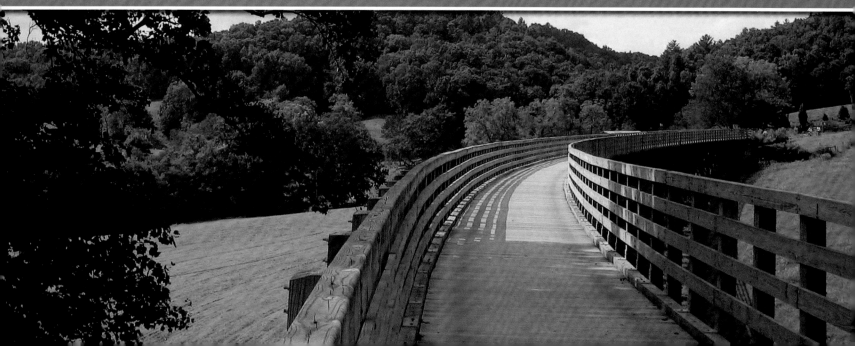

Restaurants & Cafés

The Tavern Restaurant

If you're looking for a dining experience that is as steeped in history as the food is in flavor then head for The Tavern Restaurant in historic Abingdon. The Tavern is housed in one of the oldest buildings west of the Blue Ridge Mountains, which is also the oldest historical building in Abingdon and has been used primarily as a tavern and overnight inn since its construction in 1779. This classic old building has played host to many famous travelers over the years including Henry Clay, Andrew Jackson and Pierre Charles L 'Enfant, the famous French designer of Washington D.C. Over the past two centuries this grand dwelling has been home to everything from a stagecoach stop and post office to a bakery, cabinet shop and private residence; it even did a stint as a hospital during the Civil War. Today, this stately building is owned by Max Hermann, a native German and retired United States Air Force officer. Hermann moved to Abingdon in 1994 after a 20-year service career and took over management of The Tavern, which is known for its fabulous service and superb cuisine. Max's goal has always been to preserve the history of the building while introducing an international menu and he has met this goal beautifully. Patrons are offered a wonderful selection of perfectly prepared dishes that range from succulent steaks to classic German dishes such as *Wiener schnitzel*. Become a part of living history while enjoying a fabulous and relaxed meal at The Tavern Restaurant.

222 E Main Street, Abingdon VA
(276) 628-1118 *www.abingdontavern.com*

Alison's Restaurant

Alison's Restaurant is currently one of Abingdon's most popular spots, just as it was in the 1950s when it was known as the Bar-B Burger Drive-In. It was sold several times until the early 1990s when Alison and Marvin Gill bought the building and opened Alison's Restaurant. Lanny and Patty Stoots acquired the restaurant in October of 2001, but continued to keep its charm and traditions alive, including continuing to serve its world famous baked potato soup, a local favorite known throughout the county. Lanny introduced some of his own recipes such as the house barbecue sauce that is used to baste their smoked ribs. Alison's was awarded Best Overall Restaurant in 2005, Best Ribs for three consecutive years and Best Soup for two years in a row by the Washington County News. Alison's catering business is well known for accommodating residents, church groups, businesses and weddings. The staff at Alison's keeps up the task of creating wonderful food and offering warm, friendly service. Many of the restaurant's employees have been with Lanny and Patty for years, making the restaurant very family-oriented. Tragically, Lanny Stoots passed away in 2003, but Patty carries on his work and the staff keeps his memory alive in the great food they serve. While traveling through southwest Virginia, stop by Alison's Restaurant and enjoy the wonderful food, friends and feeling it has to offer. Patty and the staff will welcome you just the way Lanny would have.

1220 W Main Street, Abingdon VA
(276) 628-8002

Withers Hardware Restaurant

With a name like Withers Hardware Restaurant, you just know there has to be a story behind it. In 1885, Withers Hardware actually was a hardware store operated by Salmon M. Withers. When Hazel Ramos-Cano and her husband Richard Cano bought the place in 2002, they renamed their restaurant in honor of the original owners. Withers Hardware Restaurant serves a combination of American and fine international cuisine. While the food is every bit as good as other fine dining to be found in the area, the atmosphere is much more relaxed, as is the wonderful waitstaff. Antique signs from the 19th century and exposed brick and rich woods match the history and charm of this place. One of best things about Withers' menu is its diversity. You can go simple and inexpensive with soups and sandwiches or all out with filet mignon. Either way, the food is terrific. Everything is fresh and made from scratch so you are bound to enjoy all aspects of your meal, including the bread, appetizers and side dishes. You simply cannot go wrong with entrées like ribs, rib-eye steaks and salmon Rockefeller. Withers closes only two days out of the year, Christmas and New Years, so chances are you won't miss it. When it comes to visiting Withers Hardware Restaurant, that's a good thing.

260 W Main Street, Abingdon, VA
(276) 628 1111
www.withershardwarerestaurant.com

Shopping & Antiques

Fandango Unique Gifts and Art

When two jewelry designers combined their creative talents to create the ultimate gift and art store, the result of their efforts was bound to be as lively as the fast paced Spanish fandango. Fandango Unique Gifts and Art, on the Virginia side of State Street in Bristol, is eclectic, non-traditional and devoted to gift-giving. It is the brainchild of owners Cindy Samuel and Landy Adams, who met after Cindy's husband delivered two of Landy's children. The pair share jewelry designing skills, resourcefulness and an understanding of customer needs. Your odds of finding and giving the perfect present improve at Fandango, with arts and crafts, home accessories and items suitable for just about any occasion, including baby or wedding showers. The shop's custom designed jewelry, local artwork and other singular merchandise assure your gift will be a standout. Cindy, Landy and staff can help you find the right gift for any occasion. They also provide gift-wrapping and domestic and international shipping. For corporate gift giving or gifts requiring personalization, the Fandango staff is always happy to create a gift basket or assist in choosing a promotional product with your corporate logo. While the store is well stocked for handling gift basket requests, customers are also free to bring items purchased elsewhere to add to the gift mix. When you need a treasure for yourself or someone in your life, turn to Fandango Unique Gifts and Art.

511 State Street, Bristol VA
(276) 669-4448

Zephyr Antiques

When Zephyr Antiques opened its 8,000-square-foot facility in 2000, Abingdon didn't have an antiques market of this size. Today, tourists seek out Abingdon's antique shops and Tim Morgan's store is an integral part of the downtown scene. Over 20 dealers sell their wares from Zephyr, a mix of well-displayed items in a variety of price ranges. Pat Miller, who keeps a booth on the first floor, predates Tim in the shop and has been his mentor in the antiquing business. Formerly the Zephyr Theater, owned by the Lincoln Theater Company, the building was converted into a furniture store in 1966 following a fire that permanently closed the theater. The shop is named Zephyr after the popular Lincoln Zephyr car model. The beautiful and historic town of Abingdon lies just to the west of the Blue Ridge Mountains in the rolling foothills of the Appalachian range. Abingdon's rich history, old buildings and brick sidewalks contribute to its charm. Daniel Boone first named the area Wolf Hills in 1760 after a run-in he had with wolves living in a cave. In 1774, Joseph Black built a fort here to protect residents from Indian raids, so the community became known as Black's Fort. In 1778, Black's Fort became the incorporated town of Abingdon, named after Martha Washington's British home. A walk down Abingdon's Main Street takes you past many historic structures. Be sure to put Zephyr Antiques, open every day, on your itinerary.

270 W Main Street, Abingdon VA
(276) 628-6115

Abingdon Celtic Cottage

The cultures of both Ireland and the deep South are known for their charm, kindness and congeniality and so is the beautiful town of Abingdon set in the rolling hills of Southwestern Virginia. Coincidentally, Scotch-Irish colonists first settled Abingdon in the 17th century, so that just might be why. Whatever the reason, Mary Eileen Osborne, owner of Abingdon Celtic Cottage, has that same gracious hospitality in her blood. The 125-year-old Victorian gingerbread cottage that she found in Abingdon's historic district emanated all the charm of the Old World cottages she knew so well in western Europe, so she decided to bring both her worlds together by opening Abingdon Celtic Cottage in 2001. Here you can find high-end European designer apparel, gourmet foods, jewelry and beautiful gift items that can't usually be found in the United States. Abingdon Celtic Cottage is right in the middle of the delightful historic district of Abingdon just a few doors down from the Barter Theatre. The entire district offers a wonderful combination of lifestyles and customs and the kind of warm, welcoming atmosphere for which the Irish and Southerners are so well known. Come in and let Mary Eileen help you find your own sense of home and connection to Ireland and the British Isles at Abingdon Celtic Cottage.

239 E Main Street, Abingdon VA
(276) 623-2311

The Cave House Craft Shop

The Cave House Craft Shop has been around since 1971. It is a co-op consisting of 110 craftspeople who market their mostly traditional crafts to the public, and 95 percent of the people who sell their crafts live within 50 miles of the co-op. The co-op began to help the Appalachian craftspeople market their work back in the 70s, and has been going strong ever since. The longevity of this co-op is very rare, and can be attributed to the fact that the Appalachian people are very easygoing and work well together. Native Appalachian hardwoods are used in crafts to produce beautiful pieces that fit into the décor of modern people's homes. Another key to the Cave House's success is that all the artists bring truly original and intriguing items to the store. The co-op is called the Cave House because of the cave on the back of the property. It is said that wolves living in the cave attacked Daniel Boone's dogs on one of his first trips through this area. The cave is 300 feet long with the main shaft taking you to a large room that has many crawling tunnels that lead to different spots in town. These tunnels were used to hide slaves as part of the Underground Railroad. There is a lot of history from different eras of America all in one spot, so come see for yourself at the Cave House Craft Shop in Abingdon.

279 E Main Street, Abingdon VA
(276) 628-7721

Index by Treasure

Index by City